MY CHILDREN
or the
CROSS

MY CHILDREN
or the
CROSS

One Woman's Sacrifice in
Pre-Communist China

–MIRIAM DUNN–

mother of Peter Graham Dunn, founder of P. Graham Dunn

PUBLISHING
Dalton, Ohio 44618

First Printing: March 2011
Second Printing: July 2013

© Copyright 2011 P. Graham Dunn Publishing
All rights reserved. No part of this publication may be reproduced,
stored in a retrieval system or transmitted, in any form, or by any
means, electronic, mechanical, photocopying, recording, or otherwise,
without the prior permission of the publishers.

ISBN 13: 978-0-983-41310-3
ISBN 10: 0-983-41310-X

P. Graham
DUNN
PUBLISHING
Dalton, Ohio
www.pgrahamdunnpublishing.com
E-mail us at: peter@pgrahamdunnpublishing.com
www.pgrahamdunnpublishing.com/facebook

Printed in the United States of America by:

Carlisle Printing
OF WALNUT CREEK LTD
800.927.4196

Design & Layout: Rosetta Mullet

Contents

Preface

OUR PARENTS' EXPERIENCES in China during World War II and leading up to the takeover of Mainland China by Mao Zedong and the Communist Party occurred during a climactic historical era of the twentieth century. Not only did Eric Liddell of the *Chariots of Fire* fame attend our mother's baptism, our mother also happened to be in the area where one of Lt. Col. Jimmy Doolittle's bombers on his return flight from Japan parachuted to safety and ended up donating his parachute for a wedding dress. Our father visited the location of the murder of John and Betty Stam on December 8, 1934, and was on the scene when the coffins for their funeral were delivered.

Mother journaled extensively throughout her life. Upon her and our father's retirement as missionaries in 1974 with the China Inland Mission (now known as the Overseas Missionary Fellowship), she was afforded the time to reflect on those entries resulting in this book.

Another passion of our mother's was the *Daily Light*, a one-year devotional. The *Daily Light* provided her with inspiration before she started each day. When writing her memoirs she chose to start nearly each chapter with a verse from the *Daily Light*. Our mother's love for her heavenly Father is readily apparent in each chapter. She served a God she loved, and gave of her life and family to further the cause of the kingdom.

Each of us four children received a Xeroxed double-spaced copy of this memoir, all carefully typed out on a typewriter. She drew her own maps, which are reproduced in this book just the way she drew them.

I have personally read through her memoirs countless times. Each time I read them, I am impressed anew by the strength of character my mother displayed, especially during those years in China when she served as a missionary while at the same time raising a family of four. Hers was not an easy life. Yet she responded to each adversity almost with a sense of adventure.

Although I was born in China and lived there my first five years, I believe that reading Mother's journal impacted my love for China and the Chinese people as much as, or more than, my having lived in China. I studied Mandarin avocationally for three years. I have traveled to China over a half dozen times in the last six years.

In 2008 I was able to return to Leshan, a city in Sichuan province, where I was born. I visited the site where the hospital once stood where I took my first breath. We worshiped in a house church. The hymns were the familiar hymns we all know in America, but they were sung in Mandarin.

On another occasion while in Hong Kong, I visited the large Baptist church located in Kowloon. The service was conducted in Cantonese (in the Coastal South they speak Cantonese rather than Mandarin), so I understood very little of the service. Regardless, I was overcome with emotion as I looked around the congregation and reflected on how many of these Chinese worshiping with me may have been the direct result of efforts of the China Inland Mission prior to 1949 in Mainland China.

While LeAnna and I were raising our own brood of four, we would often use Mother's memoirs as a devotional. If the particular chapter was not too long, we would read a chapter each evening. If the children would start to lose interest, we would finish the chapter the next evening. We will never know the seeds that were planted in the reading of this book with our children, but suffice to say that they were left with an impression of a grandmother who knew what it meant to put God first in her life.

Some of the chapters actually read like a modern-day thriller; other chapters move more slowly. Throughout, however, we believe you will be inspired by our mother's life and her writing style.

Children are hardly objective when it comes to their mother's memoirs, but for years we have felt that they needed to be reproduced in book format. We procrastinated for a number of reasons, not the least of which was that we wanted this to be done right the first time. We were not going to rush into this publication and then regret that it was done in a shoddy manner.

We trust that you will be challenged personally as you read about the life of our mother. A life of service for Christ is a life God blesses. We want you to be blessed as you read.

A final comment on the Chinese spelling style used by our mother. She was creating these memoirs before Mao Zedong and the Communists took over Mainland China in 1949. Prior to 1949, Chinese words were phonetically translated using a system established by the Russians, and later refined by the British called Wades-Giles. Mao Zedong and members of his regime chose to replace the Wades-Giles system with a new spelling system referred to as Pinyin, or language of the people. The Communists under Mao Zedong felt that the Wades-Giles phonetics were tainted by the Western cultures, and did not accurately reflect the phonetics or culture of the Middle Kingdom. We debated as to whether or not to go through Mother's book and change all of the spellings from Wades-Giles to Pinyin, but decided to leave the book the way she wrote it.

Peter Graham Dunn

Summary of a Life

MIRIAM JESSIE TOOP was born in Kuling, Kingsi, China, on Saturday, January 11, 1913, the daughter of Rosetta and Joseph Toop, missionaries with the Old Baptist Union. She grew up in China, going to school at Tientsin Grammar School. At the age of eighteen she left for University College in London to take up nursing and midwifery.

In 1940, when twenty-seven years of age, she returned to China as a missionary with the China Inland Mission (now known as the Overseas Missionary Fellowship). On July 2, 1943, she married Marvin Dunn, a Canadian, after a romance started by bandits and brigands.

Marvin and Miriam returned to China in 1949 after a furlough in England and Canada meeting each other's families. They became houseparents for forty-nine new missionaries who were learning various Chinese dialects. This group became known as the "Forty-Niners."

In 1951 Communist rule took over China, and missionaries were forced to leave. Marvin and Miriam went to Hong Kong. By this time there were four children. They spent the next twenty-three years doing mission work in Southeast Asia—Hong Kong, Singapore, and Malaysia.

In 1974 they "retired" to Calgary, Alberta, Canada. They both continued to be involved with the OMF, book selling, prayer meetings, and hospitality. In 1985 they moved to Abbotsford, British Columbia, to take advantage of the milder climate. Marvin died on December 23, 1989. Miriam continued to live in Abbotsford until a broken hip forced her to move to Vancouver. She passed into the presence of her Lord on Wednesday morning, December 5, 1999.

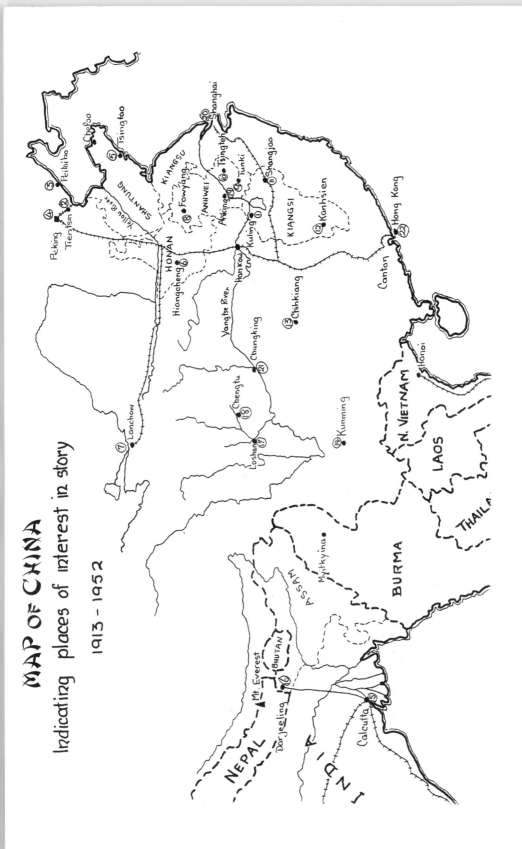

MAP OF CHINA

Indicating places of interest in story

1913 - 1952

Peitaiho
Chefoo
Tsingtao
⑤
Peking
Tientsin
④
②
③
SHANTUNG
Yellow River
Fowyang
⑧
HONAN
Hiangcheng
⑥
KIANGSU
Shanghai
⑳
Tsingleh
⑩
Tunki
⑨
ANHWEI
Anking
⑲
Shangjao
Shangjao
⑪
Kanhsien
⑫
KIANGSI
Hong Kong
Hankow
Kuling
⑦
⑪
Yangtze River
Chihkiang
⑬
Canton
Hong Kong
㉒
Chungking
㉑
Chengtu
⑱
Kunming
⑭
Lanchow
⑰
Loshan
⑰
N. VIETNAM
Hanoi
LAOS
THAILA
Myitkyina
BURMA
ASSAM
Mt. Everest
BHUTAN
⑯
NEPAL
Darjeeling
Calcutta
⑮
INDI

Legend for Map of China

1. I was born here – January 11, 1913

2. Where I spent my childhood

3. The vacation resort where I was baptized in 1929

4. Stayed here with my parents in 1940 on my return to China as a missionary

5. Here I began Chinese studies – 1940

6. Language study and orientation to Chinese rural culture

7. Where I had wanted to work in the Borden Memorial Hospital

8. My location as a district nurse in North Anhwei – 1942

9. Marvin and I married here – July 2, 1943

10. Our first home – 1943

11. Moved here to escape advancing Japanese. Engaged in church planting – 1944

12. USAF airfield to which we traveled to fly to Kunming to escape advancing Japanese – 1944

13. Where the plane carrying Mr. and Mrs. Hutchinson and Miss Loosley crashed – 1944

14. We flew from here over the Hump to Calcutta, India – December 1944

15. We arrived here as refugees. Rosemary born – February 5, 1945

16. Saw Mount Everest – 1945

17. Houseparents of first post-war Language School. Peter born – September 17, 1946

18. Beryl Weston died in jeep accident – 1945

19. Worked in first coed Language School from 1946-1948. Jennifer born – February 4, 1948

20. CIM International Headquarters. Left from here for furlough – 1948

21. Lived here with the "Forty-Niners" under Communism – 1949-1951

22. Worked with Christian Witness Press producing Chinese Christian literature after evacuation from Chungking. David born – July 5, 1952

Introduction

ONE OF THE most exciting things in the Christian life is to discover that God, the Almighty, the Creator of the universe, wants to communicate with His children. He does it in the letter He wrote centuries ago: the Bible.

Through the years, my heavenly Father has spoken to me to encourage, rebuke, guide, comfort, or just to show His love. I wondered if He wanted me to share some of these experiences, and perhaps encourage someone else. A number of years ago, a friend enclosed a bookmark with a Christmas card. It depicted a lighted candle and a Bible. Printed above the picture was the verse: "Thy Word is a lamp unto my feet, and a light unto my path" (Psalm 119:105). As I put it in my Bible, I wondered if God was trying to say something to me.

Morning by morning, as I had my quiet time at the green-topped table in our little kitchen in Kuala Lumpur, Malaysia, the bookmark moved steadily from chapter to chapter. Gradually, the feeling grew stronger that I should share the record of some of God's dealings with me. I thought back to stories my parents had shared with me, looked through an old diary, and reread dozens of hoarded prayer letters.

At that time, my husband was Field Director of the Overseas Missionary Fellowship work in Malaysia. Our days were full, but I managed to put some of the story on paper. In 1974 we retired to Calgary, Alberta, Canada and I continued writing.

The setting of this story may be unfamiliar, but missionaries are ordinary people, with foibles and problems like everyone else. I found that God's Word met my need in many different circumstances.

However, His message was not always what I wanted to hear, and I had to learn to accept what I did not understand. Some people may feel this story is too simplistic. I do not think so, and have written events as they happened.

Nearly every chapter is headed with a verse of Scripture (or hymn) that God used at that time, often the same day, in relation to a special circumstance. This was not coincidence. This is what has made me desire to share what He has been able to communicate to me. What He has done for me, He can do for you—and probably has.

As you read this story I hope you will get a message also—and pass it on!

Miriam J. Dunn
Calgary, 1978

PART I

Checkmate
1942

Chapter One

Whoso hearkeneth unto Me shall dwell safely,
and shall be quiet from fear of evil.
Proverbs 1:33 KJV

WE HAD REACHED a crucial stage in our journey—a journey that was to change the direction of my life. The Dunn brothers, Gordon and Marvin, were returning to their missionary work in the southern part of Anhwei province in China, having come north to attend a conference. I was traveling back with them.

It was November 23, 1942. China and Japan had been at war for five years. Since Japan's attack on Pearl Harbor in December 1941, any Canadian, American, or British national captured in areas of China occupied by the Japanese became a civilian prisoner of war. Today we were to venture into enemy territory, situated about 350 miles west of the metropolitan city of Shanghai.

A few miles to the south of us flowed China's famous Yangtze River, a seemingly insurmountable barrier to our advance. Japanese gunboats patrolled it regularly. Japanese troops were stationed along its banks in the larger cities. A dangerous no-man's land stretched for miles north and south.

Chinese quislings (traitors), bribed or forced by their Japanese masters, attempted to guard the approaches to the river. But hard-nosed Chinese merchants had gradually established regular convoy routes through the area. Carrying goods back and forth across the Yangtze was a profitable venture; week after week, long trains of coolies and businessmen wormed their way through enemy lines for monetary gain.

The night before, having already traversed some three hundred miles down the length of North Anhwei, we had reached the border town of Ho Pu Lin. Today our negotiations with the Travel Bureau (who had inaugurated this convoy service) had been completed, and coolies had been hired.

"Only a few more days and we should be home," remarked Gordon as we packed our cases. He had left his wife, Vera, behind with friends in the South about two months earlier. She was expecting their first child in early December and had been unable to accompany him north. His impatience to get going was understandable. As there was no missionary nurse in South Anhwei, I was going back with him, but time was running out on us.

We left Ho Pu Lin at nine the next morning with six armed soldiers leading the way. Behind them was strung out a long line of coolies. Interspersed were merchants, keeping an eye on their goods, about eighty men in all. We three were the only Caucasians and traveled toward the end of the line. The guide in charge, provided by the Travel Bureau, brought up the rear with the two plainclothes men.

A long and arduous twenty-four hours lay ahead. Gordon and Marvin decided I should save my strength as much as possible. The only available conveyance was a wheelbarrow, its huge, squeaking wheel dividing the two slatted wooden seats. I sat on one side of the wheel and some suitcases were tied on the other side to balance, while a puffing barrowman pushed from behind. He gripped the two smooth handles, while a three-inch web of canvas, attached to each handle, rested on the back of his neck. The barrow had no springs; I jerked with every bump on the dirt road.

Five miles farther on, we approached a stockaded village, where a group of armed men halted our convoy. Gladly, the coolies lowered their burdens and sat around smoking and talking. The soldiers wore no uniforms. Soiled turbans covered their heads, cartridge belts hugged their hips, and rifles were slung on their backs. Apparently, this was an informal military headquarters. They kept us there for several hours. Suddenly the message came, "Get moving!" and off we went. The line of men lengthened out as before, over the hills, through a village or two, until we reached a large green plain where cattle grazed.

We were ordered to halt while the guide and several soldiers went ahead to investigate. Soon a signal was relayed back and the convoy jogged into life once more.

Bordering the plain on the farther side was a narrow river. One little sampan (wooden rowboat) ferried us over, carrying only six people at a time. It seemed slow and inefficient to us, but we had forgotten that there was no point in hurrying; we could not move into no-man's land that bordered the Yangtze until dusk.

In an hour or two, we reached another village. It was time for the evening meal, but there was no inn to cope with this influx of people. Everyone prepared to cook the rice they had brought. The soldiers walked unceremoniously into dark houses demanding the use of pots and fires. As one of them dipped water out of a family crock to wash his own rice, Gordon gave him some of ours to rinse at the same time. When he had cleaned it to his satisfaction, he boiled his and ours in the black iron pot.

We were given coarse blue bowls and wooden chopsticks, the steaming rice was spooned out, and we began to eat. The rice with a little soya sauce, some scrambled eggs, and pickled shredded turnips made a good meal. We had just finished when other soldiers shouted from the street. It was time to go.

No-man's land, partly controlled by a notorious Chinese officer who had turned traitor to serve the Japanese, lay ahead. As our escort of soldiers would be useless in this situation, they returned to their headquarters, taking my barrowman with them. The two plainclothes men, wearing long dark gowns and white straw hats, with revolvers swaying from straps slung over their shoulders, forged to the front. They cautioned us all to be absolutely quiet, and we proceeded slowly. Occasionally, the column was halted while someone reconnoitered our position. At such times, we stood in eerie silence, waiting until the all-clear signal was passed down the line. Then we moved forward again.

The sun set in a blaze of golden light and dusk fell. Before us loomed the dark outline of a massive dike, and as we clambered up its side, a rose-pink moon pushed out of the gray mist. Climbing into the sky, its silver light illuminated the country around us, outlining the path at our feet, and also the dark figure of the person walking just ahead.

We traveled along the dike in a southeasterly direction. The only sound was the soft pad-pad of the coolies' sandaled feet and the rhythmic creaking of the carrying poles.

Suddenly, a bright light shone for an instant in front and to our right.

"I think that comes from a Japanese boat in the Yangtze," Gordon whispered, "which means we must be getting near the river."

The light flashed again. A gleaming ray shot into the sky, swooped down, and swept over the countryside. It was a searchlight.

The whole line stopped short as one. Coolies dropped their loads. Footsteps came swiftly in our direction. A Chinese spy ran up with news that three Japanese gunboats were anchored at the very place where our convoy had planned to cross!

Our guide, some merchants, and the plainclothes men huddled together in hasty consultation. We prayed for God's guidance and His protection from danger. If Japanese soldiers discovered us, we would be interned in a concentration camp in Shanghai until the end of the war. The leaders made their decision and relayed it quickly. Because there was no chance of crossing the river that night, the whole convoy was to retrace its steps to the military headquarters where we had rested that morning—a forty-*li* hike in the dark (three *li* = one mile).

Back we trudged along the path over which we had walked with such hope a short time before. The moon floated behind us now, casting long shadows at our feet. The leader decided to stay and gather more information. The two straw-hatted escorts took charge. They pushed ahead, and our little group was again at the rear. Naturally, we were disappointed, and rather dismayed, but the verses of *Daily Light,* which I had read that morning, came as God's message of encouragement: "Whoso hearkeneth unto Me shall dwell safely, and shall be quiet from fear of evil." His ways were beyond our understanding, but His love that night was real.

After a nerve-wracking couple of hours scrambling in the dark, we were allowed our first rest on a mud-packed threshing floor. I curled up on some fragrant straw and fell asleep. Suddenly a voice pierced my dreams, "Wake up, Miss Toop. It's time to go again." I jumped up, brushed off the dust and chaff, and joined the cavalcade that was slowly regrouping in a ragged line.

We were very tired, and the miles seemed to drag by. At one in the morning we recrossed the small river, having been on the go for sixteen long hours. It was not only the physical exertion, but also the tension from this setback, which made us feel exhausted. Brigands were also active in the area and would get a good haul if they attacked our convoy. The leaders kept pushing us on and somehow managed to obtain a small military escort.

We plodded on, one behind the other, in the moonlight. At last, a huddle of buildings loomed before us, dark and silent. The soldiers went from house to house, banging on doors and demanding shelter. Fearful voices replied from within. But when the peasants realized we were just a band of peaceful travelers needing rest, they kindly pulled back the bars from their heavy wooden doors and took us in.

The old man to whose house we were taken lit a small oil lamp for our coolies and us. The soldiers kindled a fire and boiled some water while Marvin and Gordon untied my bedding roll and spread it out in the side room where the baggage was stacked. They slept on the floor with the others. By three in the morning all was quiet.

Five hours later we were on the road, heading for the safety of the military headquarters. The stockade came in sight, and before long we were sprawling on benches, desperate for something to eat. The two men inquired around and returned with bowls of rice, dotted with lumps of sweet potato, which we wolfed down.

At four that afternoon our chief guide returned. His news was depressing. Japanese ships were still anchored at the crossing, and we would have to remain where we were until they steamed off.

Questions flooded my mind. Where could we stay? This was a soldiers' encampment; there was no inn. Had God forgotten us? Of course not. With rough courtesy, an officer cleared a room for me, and found accommodation for the men.

Before I tumbled into my bedding roll, I reviewed the situation:

one white woman among many men, surrounded by uncouth soldiers, and facing physical danger and an uncertain future. Yet I felt so secure in that little room. Had not God given me His word that I should "dwell safely" and fear no evil?

I did not know it then, but we were to spend five days in that unlikely refuge. This gave me time to think back on the events that had led me there.

PART II

Roots and Childhood
1911

Chapter Two

ITALIC RECALLED WHAT my parents had told me about their families and
their friendship. Father's parents (Toop) were Baptists and owned a
small business. He was born in London within the sound of Bow Bells,
which made him a true Londoner. When he left school, he helped in
his father's store.

Mother's parents (Holmes) were involved in the Salvation Army and
lived in a seaside town near the mouth of the Thames River. They were
a happy family of boys and girls, hardworking and poor. Her father's leg
had been amputated, but this only served to deepen his spiritual life and
his trust in God. This brushed off on his family also.

Rose, a pretty, curly-haired country girl, found a job in London and
attended a prayer meeting in a Baptist church. There she caught the eye
of a young, dark-haired salesclerk. Gradually, a friendship developed,
and then an engagement was announced: Rosetta Holmes to Joseph
Toop.

One Sunday evening the preacher told of the spiritual needs of the
Chinese people, and God's call came to Joe and Rose. They realized they
did not have much to offer to the Lord, but they responded with love
and unquestioning obedience.

In 1911, the traumatic year of China's Revolution, they became
members of the Old Baptist Union Mission. From England they sailed
to the continent and then traveled by train to Russia. In Moscow
they boarded the train, which carried them for days through the Ural
Mountains, over the wastes of Siberia, and along the shores of Lake

Baikal to North China. In the central province of Hwpeh they began to study the Chinese language, delaying marriage for a year in order to become more proficient in speaking. March 19, 1912, was their wedding day. Their first home was a grimy, unused temple in a country town. It was infested with rats, but Rose washed and scrubbed while Joe slapped on the whitewash.

God blessed them in that inland town in spite of loneliness, poverty, and the lack of English friends. They had each other, and around them were Chinese people living in gray-tiled, mud-brick houses, whom they came to love. God kept them safe in times of danger and upheaval. He gave them a deep love for each other and for Himself, which never wavered. Their joy became full when they knew their first child was due in January.

The nearest missionary doctor lived in Kuling, a summer resort nearly three hundred miles east of them, on the Yangtze River. As the time for the birth of their baby drew near, the young couple made excited preparations. The last half of December was cold but sunny. Rose rode in a sedan chair for three miles to a small river market town, and Joe walked behind her with the coolie who carried their suitcase and the multipurpose Chinese *p'u-kais* (thin mattresses). China's inns were known to harbor fleas and bedbugs and most travelers provided their own bedding.

At the market town, they boarded a small boat for Chichow where they would embark on a big steamer to take them down the Yangtze to Kiukiang, the disembarkation point for Kuling. But when they reached Chichow, they found the steamer was not due for another two and a half days.

There was no inn in the village. The only place where they could stay was a boathouse, drafty and cold, right beside the river. There were no beds in the huge shed, so the bedrolls were spread out on benches. Fortunately, Rose was healthy and eagerly looking forward to the birth of her baby. They walked, talked, wondered, and prayed, committing themselves again to the God who had guided them thus far.

About three o'clock on the third morning, a man rushed in. "Be quick! The steamer is here! Get up quickly!"

In the light of a smoky oil lamp they hurriedly dressed, packed the suitcase, and rolled up the bedding. Stumbling in the dark, they hurried down to the water's edge and scrambled into a sampan. The boatman rowed them out to the steamer—a dark mass in the middle of the swift-flowing water. It was moving!

"Oh, Joe," cried Rose. "We're too late! Look, the steamer's going!"

Joe called on the boatman to row harder. "We must catch the steamer!" he exclaimed.

"Don't worry," replied the man, steadily plying his oars. "The steamer is waiting for you. You have to climb up the ladder while it is moving. It isn't going fast."

Joe and Rose had not realized that at such small stopping places these ships merely slowed their engines, flung out a ladder, and continued gliding downstream. Poor Rose! Her heart sank as she saw the small ladder dangling above the sampan. How could she possibly climb it in her condition: her body swollen with child, her dress clinging to her ankles, the dark night, the swinging ladder?

"Hurry up!" yelled the sailors on the deck above. "We can't wait much longer."

Suddenly two pairs of Chinese hands groped down out of the darkness toward Rose, grasped her wrists, and helped her up. She could never have made it on her own. Joe had as much as he could do to get the suitcase and bedroll and himself up after her. It was a terrifying experience! They were thankful to learn that at the important port of Kiukiang the steamer would tie up at a wharf, where it would be easy to disembark.

From Kiukiang, Rose was again carried in a sedan chair up the winding mountain road to Kuling. At times, when she looked over the edge, she saw nothing but space, though the tops of trees were visible far below. Jog-jog went the carriers, jog-jog—and the chair swayed and bounced to an irregular rhythm. Would this uncomfortable journey adversely affect their unborn child?

In Kuling, the lady doctor was waiting, and on January 11, 1913, I made my appearance. The few missionaries resident on the mountain during the winter season were very kind to us. My parents waited there for a full month, adhering to the custom, which Chinese culture prescribed, that a new mother does not leave the house until a month after the birth of her child. On the return journey they traveled back down that same tortuous road to Kiukiang. There they boarded the upriver steamer for home.

When they came in sight of Chichow, the ship slowed down, but it did not stop. A ladder was dropped over the side and a waiting sampan shot out from the bank and was hooked to the steamer.

This picture was taken by Marvin Dunn in 1948 on the Yangtze when they were transferring from the main ship to the boat that would take them to shore. The two boats did not stop, but floated alongside each other while passengers and cargo were transported back and forth. It was on a boat similar to this, that Miriam was dropped by her mother to a waiting coolie below when Miriam was just months old.

"What am I going to do with the baby?" Mother asked herself as she was helped over the side and her fumbling feet found the ladder.

My father held me in his arms, ready to hand me over, but Mother knew she could never make it. "Joe, I can't do it!" she cried.

"Hurry up!" yelled a sailor. "Drop the baby to the man in the sampan. She'll be all right. He's used to catching things dropped from the ship."

Mother was horrified, but in the end she had no choice. She could not carry me down that swinging ladder. Father leaned over and dropped me, a white woolly bundle, into the arms of an old Chinese man in the bobbing boat below. Mother did not remember how she got down that ladder! Once in the sampan she grabbed me from the old man and hugged me tightly. I was none the worse, but it had been traumatic for her.

Fortunately, the journey ended with no further painful incidents. In my temple-home, I became the center of attraction: the first white baby the peasants had ever seen.

My father's patient teaching of God's Word bore spiritual fruit in Chinese lives. He was thrilled to baptize a few who had accepted Christ as their Saviour. When I was twenty months old, my twin brothers, John and Billy (1914), were born. In 1917 my sister Peggy completed our family.

England was at war, and money sent from London sometimes failed to arrive. Life became more and more difficult. Four small children took all of my mother's time and strength. Late in 1917, we had to move to the international city of Shanghai, where my father joined the staff of the British and Foreign Bible Society.

I was a terribly shy child, probably because of the change in tempo from life in a quiet inland town to that of a hustling, crowded city. When I learned I had to go to school, I was terrified and cried uncontrollably. But when someone suggested that the twins start school with me, everything changed. On their fourth birthday, the three of us began a new stage in our lives.

Chapter Three

IN THE LATE fall of 1919, my father was asked to move north to Tientsin to take charge of the Bible Society agency there. One evening we boarded the coastal steamer for Tangku, the port of Tientsin. It was due to sail very early the next morning, but around midnight a sailor raced through the ship, hammering on cabin doors. "Anyone inside? If so, get up!" he shouted. "The ship is on fire. Hurry!"

Father sprang out of his bunk and threw on his clothes. Mother did the same.

"*Ku'ai 'ku'ai-ti!* (Hurry!)" called another urgent voice. "Get off the ship at once! Don't wait for anything!"

Father unlocked the cabin door and saw a crowd of Chinese coolies in the passage. "Come," he cried, "help carry the children to the wharf."

Mother bundled us up in blankets and handed us over to those rough men, who ran with us to the quay. Mother found a sheltered corner in a narrow passage between the big godowns (warehouses) that towered above us. It was a bitterly cold night. The four of us, wrapped in rugs and blankets, huddled together in a daze.

Suddenly there was the roar of a powerful motor, the urgent clanging of a bell. A bright light blazed around the corner and dazzled us. A fire engine was swinging into our narrow passage. If it kept coming we could be crushed. Quick as a flash, Mother jumped into its path. Her body was silhouetted against the glaring light. She stood waving her arms and shouting, "*T'ing-chih! T'ing-chih!* (Stop! Stop!)." Just in time, it did.

Father, meanwhile, was still in the cabin rescuing as many of our things as he could. Those wonderful coolies, uncouth, coarse, and dirty

17

though they were, brought every one of our belongings off the ship, even down to a bag of peanuts!

The China Inland Mission home kindly took us in for the next few days, after which our passages were booked on another ship sailing north. But Mother objected! She and Father went to see their superior to discuss the whole matter together.

"But, my dear Mrs. Toop, what are your reasons for not wanting to sail on this ship?" Mr. Gould asked patiently.

"I have no valid reasons," Mother replied, "but I also have no peace at the thought of going by ship. I believe God has other plans."

"It is possible to travel to Tientsin by train," he volunteered, "but it would be very inconvenient with four small children in this cold weather."

"If you don't object, I'd be much happier doing that," she said. "What do you think, Joe?"

Father was in a quandary. He did not mind going by steamer, and guessed that Mr. Gould thought his wife was being unreasonable. On the other hand, he knew she would not act in this way unless she felt it was the right thing to do. He was usually the decision-maker in the family, and she accepted his judgment.

"Well," he replied slowly, "if the Bible Society has no objections, perhaps we should go by train."

"All right, Mr. Toop. If that is how you feel, we'll cancel your passage on the steamer and buy tickets for the train," Mr. Gould replied. "However, I must say I think it would be a strange coincidence if the *second* ship caught fire also!"

Thus, our family traveled by train to Tientsin. A few days later, the paper carried news that the very ship on which we had been booked to sail caught fire in the Yellow Sea en route to Tangku. Passengers and crew were saved, but all cargo was lost.

(There is an explanation for these fires. They occurred during a Chinese boycott of Japanese ships carrying cargoes up and down the China coast. Irate Chinese sailors sabotaged many steamers before a settlement was reached.)

In Tientsin, the big old-fashioned brick house, with the office and Bible showroom opening off the dining room, became home for us. Winters were bitterly cold with icy, northern winds howling in from the Siberian wastes. Each spring brought the fragrance of lilac and the delicate beauty of wisteria. It was also the season when dust storms raced in from the Gobi Desert, darkening the sky and filling the air with gritty sand.

Across the road were the officers' quarters of the resident British garrison. We lived in the British Concession, under the protection of British guns. Daily, the wail of bagpipes announced the changing of the guard, as soldiers, kilts swinging, marched from their barracks.

Each morning, Father conducted family prayers, on holidays and school days alike. As we each learned to read, we took our turn around the circle: our loving yet authoritarian father, our attractive mother with blue eyes and curly brown hair, the mischievous twins, pretty little Peggy, and myself, a rather sober big sister who took her responsibilities seriously. This principle of daily family worship, which included singing the old-fashioned hymns, inevitably made a lasting impression on us all.

We attended the Tientsin Grammar School, and thus escaped the trauma many missionary children had to face of leaving home and going to boarding school. Our classmates were multinational: White Russian refugees, Americans, Canadians, English, and French. The principal stalked the halls, cane in hand. No rudeness, no laziness, and no cheating were allowed. Because we studied for the Cambridge University external exams, the standard of education was good.

Procrastination was a weakness of mine, and my little sister suffered as a result. When we were old enough, we cycled to school. John and Billy each had a bike, and I took Peggy on the back of mine. Many mornings I would still be working on some homework (or reading an exciting book) when Peggy's voice would ring up from the garden, "Miri-YUM! Hurry up! John and Billy have gone and we'll be late!"

"Coming!" I would cry.

A little later, she would call with greater urgency, "Miri-YUM!" Because of my dilly-dallying, more than once we had to slink into the Big Hall and join the last class filing in for morning prayers.

In winter, we skated and played field hockey. In summer, we swam and played tennis. Our good friends, the MacKenzies, had a court in their big garden to which we gravitated. The adults always played first, but the long summer evenings gave us many hours of exercise.

Mother always tried to dress us in pretty clothes, and great was our excitement when a parcel arrived from Montgomery Ward. New dresses, coats, shirts, and suits were pulled out, held up, and gloated over. The mail-order houses were a boon to us. But oh! How I hated my button boots and the struggle to fasten the long row of buttons with the special hook! How glad I was when spring came and those wretched boots could be stored away until next winter.

Our church home was the Union Church. When we were small we attended the morning service, and in the afternoon we bowled along to Sunday school in rickshaws. Latterly, our superintendent was Eric Liddell, a former Olympic gold-medalist from Scotland, and now a missionary. He was a great favorite at athletic meets, and seemed to fly over the ground with head flung back, arms bent, and legs stretching like young Mercury. Amazingly, he was a humble man of God, gentle and with a great sense of humor.

My parents were very hospitable and our home was open to many transient missionaries. For instance, because of widespread anti-British feeling in 1927, hundreds of missionaries from the interior of China had to evacuate to the coastal cities. The China Inland Mission home in Tientsin was full to overflowing; as a result various refugee couples stayed with us.

Christmas was always a happy time. The Parrys, the MacKenzies, and our family celebrated together. Mother's pastries and pies were meltingly good; Father's jokes and riddles were famous. Always, the evening ended with prayer and thanks to our heavenly Father for His goodness to us.

But times were not always so prosperous. Our parents were hard hit when a bank in which they (and many other missionaries) had invested their little bit of savings went bankrupt. Bread and butter *or* jam—not both—was the order of the day for a long time.

In the course of his work, Father periodically visited cities hundreds of miles away where the Bible Society had branch offices. Travel in the interior was rigorous, but he loved to go and see how the men were faring. Bible Society colporteurs tramped to outlying villages and towns, witnessing for the Lord and selling Gospel portions and Bibles. What we children enjoyed when he returned was to eat up the leftover sweetened condensed milk that he always managed to bring back with him. We rolled the sweetness around our tongues and enjoyed it to the full.

When not on these trips, my father ordered Bibles from Shanghai and supervised their shipment to inland cities or sold them locally. He was active in church and Sunday school, and also in evangelistic work among the many British soldiers quartered in our city. He was a man who always threw his weight on God's side of the scales of life.

Chapter Four

*Trust in the Lord with all thine heart, and lean not unto
thine own understanding. In all thy ways acknowledge
Him and He shall direct thy paths.*
Proverbs 3:5,6 KJV

SUMMERS IN TIENTSIN were sweltering, with temperatures in the
hundreds. Unfortunately, the Cambridge exams were always held at
the end of the summer term, the hottest time of the year. To cool things
off, big blocks of ice were placed on the windowsills, while hoses played
outside on the slatted blinds, which hung at every window to exclude
the sun. Fans whirled overhead in every classroom, but it was still HOT.

As soon as school was over, we escaped to a beautiful holiday resort
called Pei Tai Ho for two and a half glorious months of vacation. Dad
and Mother would spend days packing, and very early in the morning
our cavalcade of rickshaws, loaded with children, trunks, and baskets
of provisions, set off for the station. Dad would help us to settle in our
little bungalow at East Cliff, and return to Tientsin to work in the office
and live alone until August, when his vacation began.

Blue skies and clear water: Every morning except Sundays, dressed
in our swimsuits and draped with towels, we ran down the little path,
trampled smooth by many feet that led from the bungalow to the beach.
By the end of the summer we were deeply tanned, and our hair bleached
blond. Golden sand, gently lapping water, jellyfish, jagged rocks to
avoid, ducking, diving, swimming, splashing—this was our life.

Picnics and donkeys: One favorite picnic spot was the Lotus Hills, some miles to the south, which included a donkey ride. A noisy, motley collection of boys and their animals would gather at the back gate when they heard that donkeys were wanted. Our cook's call of "*Lu-ah!*" (donkeys!) brought them running. We children each chose the beast we wanted, and then the fun began. The boy would run behind, shouting, while we would shake the reins, dig in our heels, and yell. If one donkey began to hee-haw and set another snorting, that made it all the more hilarious. Mother usually rode in a rickshaw with the picnic basket, which contained huge slices of sweet red watermelon. At the top of the hill, sitting on rocks, we would bite into them, spitting out the seeds, pink juice running down our chins.

Another treat every summer was taking a breakfast picnic to the rolling sand dunes that beckoned to us past Eagle Rock, across miles of sand flats. Some riding donkeys, some walking, we set off very early when the tide was almost out. Sparkling on the wet sand were shells of diverse shapes and colors: long "Chinamen's fingernails," tiny cat's eyes, and vivid fan shells. At the start we would be full of energy, but after climbing the dunes and sliding down their smooth, warm sides, and running around on the flats looking for starfish and shells, our vitality began to drain away. Dad kept his eye on the time, and got us moving east before the incoming tide could cut us off. All we wanted to do when we got back was to dash into the white-lipped waves and cool off.

Sundays: In the mornings Mother and Father often attended a Chinese-speaking Brethren service. Every Sunday evening we went as a family to a community service held on the wide veranda of a huge stone bungalow built on the crest of a hill near our home. To this day, when I sing "Day Is Dying in the West," my thoughts fly back to that meeting place. The setting sun filled the western sky with glory, and below us was the vast blue-green ocean, gently lapping against the golden sands.

It is great to have lovely memories, but memory is fickle. Of most lasting spiritual blessing to me personally were the informal children's meetings, which God used to make the Bible come alive. A Brethren missionary, Frances Wilkes, came one summer to Pei Tai Ho. She loved kids, even missionary kids! So she taught us each week, sometimes on the verandas of different homes, sometimes on the beach. We learned new choruses; we dramatized stories. At the end of each session, she gave us a verse to memorize, and also to illustrate for the next meeting, using shells, flowers, feathers, and grasses. Her love for Jesus Christ came through to us. God used her, and also the teaching and example of my parents, to lead me to know Jesus Christ as my Saviour, though I cannot pinpoint the day.

The summer of 1929 was the last one I spent in Pei Tai Ho for some years. Before I left China for further education, I wanted to be baptized. John, Billy, and I decided to take this important step together. We wanted others to know that we loved the Lord Jesus, and that we were following Him. On the beach one August afternoon, a group of missionaries and Chinese believers stood singing and praying. Curious onlookers loitered not far away. Mr. Tharp, an English missionary, led us into the warm blue sea. One by one, we were immersed as he baptized us in the name of the Father, the Son, and the Holy Spirit. For me, this act crystallized my faith in Jesus Christ. The easy belief of childhood blossomed into

a deep reality. That afternoon, Father gave us the two verses from Proverbs that have held a special meaning for me ever since: "Trust in the Lord with all thine heart, and lean not unto thine own understanding. In all thy ways acknowledge Him and He shall direct thy paths."

Eric Liddell, our friend and Tientsin Sunday school superintendent, was also in Pei Tai Ho that summer. Hearing that we were to be baptized that afternoon, he cycled a number of miles to be with us. Later, in Tientsin, he bought three leather-covered Bibles from my father and gave us each one, inscribing

Eric Liddell, the Flying Scotsman,
at the Paris Olympics in 1924.

the flyleaf with his neat, meticulous writing.

Very soon, the truth of the above words was to be tested. I thought I would like to be a doctor, but in my heart I knew this could not be. For many years, my twin brothers had geared their ambitions to medicine, and this would strain my parents' resources to the limit. So I decided to become a nurse. My best friend was going to Canada, and her sister was planning to enter nurse's training. To my way of thinking, the obvious thing was to go with them. However, my parents felt strongly that I should go to England, where *their* relatives were. But these aunts, uncles, and cousins were complete strangers to me. It was a tremendous struggle to give up *my* plans and follow the wishes of my parents. They did not force me, but they did pray. The verse my father had given me held new meaning as I trusted Him in this situation and relinquished my own desires.

Nearly twenty years earlier, my parents had journeyed to China via Russia. They thought it would be interesting for me to travel to England the same way. Since then, of course, the 1917 Communist Revolution had transformed the land and the people. We heard of a lady leaving for England in the spring who wanted someone to travel with her and her

Eric Liddell, serving as a missionary in China, under the
London Missionary Society from 1925-1943.

two children on the Siberian train. I was a naïve eighteen at that time, shy and retiring, apprehensive of journeying alone. I was relieved to link up with someone else. She would pay my fare if I would help entertain the children during what could be a tedious trip.

Too soon the day of my departure arrived. For the last time, I rode in a rickshaw to the station, bowling through the familiar streets. This was

Dear David—
   In 1931 my twin brother and I travelled from our home in Tientsin, North China (via Japan, Vancouver, Toronto, & Quebec City) to England with our Sunday school teacher, a vibrant 29-year-old missionary who was going on his first furlough to Scotland. Our families had been friends for years, and he had himself been born in Tientsin (now Tianjin), where we had lived from about 1919 to 1931. He was a keen Christian and a first-class athlete, and Olympic champion! He died in February 1945 of a brain tumour while in a Japanese Internment camp in North China. Many years later his story was, in part, told in the motion picture 'CHARIOTS OF FIRE'. His name? ERIC LIDDELL. This picture was taken on our last day on board, steaming up the English Channel. (I'm the one who is holding the ship steady!) John

Miriam Dunn's twin brothers, John and Billy Toop, accompanied Eric Liddell from China to England on this ship in 1931. Eric was returning to Scotland for his first furlough. The Toop brothers traveled to England to become medical doctors, later returning to serve as missionaries in China.

the first break in our family, but I was somewhat comforted by the fact that the twins would be arriving in England a year later. However, one year seemed an eternity to me that night. We kissed goodbye, the train jerked forward, and the well-loved faces faded from sight. Frightened and tearful, I crawled into my berth. The train chugged relentlessly forward, taking me away forever from a happy home and the security of my parents' care—but not from their love and prayers.

We rattled north to Harbin, and then proceeded westward to Irkutsk, Omsk, and Moscow. The Russian steppes seemed endless. Thick pine forests and deep virgin snow formed a monochrome of black and white. Tiny settlements sprouted in the middle of nowhere. When the train stopped at stations, we dashed out like everybody else to fill our thermos flasks from boiling samovars (hot water urns). We made simple meals in our carriage with the food we carried with us. No one else spoke English, though the other passengers tried to be friendly.

In Moscow, we tramped the streets, enjoying the exercise after being confined to the train for so long. There were no cars, there was no color, and there were no smiles. Pedestrians in drab clothes hurried along the sidewalks with sober faces. In Red Square, the ornate, domed churches jolted us by their incongruity in this atheistic city. At Lenin's Tomb, we joined the queue moving slowly past the glass casket. With an upsurge of joy, I realized the contrasting wonder of Christ's resurrection! I belonged to a *living* Lord.

Crossing the border into Poland, we breathed the air of freedom and were thankful. Traveling through Germany and Holland, I was in a dream. After a rough passage across the Channel, we reached England at last. A train disgorged us and other weary travelers on a smoky, gritty London platform, where kind relatives met me and whisked me off to their city home.

PART III

Preparation
1923

Chapter 5

Ye have not chosen Me, but I have chosen you.
John 15:16 KJV

I STILL WANTED to become a nurse, but needed some adjustment to life in England before entering a big London hospital. A friend suggested I apply to the small children's hospital connected with Dr. Bernado's Homes. There I learned how to sweep and clean and polish brasses—as well as look after the ill orphan boys. In time, I rose above the bedpan-emptying duties to taking temperatures, keeping charts, giving injections, and doing dressings.

My first day in the operating room (O.R.) was a near catastrophe. About eight tonsillectomies were scheduled. The first snoring patient was rolled in. Snip! Onto his tongue went a pair of tongue forceps. *Horrors!* I thought. But there was more to follow. The suction pump gurgled away and bloody sponges flew right and left. It was more than I could take, and I made an ignominious retreat to the anesthetic room. There lay another small mound under a sheet, and the sickly smell of ether drove me into the corridor. Nursing was not for me! However, the next time was not quite so bad, and soon I even began to enjoy the O.R.

Infectious diseases were very common among the children, and we early learned the routine of absolute isolation: masks, gowns, and disinfectant for the hands. We nursed small boys with measles, scarlet fever, and diphtheria. Two or three times, a tracheotomy had to be performed because the gray membrane of diphtheria had closed the trachea. I was always frightened when caring for these patients. The horrible suction and rattle as air was forced through the silver tube; the

29

cleaning out of sticky, glutinous phlegm; the terror that filled a child's face as suffocation seemed imminent: these filled me with dread.

In 1932, Matron Phillips asked if I and another student nurse would like to help as nurses in a Christian Business Girls' Conference to be held at High Leigh. This was an old country house set in well-kept grounds. As we had few calls, we were able to attend all the meetings. It was the missionary meeting that redirected my life to China. We thought the missionary speaker, Mrs. Bird, was old-fashioned with her white hair pulled back into a bun, her long dark dress, and her gaunt features. However, as she spoke to us that afternoon, her face lit up with an inner glow and we forgot her appearance in the power of her message. She told us of the country women in China's Honan province where she had worked for many years: of their poverty, their unhappiness, and the droughts and resulting famines which brought unbelievable hardship to them and their children. She mentioned the many boys and girls who died of hunger and malnutrition. Finally, she gripped us with stories of their spiritual need—of the idol worship, the power of the temple, the fear of spirits, and how so few had the chance to hear the Gospel.

A pregnant silence filled that lovely room as she finished. Then a sweet voice rang out in the following chorus:

> *"I heard the call, 'Come follow!' That was all.*
> *Earth's joys grew dim; my soul went after Him.*
> *I rose and followed—that was all.*
> *Will you not follow if you hear His call?"*

Mrs. Bird suggested we take a few minutes to ask God to show us His will. She challenged us to be honest before Him, ready to go or ready to stay. It was during the time of soul-searching that followed that I knew, beyond the shadow of a doubt, that God wanted me to go back to the land of my birth to share Jesus' love. When we sang the chorus together at the end of the meeting, I made it my own response to Christ's call for service.

Later, I told Mrs. Bird what had happened, and she promised to pray for me. That day Christ's words to His disciples came as a personal message to me also: "Ye have not chosen Me, but I have chosen you."

Chapter Six

I will restore to you the years that the locust hath eaten.
Joel 2:25 KJV

IN 1933, I left the security of Bernado's for the unexplored happenings of a big London hospital. At University College I was thrust into the maelstrom of life and death. I knew the agony of helplessness when nursing terminal pneumonia patients. I felt the quick stab of apprehension when accident cases were rushed into the O.R. I enjoyed the fun on the men's surgical ward, and was amazed at the gallantry of some who faced wearisome disabilities. I lived and worked with student nurses, some of whom were keen Christians, and a few who were confessed atheists. I was also free to indulge in a side of life from which I had been sheltered until then: movies and the theater. But as the ten-hour stretches of duty reeled by, sometimes on days and sometimes on nights, I found that physical weariness began to take a spiritual toll. My Bible lay unopened for days at a time.

My testimony lost its sparkle, and that vital contact with Jesus Christ had gone. I was spiritually dry—dry and thirsty, yet aloof and self-sufficient, too proud to ask for help. Was not I looked up to as one who was going to China as a missionary? How could I admit defeat?

At last, the day came when I received the coveted S.R.N. (State Registered Nurse) diploma. Six months and twenty baby deliveries later, I won the hard-earned S.C.M. (State Certified Midwife). This had meant living at the end of a phone, dashing out on my bicycle at midnight, climbing tenement stairs, and then delivering a baby. And always I lived with the nagging worry that all was not well with my soul. (Did I secretly hope that my parents were praying for me in far-off Tientsin? Perhaps they could read between the lines of my letters.)

There followed some interesting experiences in private nursing. I also made more money than I had ever seen before. It was while I was looking after a private patient that my brother John wrote, inviting me to stay at the Scottish University house party at the Keswick Convention. I grasped eagerly at this opportunity. If anything could help me find my way back to God, surely this was it. Immediately I wrote to say yes.

The beauty of the Lake District where the Convention is held each year, and being with my brothers again, did something for me. Added to that was the stimulus of living with a group of keen Christians. It opened my eyes to my own need of spiritual renewal. The very first night in the big tent on July 19, Mr. Lindsay Glegg spoke to the huge crowd. His subject was SIN. The Holy Spirit was already working in my heart, and as I listened I knew his message was for me. He described my state of mind exactly: dissatisfaction, unhappiness, insecurity, questioning, cut off from fellowship with God.

"Young man, young woman," he cried, "if this is your experience tonight then there is some hindrance between you and God. When you leave this tent, go to a quiet place, get down on your knees, and ask Him to show you what it is. Don't let anything stop you from getting right with the One who loves you so much."

Stillness reigned in the tent; the Holy Spirit was there. Quietly the big crowd filed out. My own heart was heavy, and conviction from the Spirit bore in upon me. I *must* talk to God—that very night. Quickly I ran to my room, knelt by my bed, and waited for God's finger to uncover the hindrance. He exposed this sin and that, and probed ever deeper.

Eventually, I saw myself as God saw me—concentrating on *my* plans, *my* time, *and my* ideas. Yes, I was going to China as a missionary, but with the society of *my* choice, and after I had earned a lot more money. As God revealed my self-will, I confessed I had wanted to be the architect of my own life, asked His forgiveness, and committed myself to Him in totality. A wonderful release came. The responsibility passed from me to Him forever! I was free!

The Missionary Meeting was held near the end of the week, and the chairman asked those who were ready to obey God and trust their future to Him to stand. Many young people rose to their feet, I among them. This was my solemn affirmation before God's people of the committal I had made just a few days before.

As the meeting ended, Mr. Aldis, the Home Director of the China Inland Mission (CIM) and a friend of our family, came up and shook hands. "It was good to see you standing with the others, Miriam," he said quietly. "God must have been speaking to you. Do you know what He wants you to do?"

His kind inquiry broke me up. I, who never cried, and prided myself on my self-control, burst into tears. All the pent-up feelings boiled out. He led me to a nearby chair, and sat beside me with his hand on my arm until I grew quieter. I told him the story of my spiritual failure, my unhappiness, my repentance, and my desire to serve God for the rest of my life.

"I have just the verse for you," Mr. Aldis said. "Perhaps you know it. It is found in the book of Joel, and seems to fit your situation exactly: 'I will restore to you the years that the locust hath eaten.' I wonder what your next step will be."

"If they'll have me, I am going to apply to the CIM," I replied.

His face broke into a beaming smile. "Good! I was hoping you'd say that. I think you'd better write to Miss Bond at Aberdeen Park as soon as you get back to London. It's best to keep moving with God. Here is the address." And with a twinkle in his eyes he handed me a card and said goodbye.

That is how I, who had made up my mind long ago *never* to join the China Inland Mission, went to the Ladies' Training Home in London. God had His way, and this was it.

Chapter Seven

Have faith in God.
Mark 11:22 KJV

SET IN A redbrick building in Newington Green, darkened by London's smoke and grime, is a narrow archway. It spans the entrance to the London Headquarters of the CIM, built in 1895. Behind it looms the big old-fashioned house, which for many years has been the hub of our mission in England. Above the door of the Prayer Hall a short sentence from the New Testament is carved in stone: *HAVE FAITH IN GOD.* It throws out a challenge to the materialism of the twentieth century.

This truth—of simple faith in a mighty God—became real to Hudson Taylor, the founder of the China Inland Mission, even before he went to China as a missionary. He proved that God, in answer to the prayer of faith, miraculously supplied his various needs. Therefore, when he founded the CIM in 1865, he and those who joined him laid their lives on the line as far as this principle was concerned. For those of us who were now in training, this text was a constant reminder of the steadfast faithfulness of God, and the wonderful heritage of the past. We too learned new lessons of faith and trust. We also were to see God provide for us in many ways.

The Ladies' Training Home was situated in a quiet backwater called Aberdeen Park, about half a mile from Newington Green. In Hudson Taylor's day, there were no Bible schools; all new missionaries were given Bible instruction and practical training in the London headquarters before being sent out to China. This practice was still followed in 1938, and the training periods normally lasted two years, although exceptions were made. The group that I joined that fall turned out to be the last one to live in A.P. (as Aberdeen Park was affectionately referred to): World War II brought drastic changes.

Miss Bond was our spiritual leader, appointed to train and discipline the women candidates. We learned to get up when the bell rang at six, have our daily quiet time, shut doors quietly, be punctual, and finish all the food served on our plates. She initiated us into the practice of tithing: one-tenth of *everything* we were given, whether in money or in kind, should be set aside for God's use. She guided us in our times of prayer. She gave us much information about China and its customs. She was tough with herself and expected us to exercise the same self-discipline. Her brown eyes were sympathetic behind her glasses, but she did not find it easy to communicate. Because of this, it took time for me to love and appreciate her. When I did, I found her a faithful friend and prayer partner.

Working with her that year was Miss Jessie Gregg, a vivacious, white-haired dynamo of seventy years. She was amazingly young in heart, and provided the balance needed against Miss Bond's more strict and intense way of life. Often at meals, gales of laughter would explode from Miss Gregg's table. At other times, there would be deep silence as she told us some of the fantastic miracles God performed in 1900 during the Boxer uprising, when many missionaries were killed.

Miss Gregg's greatest treasure was a pair of rather coarse white cotton stockings. In them, she had walked for many weeks during her flight on foot from Boxer killers. Yet the stockings did not have one hole. God had literally given to her the same wonderful provision experienced by the children of Israel in Deuteronomy 8:4: "Your clothing did not wear out."

Another story she told us took place many years later, when God sent her all over China as an evangelist to Chinese women. One day, brigands stopped her and her companion. There was no human help available. As the men began acting in an obnoxious way, she heard a voice say, "Take the hairpins out of your hair." She looked around but could see no one. Again the voice came, "Take the hairpins out of your hair." Suddenly, she realized it was God speaking, and she asked, "But, Lord, whatever for? What good will that do?" "Just do as I say," came the reply. So rather reluctantly, for it seemed such a stupid thing to do, she took off her hat and removed her hairpins one by one. Her white hair cascaded around her shoulders, a shining cloud. To her amazement, the men took up their guns and slunk away.

Stories such as these stimulated our faith in the power of the Lord, and only served to emphasize that I was not living in a different world. Instead of scurrying from bed to bed in a hospital ward, I found I had to adjust to life at a measured tempo, with quiet mornings given to study and prayer. Mr. Hogben, in a classroom in Newington Green, gave lectures. He was a fine Bible teacher, and made us dig into the Word for ourselves in order to find answers to the questions he set. In class, he would call on first one, then another, to read our answers. It was the way in which he did this that sent some of us into a mental tailspin.

"Perhaps Miss – er – er – Ammonds will give us her answer to Question one," he would say. During that excruciating pause we would all wonder whose name he would call!

Other men on the Home Staff taught us the principles which, under God, Hudson Taylor had incorporated into the warp and woof of the CIM. One was the extremely wise and unusual decision to establish the International Headquarters on the field (at that time in Shanghai). Another was the Biblical structure of "leader" and "team members": God would guide us through the mission directors. Yet another related to the pooling of all funds, which meant that the General Director and the newest member were on par as far as income was concerned.

I found that the CIM was a mission composed of men and women drawn from different denominations, but all desirous of communicating God's message of salvation to the Chinese people. I also discovered that this mission was not purely English. The first term, I shared a room with a Norwegian girl and a German girl. They and a few others in the house were members of European Associate Missions of the CIM. They had come to London Headquarters to learn English, not to do Bible study. Their language difficulties caused us to become sensitive to, and thoughtful of, the needs of others. The German sisters wore long, black, belted dresses and starched white bonnets, but underneath the uniforms we found they were as human as we were. Their presence opened windows on another world. One thing we could not understand was their loyalty to Hitler, in spite of his treatment of Jews. Politics became taboo.

Each week had its schedule. Knocking on doors and sharing Jesus with strangers was completely foreign to my personality, and something that I did not find easy. But it brought its own reward. Speaking at women's meetings was also a new experience, where the apathy to spiritual things chilled us. One thing I did enjoy was my Sunday school class of girls, especially when two of them opened their hearts to Christ.

For various reasons—the imminence of war, my Christian background, my age—it was suggested that I study for only one year. So in the late spring of 1939, I joined the hopeful, apprehensive, and excited group waiting to be interviewed by the men of the Home Council. As my surname began with T, I was at the end of the queue.

At last it was my turn. I entered the council room in a bad state of nerves, which Mr. Aldis did his best to dissipate. He invited me to sit down at the huge oval table around which sat the elderly men who, under God's guidance, decided the fate of the CIM candidates: to sail for China or remain at home.

To my relief, they threw no doctrinal questions at me. Instead, I was asked about my call to serve God in China, my memories of that land, and the work my parents were doing. Their sympathy and understanding steadied me for the decision that would set the direction of my life.

Afterwards, as we waited outside for the verdict (which we knew would be much prayed over), Margery, another candidate, told us her experience. "They asked me if I had read the Bible right through, and when I said I had started this term, one of them really embarrassed me with the question: 'How far have you read it, Miss Sykes?' I had to admit that I'd just finished Genesis 8. You should have seen them grinning at each other!"

Not long afterwards, we found we had all been accepted, and

could anticipate sailing later in the year. This was the early summer of 1939, and rumors of war filled the air.

Miss Bond had suggested that we exercise faith and ask God to supply the money for our passage to Shanghai, and also some extra money for incidentals along the way—approximately forty dollars. I regularly prayed about this, and was excited when gifts began to come in. But one day I suddenly realized that I had not tithed all the money friends had sent, and if I were to give God His due, the remainder would be pretty small. The temptation to do nothing was fierce; I needed that precious money! But the Lord kept nudging me about Hudson Taylor's motto: "Have faith in God." So I sent off my love gift to the Bible Society. Immediately, more gifts flowed in, and by the time I finally left England, my passage was paid and I also had just over the extra forty dollars I had been asking God for.

Chapter Eight

Thy Maker is thine husband.
Isaiah 54:5 KJV

ONE OF THE members of the Keswick Scottish house party
referred to earlier was a young doctor, an accepted candidate
of the China Inland Mission. During the week of my spiritual and
emotional upheaval, we were attracted to each other. One evening,
walking beside the softly moving waters of the lake, love came to
us. For me this was the over-and-above of God's grace. All mundane
things were touched with gold. Life was exhilarating, and seemed to
stretch before us in the brightness of joy.

However, we soon came to earth with a bump. The CIM kindly
but firmly explained their current marriage policy for new workers.
As my acceptance into the Mission was still a matter of doubt at that
time, there could be no firm engagement. *He* would sail for China
as planned that fall, and *I* would enter the Ladies' Training Home
at Aberdeen Park. After my year of study and training, the London
Council would interview me. If they accepted me, our engagement
could be announced.

A year! A whole twelve months! Could we wait that long? We
prayed about it together, and decided that God wanted us to abide by
the CIM ruling. This was difficult for us, but we had some halcyon
days together before he left for China with the other new workers.

Then I entered the doors of the Training Home with its virginal
atmosphere. I had to adjust to his physical absence and the deep

41

trauma of loneliness. However, there were letters to keep us in touch; I waited impatiently for them. They came regularly, and mine went back in answer. For some time this pattern continued. Then my lovely world fell apart.

Returning from an afternoon of visitation, as usual my glance went first to the bench in the hall where incoming letters were placed. There lay a square white envelope with a Chinese stamp, and the loved handwriting.

"Oh, look!" I cried to Emma. "A letter for me."

Snatching it quickly, I ran upstairs to the room I shared with three other girls. Throwing my hat on the bed, I sank into a nearby chair and held the precious letter in my hands, anticipating the love it contained. I ripped open the envelope and started to read the closely written pages. The first few paragraphs told of his life in Chefoo, and language study. Then my heart seemed to stop. What was he saying? It could not be true!

"I have had time to think and pray ... I feel there has been undue haste in our engagement ... It would be better to revert to being friends ... Then we can see more clearly what God has for us ..."

Friends! How could we be just friends? I loved him deeply, with a girl's first love. But as I read and reread the letter, it became obvious to me that his feelings were different. As the reality of this hit me, I grew numb.

God mercifully dulled the deepest grief of those days in later months, but at the time it was all too real—stabbing at my heart. Soon all the girls knew, and showed their loving sympathy in various ways. I rebelled. I did not want their sympathy; I wanted my love again. I was miserable and unhappy. It was unfair that this should happen to me. Just a week or so earlier, his photograph had come in the mail, smiling at me. In my drawer were the precious letters he had written. As I read parts of them again, the knife turned in my heart. How could I give him up? What could I do? God had let me down.

I was deep in a morass of self-pity, then I was shown a solution. It was drastic; it was bitter; but it was effective. The photograph was wrapped up and mailed back to Scotland. The letters were burned to ashes in the basement stove. Nothing remained—except memories.

It is strange, but in all honesty I cannot pinpoint any special word of comfort that God gave me during those days when my hurt was deepest. I knew prayer surrounded me, but I often felt that *I* could not pray. Why had God let this happen to me? He knew my loneliness, my separation from home, my shyness. And then this tearing hurt had come after such deep joy and the experience of spiritual renewal.

One day Miss Gregg invited me to her room. "Miriam, we have been praying for you these weeks," she said. "We know what a shock this has been. Now I want to share with you some of God's dealings with me.

"Many years ago, when I longed for human love, God spoke to my heart through His Word. The message He brought to my notice was this verse in Isaiah 54:5. Read it to me, will you?"

Sharing her Bible, I read, "Thy Maker is thine husband."

"Yes," she said slowly, "God showed me that day that He loved me more than any man could, and He wanted all of my heart. Foolishly, I did not surrender at once. I wanted my own way. But the day came when I said, 'Thank You, Lord, for Your love. You have said You are my Husband. Thank You, thank You.'"

Dear Miss Gregg! The tears misted her blue eyes as she lived those days again. She took out her hanky and blew her nose noisily. The creases deepened in her lined old face as she smiled at me. Her silver hair gleamed in the pale London sunshine.

"And He's just the same today, my dear, as He was then. What He did for me He can do for you. All He wants is your trust and your love."

We knelt beside her bed together, the experienced old missionary and the young candidate with the aching heart. God was with us, His love around us, and peace flowed in.

Chapter Nine

He blessed and broke the loaves.
Mark 6:41 (KJV)

DURING THE TROUBLED summer of 1939, I was busy saying goodbye to friends and packing my trunks. Neville Chamberlain's earlier conciliation with Hitler at Munich had brought an uneasy peace, but as to how it would all end, I gave little thought. My little world revolved around the conviction that God was taking me to China.

On August 16, I jumped off the bus at Newington Green and turned under the brick archway. Facing me were those stirring words: *HAVE FAITH IN GOD.* My ticket to Shanghai had been bought. My trunks were on the ship, and I was due to sail from Southampton in three days' time.

It was Wednesday, and that evening the usual weekly prayer meeting was being held. Mr. Baker, the leader that night, had asked me to give my testimony, and at the end of the service, I would be received into the membership of the China Inland Mission. I was thinking about what I would say, and was bubbling over with an inner excitement because the door to China was swinging widely open. God had heard my prayers: this was it. Thus I was totally unprepared for what followed.

As I walked up the office steps, white-haired Mr. Martin called me into his room. "Miriam," he said, "I'm afraid I've got some bad news for you. A cable arrived from Shanghai only this morning. It read: NO NEW RECRUITS THIS YEAR. I'm sorry this has come just now, but we feel we cannot let you sail this week."

Not go to China? My exciting dreams collapsed in shreds around me. What was God doing? How could I go back and tell my friends that everything was off? Mr. Martin's quiet voice went on, trying to soften the blow. But the words drummed over and over in my mind: "Not sail. No new recruits this year." I fumbled in my bag for my handkerchief as tears of disappointment filled my eyes.

"It's a quarter to six, Miriam. Do you want to go to the meeting?"

The late afternoon sun shone outside, and the sky was still blue. Had only half an hour passed since I had walked so happily under the archway? Those carved words mocked me now. Could I face the friendly, sympathetic faces, the warm handclasps? Or should I quietly make my way home?

"If you feel able, I think it would be good to stay," the kind voice continued. "God will give His balm and His guidance. You are His child."

So I tidied myself and crept into a seat at the back of the rather crowded hall, sad and dispirited. Mr. Baker led the meeting. Speaking was not his forte, and I wondered if, at this stage, I could bear to hear his hesitant delivery. He talked about Jesus feeding the five thousand. As he slowly enunciated his words, my attention was caught—and held—for God was speaking to my need.

"The loaves were broken in Christ's hands before they could be given to the hungry people," he said. "Today the Lord breaks His children— in heart, in plan, in ambition—before they can be used by Him to feed the needy."

Broken—by Christ—that others might be blessed. This was His word for me that hot August afternoon: "My child, the breaking is in *My* hands. Can't you trust Me?"

When the meeting was over, I climbed into a bus and sank onto a seat. Stopping and starting, stopping and starting, I was carried on my way: disappointed, yet comforted; sad, yet at peace.

The very next day a letter came from an ex-patient with an enclosure of two hundred dollars to pay for my fare to China. It was the biggest gift I had received. Did this mean that God wanted me to go forward on my own? After all, my passage was booked. I phoned the CIM, and they left the decision to me. However, as I prayed, I felt I should stay.

Perhaps I realized that the breaking process was not finished. My trunks were retrieved from the ship and delivered back to Newington Green.

Some days later a cable came from my parents, which drove me to God in shame for my lack of trust. There had been a flare-up of anti-British feeling in Peking, and foreigners had been advised to leave the capital. Dad and Mother had had to evacuate their home and move temporarily to our summer bungalow in Pei Tai Ho.

This was another lesson I needed to learn: God's power and foreknowledge. If He had not kept me in England when He did, I would have landed in China in the midst of a tense situation.

Chapter Ten

Present thyself approved unto God, a workman.
II Timothy 2:15 KJV

SEPTEMBER 3, 1939—the beautiful, bright Sunday morning when England declared war on Germany. I was staying with an aunt and uncle in Folkestone at the time, as the Mission had canceled the fall term, though they hoped classes would start again soon.

That morning I had gone to church alone. Rumors were rife, and everyone was wondering when and how the war would come. During the service, the churchwarden handed a slip of paper to the vicar. He read it and walked slowly to the pulpit. He told us that an announcement had just been made over the radio of England's entry into the conflict against Germany.

"We are at war," he said solemnly. "Let us pray."

As we rose from our knees, the eerie, warbling note of an air-raid siren knifed into the silence of God's house. It rose and fell in sickening, awe-inspiring cadence. The vicar quietly dismissed the congregation and we hurried out. People were in the streets, peering at the sky, but no planes could be seen. Soon the all-clear signal rang out and tenseness eased. Hurriedly, I made my way home. I wanted to be with my own folk if danger came.

Twice that night, the wail of sirens split the darkness. My pulse quickened when I heard it, my throat tightened, and sleep fled. The next day, I traveled up to London. Everywhere, there was evidence of war. In the sky, hundreds of barrage balloons bloomed like silver flowers, protecting this vital city against Nazi bombs. Sandbags were piled in front of important buildings; air-raid wardens in tin hats were on duty. Many men were in uniform; all carried bulky gas masks. The war, long dreaded, had come at last, and no one knew what lay ahead.

I made my way to my old hospital, University College, and joined the Civil Nursing Reserve. They directed me to the Mildmay Mission Hospital, known for its evangelistic outreach in the East End of London. During a ward service one day, God's message came to me: "A workman for God."

I was later posted to a small country hospital, and found that God had many new and different kinds of work for me to do: pasting paper strips on windows to prevent the glass from splintering in air raids; witnessing to other members of staff about God's faithfulness; taking prayers in the ward occasionally; coping with a sudden emergency hemorrhage; starting a small Bible study group; adapting to rationing of sugar and butter; traveling in London's blackout. I lived through high peaks of excitement some days, and low dips of monotony on others.

Being in the country, I was thankful for the delightful bonus of living near fields and woods. Glimpses of God's handiwork in nature, made all the more precious in contrast to the stark and terrible news that came from the war fronts in a mounting crescendo of horror, embroidered my days.

Fall: Pale silver birches, green lichened oak, golden beech, and a carpet of tawny leaves gleaming in pallid sunshine.

October 14—Tragic loss of the *Royal Oak* with nine hundred men on board.

Winter: Full moon shining through the lacework of leafless trees. A rising sun gilding the edges of dark storm clouds. Hoarfrost sparkling on every twig and branch. Snow blushing pink under the sun's kiss. I was reminded of Psalm 147:16: "God giveth snow like wool: He scattereth the hoarfrost like ashes."

December 2—Russia invaded tiny Finland.

March 13—The intrepid Finns capitulated at noon.

Spring: Sunshine, blue sky, snowdrops, crocuses, green spearheads of grass. Wild daffodils dancing beneath silver birches in Knighton Wood under a crimson sunset sky. Bluebells at Kew, a carpet of misty blue, beneath beech trees clothed in new green leaves.

April 9—Germany invaded Norway and Denmark.

May 10—Invasion of Holland and Belgium. Hundreds of civilians die.

Chamberlain resigns. Churchill becomes Prime Minister!

May 15—Capitulation of Holland after five days of heroic fighting.

On March 4, a letter from Mr. Hogben brought the unexpected news that a fresh term was starting in Newington Green on April 11, and I was invited to attend. I hoped this meant that the CIM was planning to send out new missionaries in spite of the war.

The very first day of the term, Mr. Aldis called me into his office. He said the General Director in Shanghai had agreed that I could sail as soon as possible. But there was a snag: I could not travel alone, and no one was returning to China in the foreseeable future. He suggested I pray about this and that the provision of a fellow traveler would be God's seal of approval on my sailing.

Days passed. I prayed and waited for news. However, Mr. Hogben gave us no idle moments. He kept the assignments rolling—Daniel, James, Hosea, Genesis, and Peter. Besides this Bible work there were Chinese characters to learn and messages to be prepared and given at weekends. We were kept on our toes and scarcely had time to think of anything else, which was a good thing.

On April 18, Mr. Aldis told me of two possible escorts for the journey, and at the same time my parents wrote suggesting yet another. Things were moving. That evening my roommate and I prayed together about my sailing. "Dear Lord," prayed Emma, "we thank You for the three 'hopes' we have of someone to travel with Miriam. We do pray that You will guide to the right one." *Amen!* I agreed. "But, Lord," she continued, "if none of these is the right one, then please make it very clear to Mr. Aldis and others who have to make this decision. We look to You to overrule, and ask this in Your name and for Your glory. Amen."

I could not truthfully say "Amen" to that prayer! This would be throwing all my chances away. *One of the three must be the one*, I thought. As I snuggled beneath the blankets, I was rather disappointed in Emma.

However, God's Spirit had indeed guided her. One by one, the "hopes" fell through, and I realized how futile it was to trust in man's plans. Four days later, Mr. Aldis told me that Miss Isabel Smith had been cleared to sail for China. She was willing to sail any time! The date was set for the end of May. A cable telling the good news went off to my parents, who were now back in Peking. When God's time came, things moved smoothly.

PART IV

Missionary Beginnings
1940

Chapter 11

What time I am afraid, I will trust in Thee.
Psalm 56:3 KJV

I WAS DEEPLY happy at the thought of sailing for China, and had a hectic time preparing to leave. All my notes, photos, and printed material had to be taken to the censor in Pall Mall for approval before they could be packed: just another reminder that England was at war. Coupons made purchasing of clothing and bedding difficult. Blackout conditions discouraged evening travel. Gas masks had to be carried everywhere.

But in spite of all the activity, there was one paralyzing fear at the back of my mind. It threatened to overwhelm me and was outside my power to control. Submarines were sinking British ships, and between China and me lay thousands of miles of ocean. As I thought of this, and of the hazards involved, my imagination began to play havoc with my faith in God's power. I could almost feel the quiver of the ship as torpedoes struck. I gasped as the icy gray water of the Atlantic swept over me. I sank down, down, down into the ocean, my lungs bursting, my eyes stinging. The final terror came when I could no longer hold out and the salty water poured in and drowned me! I prayed, but it seemed to make no difference. As the weeks passed, this fear grew to outsized proportions. I mentioned it as a matter of urgency to some praying friends (Miss Bond and Mrs. Bird were among them), but still the fear was there, waiting to pounce in an unguarded moment.

On May 22, 1940, I finally became a full member of the China

Inland Mission. It was a thrilling moment. When I looked at my membership card later, I found a text written on the back by Mr. Aldis: "What time I am afraid, I will trust in Thee." This came as a new thought. God did not expect me *not* to fear. He knew me and my imagination through and through. But He did expect me to trust Him *in* my fear.

Three days later I boarded a gray, blacked-out, nameless ship with Miss Smith, my elderly traveling companion, to sail for China via Canada. The first few days were tense. The crew would not tell us a thing. We could be headed north, south, east, or west! But on May 27, news percolated through the ship that we had finally left English waters and were zigzagging westward. That day I wrote in my diary: "Really on the way now and no turning back. We carry life belts with us everywhere, even to the dining room. There is a feeling of tension and unrest, and many are fearful of submarines. God has taken my fear away." Yes, God had given peace, and it was amazing to me. As opportunity offered, I was able to share this with others. His power was real.

On the 28th, the news of Belgium's capitulation was a shock to us all. News bulletins were broadcast from London two or three times a day, and always the lounge was crowded with anxious passengers: men and women fleeing from the horrors of war, refugees from Nazi cruelty looking for a new life, missionaries returning to lands of the East via Canada because submarines lurked in sea lanes south of England. We all strained to hear that voice from the BBC, hope or fear mirrored in our faces. Daily, Miss Smith and I prayed together in our small cabin.

When the glory and tragedy of Dunkirk hit the headlines, our gray ship was sailing into the mouth of the St. Lawrence River. The first part of the ocean voyage was safely over. That night, in towns along the riverbank, we saw our first lights gleaming in the darkness since the war started eight months earlier. We thanked God for His care.

After a few days in Toronto, we boarded the Canadian Pacific Railway train for Vancouver, and cooked our meals in the tiny kitchen in the tourist coach. We were amazed and rather dismayed by the unending, bare flatness of the wide-spreading prairies, but exhilarated by the grandeur of the Rockies.

On the morning of June 10, a railway official entered the coach. "News has just come through," he announced, "that Italy has entered the war on the side of Germany!"

We looked at each other, aghast. Then a buzz of excited comment erupted as he walked down the aisle to make the same announcement in the next coach.

In Vancouver more bad news flashed over the air: Paris had fallen to the Nazis! Our world seemed to be falling apart. But God's Word brought comfort, "What time I am afraid, I will trust in Thee."

On June 15, we embarked on another gray ship, the *Empress of Asia*. Plowing through the sea-green waters of the Pacific with a few passengers, we sailed steadily westward. Bulletins were posted twice a day. News grew progressively ominous. Finally, on Sunday morning, the 23rd, we heard that France had signed an armistice with Germany, handing over her fleet, munitions, and the use of all her ports to Hitler. England stood alone.

My voyage ended temporarily at Yokohama, Japan. Here my parents met me. There was so much to share with them—my broken engagement, conditions in England, news of my sister and brothers who were all studying there. It was good to be able to talk face to face after years of writing letters. We had a wonderful vacation— viewing the Daibutsu statue in Kamakura, walking through Nikko's marvelously carved temples, sitting on the floor in a restaurant eating sukiyaki (a tasty Japanese dish), sailing on beautiful Lake Hakone, and traveling through the Inland Sea dotted with islands of all shapes and sizes.

July 12 saw me home in Peking at last, thankful to God for His many mercies and for His faithfulness. The long, dangerous journey was over. God's hand had guided and His love surrounded me. The verse from the Psalms, written by David many centuries earlier under the guidance of the Holy Spirit, had more than met my need in 1940.

Chapter Twelve

Behold, I will do a new thing... I will even make a way
in the wilderness and rivers in the desert.
Isaiah 43:19 KJV

WHEN I ARRIVED in the temporary Language School in Tsingtao on October 3, I found the above verse on my desk. That afternoon everything was new, exciting, and a bit overpowering, but for the first time I felt I was really in the CIM.

Dad and I had left Peking early the day before, traveling south by train to Tsinan. There we had changed trains at nine that evening, and spent the night trying to sleep sitting up in a jolting carriage, suitcases under heads, and our legs curled around a few more. We were rather bleary-eyed when the train eventually pulled into the Tsingtao station.

Normally, the Ladies' Training Home and Language School was located in Yangchow, not far from Shanghai, while the men went to Anking. But since the 1937 "China Incident," conditions had been very unsettled. Fighting flared sporadically between the short, squat soldiers of Nippon and the ragtag army of Chiang Kai Shek. Our CIM leaders decided that the new lady recruits should go to Tsingtao, living in the family home of Betty (Scott) Stam. This seaside town, with its backdrop of hills, is situated on the southern edge of the Shantung peninsula, which juts into the Yellow Sea like the head of a puppy. On the northern edge, just about where the puppy's eyes would be, is Chefoo. The Men's Training Home had been transferred there two years earlier, near the Chefoo School for missionaries' children.

That same October day of my arrival, the 1940 group of North American girls sailed into the Tsingtao harbor, traveling third class on a coastal steamer from Shanghai. There were ten of them plus nine other missionaries. Six droskies (horse-drawn carriages), piled high with ninety-nine pieces of luggage, labored up to number sixteen Hsien Yang Road in the Iltis Huk area. Confusion and disorder followed as the girls and coolies poured into the house and then fanned out to different rooms. Little did I dream that day that the coming of this group was to have unthought-of repercussions in my own life. God's "new thing" was beginning.

One "new thing" was the serious study of the Chinese language, which began almost immediately, and which I thoroughly enjoyed. Having been born in China, the soft *shih* and *hsu* sounds held no difficulty for me, nor did the rhythm. But the tones wore me down. We were each given a big red *Matthew's Kuoyu Primer*. Lesson 1 contained our first vocabulary, two columns of Chinese characters, giving sounds and meaning. The first class with my teacher was fun. Mr. Chao was a born actor. Hands, shoulders, facial expressions—all were thrown into the battle to enlighten my understanding of things Chinese. Day after day, instruction continued. Gradually, the tones came more naturally, words and phrases fell into the right order, and comprehension grew. But always there was new vocabulary to master, new combinations of characters to learn, and flash cards to prepare ad infinitum.

On October 30, the first party of my friends from England arrived by ship from Shanghai. I did not realize how homesick I was for English voices until then, nor how I was longing to hear news from England firsthand about how England was suffering under Nazi bombs and gradually being strangled by the torpedo war.

The big piece of news they brought, which was to have an immediate impact on us all, was a decision recently made by the China Council of the CIM—new lady workers for the first time for many years were not to remain at the coast for language study, but were to travel at once into inland China. One reason for this was the deterioration of the political situation. American Consuls had already circulated notices warning their citizens to prepare for evacuation. The Japanese were getting more and more autocratic in their areas of civil occupation (of which Tsingtao was one). Japanese armies were on the move in many areas, and the future was extremely uncertain.

Group after small group of new missionaries and their senior escorts soon began to move out from the comparative comfort and stability of Tsingtao into the fluid military and political situation of the hinterland. We newcomers did not realize the possible danger. To us it was an exciting adventure.

When the security of the coastal administration was left behind, unknown factors loomed large: bandits, uncooperative officials (Japanese or Chinese), political changes, and physical danger. Doors into the interior were closing, leaving only one route into Anhwei and Honan provinces. It was along this way that the various parties traveled by rail and boat into Free China. Yet we believed this decision was from God and that we could leave the working out of it all to Him.

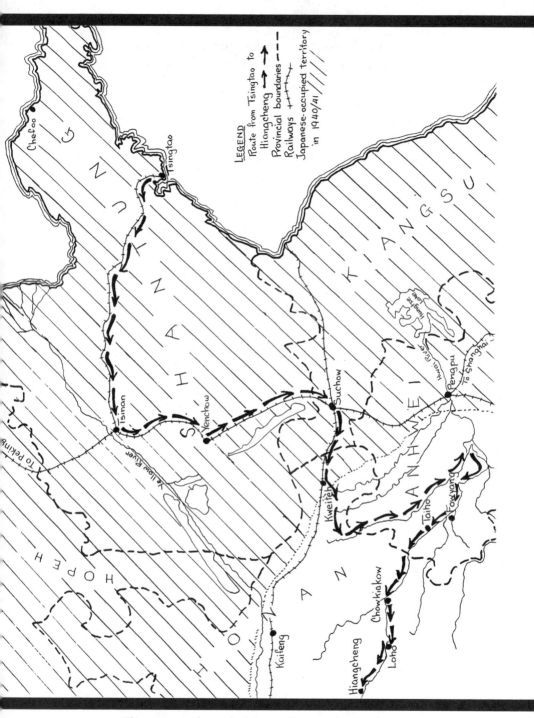

LEGEND
Route from Tsingtao to
Hiangcheng
Provincial boundaries
Railways
Japanese-occupied territory
in 1940/41

*This map was drawn by Miriam Dunn indicating her
travels as a single woman when first returning to China,
the land of her birth, as a missionary in 1940.*

Chapter Thirteen

Behold, I have set before thee a door
opened, which none can shut.
Revelation 3:8 ASV

NEARLY ALL MY former friends from England had come and gone. As I had begun my Chinese studies with the American girls, it was decided that I should remain with them and head for the small Language School in Honan where Henry and Mary Guinness were to be in charge. As I have already mentioned, there was now only one travel route by which missionaries could enter the interior. The Japanese had closed all others. To avoid a concentration of Caucasians in the small town where Japanese jurisdiction ended, the travelers left Tsingtao in small parties. Only as one group was given permission to pass into Free China did the next group leave Tsingtao. A bottleneck could have built up otherwise, raising suspicion in the minds of Japanese officials, and causing the one vital escape route to snap shut.

I did not find the waiting easy and began to chafe at the delay. On December 13, God gave me the above message during my quiet time. I believed something was going to happen. That very day a telegram came saying the previous group had left the small town of Kweiteh. This was the signal we were waiting for.

Two days later, we boarded the train to begin our six-week trek inland. We were dressed in long wadded gowns, such as the Chinese wore, to identify with the people and to keep warm. Miss Standen, our escort, was a gentle, white-haired lady, my ideal of a missionary.

We were thankful to reach Kweiteh without incident. Here we switched from train travel to rickshaw cart, an ingenious Chinese contraption. The comfortable upright seat had been removed from the rickshaw frame and replaced by an oblong, slatted wooden structure attached to the axle of the big wheels. Shafts were fastened to one end of it, which were held by the puller, with the frame sloping backwards behind him. Usually these carts were loaded with merchandise, but they could also be adapted to carry people. Blue- and red-striped Chinese bedding rolls, six feet by eight feet, were part of a missionary's standard equipment for inland travel. With this folded and laid on the frame along with pillows and warm rugs, we traveled quite comfortably.

Winter weather meant cold winds and low temperatures. These were compensated by blue skies and bright sunshine. For the next three days, a string of thirteen carts swung out across the Honan plain to the accompaniment of Honan dust and the songs of Chinese carters.

Our passage through a village was the signal for every inhabitant, from grandpa to baby, to stand and stare. When we stopped to eat in the village inn, first the children, then the adults pressed in to watch us. Those who were unable to get inside spat on their fingers and rubbed spy holes in the paper windows.

On the third day of travel, the road had been dug up at intervals in an effort to prevent the Japanese army from advancing. This meant a long, hard pull for the carters.

The next leg of our journey was by boat, due to flooding ahead. Months before, the dikes along the Yellow River had been breeched by order of the Chinese High Command. Swirling, angry water had spilled out over the surrounding countryside, carrying destruction in its wake. What had been intended to hinder the enemy had backfired, for Chinese farmers suffered more than the Japanese. The entire course of the river was changed and vast areas of land flooded, necessitating the use of wooden boats for transportation.

It was dark when we finally reached our destination of Shih Tzu Ho. Heavy rain was falling. This did not dampen the cheerful spirits of our carters who unloaded the vehicles by the light of oil lanterns and flashlights. Slipping and sliding down the muddy bank, they hauled our boxes and trunks to the two boats that had been hired for our travel. First, the holds were packed with our boxes with yellow waterproof oilcloth spread over them. Then the boards that formed the decks of our craft were pushed into place. When all was shipshape, we literally crawled into our cabin: three girls into a space six feet long, three feet wide, and two and a half feet high.

The next day it was decided to hire another boat, and the cabin of this one was twice as large: six feet long, seven feet wide, and three feet high, and five of us girls found that it could be made quite comfortable with our soft bedding rolls. We had to wait for others to join our party and were glad to stretch our legs along the bank after the days of inactive cart travel.

The three boats finally set sail on Christmas Eve at three-thirty in the afternoon, loaded with thirteen passengers, their many boxes, and the crews and their families. Sometimes poling, sometimes hauling, we made ten miles that evening before tying up at a small market. After supper in an inn, the whole party gathered on the deck of our boat. Stars shone brightly in the winter sky. By the light of a storm lantern hung from the mast, we read the story of the first Christmas. It was most moving in such surroundings, and Jesus' presence was very near. The noises of boat life flowed around us, and dark water slapped against the boat's wooden sides.

Every day something new gripped our interest. One day when the wind was favorable, huge patched sails were raised. With much squeaking of gear, we fled swiftly upriver in bright sunshine. At other times, we were laboriously poled along near the bank. Sometimes we traveled to the creak and splash of oars as one man stood in the stern. Facing the way we were traveling, each sinewy hand grasped the short crosspieces at the ends of the long, wooden oars as he rowed the boat slowly forward.

At one stage of our journey, we heard that bandit-infested country lay ahead. For three days our boats and a number of others were tied together in midstream while we waited for an escort of armed soldiers to scare off any would-be attackers.

It was during this waiting period that God impressed the following two "happenings" indelibly on my heart. They took place on Sunday, December 29, which was the first day of the last month of the Chinese year. (They calculate by the moon, so our calendars are different.)

The first episode underlined the fact that the fear and worship of evil spirits are woven into the very web of Chinese life. From many of the boats tied around us came sudden sharp bursts of sound as dozens of red Chinese firecrackers blazed out. This was a feast day. We watched with interest as the small son of the owner of the boat next to us made his way along the gently rocking deck. He wore thick-wadded clothes (as we also did), and in his hand he carried a square of burning yellow paper. When he reached the prow, he stood waving it to and fro. As it curled to ash, he threw it to the wind, which caught and flung it into the water. His other hand tightly clutched some sticks of burning incense. These he stuck in a special place in the prow, and as the blue smoke curled lazily into the air, he knelt and prostrated himself. Three times he banged his head against the deck. With his "worship" over, he jumped up, grinning in anticipation, to set off the firecrackers that would scare away the evil spirits.

The second incident followed later in the day, and illustrated to us our responsibility in communicating God's love. Miss Standen sat on the deck, the sun shining on her silvery hair, the love of Christ lighting up her face. Grouped around her were the boat people—men, women, and children, reminding us of the love Jesus Himself showed to fisher-folk. A man in front leaned forward, engrossed in the story of the Prodigal Son. Another forgot to pull on his long-stemmed bamboo pipe as he sat in the prow. Behind her were the women, the forgotten people of Chinese culture. One listened hungrily, her dark eyes fixed on Miss Standen's face. She had never heard this good news before. The children, with dirty noses and tousled hair, dressed in warm wadded outfits, squatted in front. That evening, too, by the light of a small vegetable oil lamp, the seed was sown in other hearts as Miss Standen visited the smoky, dark cabins at the stern of each boat. One woman believed! "Instant in season, out of season" took on a new meaning for us girls at the outset of our missionary careers.

On the last day of 1940 (I was twenty-seven years old), we slipped from our moorings with a following wind, each boat carrying a soldier with a gun. Ever since the inception of the CIM in 1865, Hudson Taylor had set aside December 31 as a day of prayer and fasting. (This is still a loved and honored tradition.) Following the pattern set so many years before, we had times of prayer and sharing in each crowded cabin that day. This first celebration in China, in such different surroundings, was most meaningful to us.

God took us safely through the Bad Lands, but we soon found that another danger awaited us. That afternoon, wicked white water swirled and tossed around our vessels. In these notorious rapids, some boats had sunk with all on board. But once again, God's hands kept us. He had opened the door before us, and He led us forward— over flooded country, through rapids, and against the pull of strong currents. He guarded us against brigands and the petty officialdom of men in uniform, watching over us by day and by night.

Chapter Fourteen

He shall be as the light of the morning when the sun
riseth, even a morning without clouds.
II Samuel 23:4 KJV

THOSE SEVENTEEN DAYS of boat travel were interesting, inconvenient, and exciting. We tried to do some language study, but it was not easy to concentrate with so many distractions. For instance, one day we saw men using cormorants to catch fish. They were black, ungainly birds with rings fastened around their necks to prevent them from swallowing the fish they caught. Instead, the men pulled the fish from their beaks and tossed them into a basket. Another day we noticed men dressed in skins standing in shallow water spearing the fish as they sped by.

Study suffered, but we learned how the Chinese people lived firsthand. We ate with chopsticks, though slippery, tasteless noodles were hard to manipulate. We managed to wash our hands and faces, but not much else. We tried to adjust to the very primitive sanitary conditions. We learned to wriggle in and out of our wadded gowns while lying in our low-roofed cabin. We sat out on deck in the sunshine when possible, and huddled in our blankets and *p'u-kais* (bedding rolls) when the winds blew cold.

The most precious memories were of our times of prayer together. Each evening, if at all possible, when the boats tied up in some village market for safety, we would crowd together on one of the boats for fellowship and sharing. We prayed for China's people, for the loved ones we had left behind, for war-torn England, for the places to which we were journeying, and for our Chinese studies.

On January 7, 1941, with a following wind, we sailed into the town of Chow Kia Kow in Free China. Our boat journey was over. When we climbed on shore we had to pass through customs, but there was no trouble. The next day came the great washing: hair, clothes, and bodies! We felt like new persons afterwards.

Our party broke up here. It was hard to say goodbye. Those of us going to Hiangcheng still had a few days' journey before us. This time we traveled in rickshaws, rather dilapidated but functional, and much more comfortable than the rickshaw carts. It was as we began our second day's journey that God's Word came alive to me again.

We started early that morning in the crispness of a new day. We followed a cobbled street through the ten-foot-high city gates and walked along a road that hugged the old stone wall. A waning moon, battling the faint luminescence of the dawn, softly lighted the sky.

Gradually the road sloped toward some temple buildings on the hill outside the city. As this was a famous place, and we had time to spare, we decided to look around. Within the encircling walls were ancient cypress trees, towering above the temple itself. Early though it was, incense was already burning. Ferocious-looking idols lined the smoke-blackened walls. One sensed the power of evil. A quick look around, and it was a relief to get out and breathe pure air again.

As we mounted the edge of the hill, the sun's rays blazed into our eyes. Immediately I remembered a verse I had read in *Daily Light* a few days earlier: "He shall be as the light of the morning when the sun riseth, even a morning without clouds." What a perfect illustration God gave me that morning. The contrast between the brilliant light of the sun and the smoky darkness of the temple, the beauty of the Lord and the fearsome idols fashioned by the hands of men.

My heart bowed in worship as we rode off in our rickshaws. Not only had He brought me out of the darkness of sin and death, but He had also called me into His service. The vision of His beauty filled my eyes, but at the same time the forces of evil had brazenly revealed their own spiritual power over souls in this land.

Chapter Fifteen

Even to old age I am He, and even to hoar
hairs will I carry you: I have made, and I will
bear; yes, I will carry, and will deliver.
Isaiah 46:4 ASV

HIANGCHENG WAS A large walled city, embracing many thousands of people. Narrow cobbled streets were lined with gray-tiled houses, huddled side by side. Each house was overcrowded, for mother and father, sons and daughters-in-law, and innumerable grandchildren seemed to live in each courtyard.

In one area, the tap-tap of hammers beating on metal told us that tinsmiths were plying their trade. Nearby, the smell of hot wax and the display of red or white candles indicated the candle makers' domain. The hum of sewing machines and snipping of scissors marked the section where tailors transacted business. Stalls, some hung with slabs of beef and pork, others overflowing with sweet potatoes, turnips, huge persimmons, and dried dates, outlined the marketplace. Each trade was confined to its own area, which we learned was a Chinese custom.

The CIM church and the big, double-story house in its walled compound had been erected in one of the suburbs across the river from the town. Here our temporary Language School was housed, with nine girls from North America and myself from England. From our upstairs rooms, we could look out over the flat Honan plain, dotted here and there with large clumps of trees that screened the homes of poor, hardworking peasants.

71

Three weeks after we had settled in, Japanese planes on silver wings zoomed out of the east to bomb our unsuspecting city. No reliable news had reached us that danger was pending, although every day rumors flew from mouth to mouth. Our first warning came when the deep notes of a huge brass gong, beaten in slow rhythm, floated across the river from the direction of the city wall.

"*Ching-pao! Ching-pao!*" (Air raid warning!), shouted one of the men in the compound. "That means that enemy planes are flying in this direction."

In a short time the rhythm of the alarm changed. "Bong! Bong! BONG!" it boomed in a quick, pulsating sound as the soldier suddenly hit it in furious haste.

"*Ching-chi!*" (Urgent warning!), came the shout. "Hurry, everyone! Get down into the cellar. Don't wait for anything."

Pell-mell, we scrambled from the rooms where we had been studying, down the stairs, out the back door, and down the cellar steps. All the time, the big gong roared its warning to people within sound of that frenzied hammering.

Our own hearts were thumping with excitement as we tried to find somewhere to sit. Outside the winter sun was shining, but inside all was gloomy and dirty. Suddenly, we heard the screaming engines of diving planes. The ground shook. Bombs were falling. The stone walls of the cellar did not look as thick and strong as we would have liked them to be. No "ack-ack" of anti-aircraft fire came to our ears. It was obvious that Japan's planes ruled the skies.

Eventually, the all-clear signal sounded and we stumbled out into the sunshine. Smoke hung over parts of the city. Some houses were in flames. But we, on the other side of the river, had escaped.

That evening rumors were rife. "The Japanese are on the run." "Planes will be bombing every day!" "The Chinese army is retreating." No one knew the truth. However, Chinese soldiers and their equipment were on the move. At night we could hear the rumbling wheels of their loaded wagons as the army trudged by. Evidently, Japanese intelligence knew these men were in our part of the province and the bombing was their answer.

The next day was quieter, but a spirit of unease pervaded the city and its suburbs. Once or twice we heard the sound of far-off planes, but none came our way. The Chinese said more bombing was inevitable, and it would be unsafe to stay at home. As Henry Guinness was away on an evangelistic trip, the responsibility of making decisions fell on Miss Standen and Miss Williamson. Some Chinese friends suggested that we should take shelter among the low hills that lay a few miles away. So at 9:45 the next morning, we set off with food and study books to spend the day there.

We were not alone in seeking refuge in the hills. Others walked with us. When seven planes suddenly appeared in the distance, flying in formation, we followed the example of our Chinese fellow travelers and flung ourselves in the ditches that lined the road. However, the planes flew on, and before we reached the hills, were dive-bombing our city. We saw smoke belching over the walls.

Most of the time we sat out in the sunshine trying to learn new words. When planes were heard, we hid in nearby caves. When the shadows lengthened and the sun dipped low, we packed up our books and hiked home. We learned that there had been little loss of life that day, as people had spewed out of the city when the alarm sounded. Wheelbarrows laden with household goods were pushed to the river's edge. Mule carts were impelled along the roads with whips and curses. However, many homes and shops had been hit.

The next day, we ate a very early breakfast and set off at dawn. Crimson clouds heralded the sun as we trekked to the hills. That day, only one plane flew over us to drop bombs on the city. With the sun setting in golden glory, we walked home. Henry had still not returned.

For a few days we followed this pattern. God kept us safe, though we felt very vulnerable whenever Japanese planes flew overhead. Sometimes we heard the staccato chatter of their guns as they swooped low, machine-gunning travelers on a nearby road. Sometimes it was the thud of bombs, falling near our city. But when military activity moved to another area, life in Hiangcheng resumed its normal course.

Later, conditions worsened again. A continuous stream of Chinese troops suddenly appeared, marching past our house and over the bridge, going north. Once again, rumors brought conflicting news, which steadily grew more serious. Our teacher fled with her family. Some doors on the compound were bricked up. Provisions were laid in. Prayer was made. Mr. Guinness felt that he should visit the single lady missionaries in small towns in his area: a visit from a man would be a shot in the arm for them, as they talked and prayed over the situation. Also, plans could be worked out in case of a possible Japanese takeover of their towns. So he set off, with his wife Mary willingly letting him go. Their self-sacrifice was always a challenge to me.

When he returned, he brought news of thousands of soldiers in the North, and rumors of further fighting. Things began to quiet down, and then suddenly flared again. Eight air-raid alarms in one day roused us to the fact that the tide of war was once again flowing in our direction. Two days later, a single bomber flew over, followed by nine planes a few hours later.

The gong beat its frenzied alarm. Once more, we fled to the coal cellar, and sat there in the dimness straining our ears. We could not see what was happening outside, but as the earth shuddered, we knew that death and destruction were raining from the sky. I felt helpless and afraid. The last time we had escaped. Was it asking too much of God to protect us again?

Suddenly a verse I had read in Isaiah that very morning came to my mind and I smiled. It was such an odd verse. It was not something I had specially noticed, nor was it familiar. Yet in that dark cellar God reminded me of it, and it did something for me. "Even to old age I am He, and even to hoar hairs will I carry you." I was young, not a gray hair on my head, but here was God promising me, "Don't be afraid, for I am going to watch over you until you are old and your brown hair turns to gray. I will deliver you." Amazingly, fear left me. God surely has His own ways of getting His message to those in trouble. When the all-clear signal sounded, I ran up the stairs to my room and underlined that verse in my Bible.

The next day one reconnaissance plane flew back and forth along the river. Chinese soldiers marched down from the north, winding below the city wall and across the stone bridge, silhouetted against the glowing river. Many were billeted all around us. They passed on. Conditions grew more normal. People who had fled returned back to their homes, and life resumed an even keel.

Chapter Sixteen

Come, my beloved, let us go forth into the
field; let us lodge in the villages.
Song of Solomon 7:11 KJV

WINTER WAS STILL king when we arrived in Hiangcheng, but we kept warm in our long wadded gowns, hand-knit woolen stockings, and padded shoes. Usually sunshine and blue skies brightened our days, but sometimes the wind howled down from the north. Snow fell once. It transformed the monotonous brown landscape, gave beauty to the city, and lingered on the hills.

Spring came. The earth stirred and shook itself. Seed planted in the fall pushed brave green spears above the ground. Soon the whole plain had lost its brown ugliness and pulsed with living green. Next to respond to the stimulus of new life were the fruit trees. Peach and apricot burst into a froth of pink and white blossoms. Winter and its rigors had died for another year.

Much of Honan is flat, even plain, so the hills to the south and west were God's beneficence. I loved to watch their different moods. When the clouds hung heavy and black, the hills grew dark too. When the wind tossed the clouds high in the sky, the far-off ridges were painted in mauve on the skyline. Their ever-changing beauty met a need in my life.

By May, the wheat was standing strong and green. Rain fell on its thirsty roots. The wind blew caressingly and the grain bent in rippling waves of color. Gradually, the green gave way to gold. The yellow heads hung heavily on their drying stalks. The words of Jesus in John 4:35

came to my mind: "Lift up your eyes and look on the fields, for they are white already to harvest." Golden fields had been a familiar sight to Him when He walked the roads of Galilee. So many of His illustrations are from nature and from man's activities on the land. This was the first time that I had seen the whole process of wheat's growth, for nearly all my life had been bounded by city streets.

The time for reaping came. Men and women cut the golden grain by hand and hauled it to the threshing floors. Each village boasted one of these on its outskirts: smooth, hard-packed earth, carpeted with the cut wheat. A cow, mule, or donkey dragged a heavy stone round and round over the stalks and ears. As they were crushed, the hard grain filtered through the strewed stalks to the ground. Men tied the stalks into bundles for kindling, and women with winnowing baskets scooped up the wheat. Holding the baskets high and gradually tipping them, the heavy grain fell like brown rain to the ground, and the breeze whipped off the chaff. We were fascinated to see such Biblical scenes enacted before our eyes.

By mid-June, the farmers were at work again. Plows of ancient design turned over clods of rich brown earth, softened by rain. Precious seed was sown. But the summer sun burned down. No rain fell. Living very close to starvation level, the country people feared the worst. Early each morning the Christians met for prayer, but still the sun beat down.

"Come to the front gate," called one of our Chinese friends one day. "Can you hear the drums?"

We ran to the compound entrance. A procession came trooping over the stone bridge from the city. Drums rolled, cymbals clanged, and flutes piped. "Whatever is happening?" Esther asked. "It isn't a funeral, is it?"

"No," came the reply, "it's a rain procession. See those red-covered bundles in the middle of the crowd, carried between bamboo poles? They are idols from the city temples, and the priests are taking them out to the country. The farmers' fields need rain, and they believe that when these idols are worshiped by the farmers on the dry, hot land, they will make the rain fall where it is needed most."

"Oh, just look at the children!" cried Helen. "Are they involved in the worship also?"

"No, they just go along for the fun of it," was the reply. But when we observed them more closely, we wondered.

A group of naked brown children led the noisy cavalcade. Green willow leaves were twisted like crowns around their heads. In their hands they carried smoking incense sticks, bound with willow twigs and strips of yellow temple paper. Red, white, and blue banners streamed overhead.

We stood watching, sad at heart, as they passed our gate and took the dusty road to the nearest village. The sound of drums and flutes grew faint; the bobbing idol chairs were hidden by the crowd; the banners blurred and disappeared from sight. The darkness and futility and power of heathenism hit us forcibly.

It was to the villages that God directed my thoughts through His Word one sunny spring morning. A young married woman who lived nearby called for Mary Guinness. She wanted Dr. Mary and the help of Dr. Mary's God. The girl's mother-in-law was a Buddhist, and had scolded her because she refused to go to the temple to ask the idols to heal a painful breast abscess. It was my privilege to accompany Mary that morning, help with the dressing of the wound, and then teach this illiterate girl a verse from the Bible to hold in her heart.

Each week Miss Standen tried to take some of us new workers out to the surrounding hamlets. The women and children pulled at her heartstrings. They would not hear of Jesus unless someone cared enough to go and tell them. Mrs. Pang usually went with us—a little Chinese lady with a happy face, dressed in a spotless white jacket and dark trousers, carrying a big palm-leaf fan and her Bible.

The country people had so little: mud-brick houses, a few sticks of furniture, a large iron *kuo* (Chinese cooking pot) set in a mud stove, fed from below with kindling used very sparingly. Noodles and sweet potatoes were the mainstay of their diet, spiced up with turnips, beans, or any green vegetables that were in season. A pig in the courtyard meant pork and home-cured ham on a feast day. Skinny hens clucking in the dirt produced small eggs.

There were children everywhere! In cold weather they wore dirty, padded jackets and trousers split up the crotch for obvious reasons. Their faces were chapped and rosy from the cold, their noses runny, their eyes showing a fearful interest in the foreigners. In summer, the toddlers wore nothing. The older boys usually sported shirts, and the girls wore loose, long pants. Poverty peered at us from these village homes, where folk lived on the borderline of starvation. One bad season could mean no food. Famine would stalk the land. Their needs tugged at our hearts.

In one home we visited, there was a woman of eighty with a seamed old face and dim eyes. Miss Standen explained God's way of salvation to her very simply, but she shook her head uncomprehendingly. Turning to the younger women crowding the small dark room, Miss Standen said, "You see what happens when you grow old. This venerable lady cannot understand the message in God's Book. Don't let that happen to you. Today is your day of opportunity."

Chapter Seventeen

He is our peace.
Ephesians 2:14 KJV

IN MARCH, A young American missionary held an evangelistic mission in the church and school at Hiangcheng. Dan was a member of a Lutheran Mission and lived a day's journey away. He was in Hiangcheng for a few days, but we scarcely saw him. I was up to my eyes in study, preparing for my first language exam. However, we all attended the evening evangelistic meetings to help in our understanding of Chinese. Then he was gone.

A few days later, a messenger arrived one evening with a letter. Mary Guinness received it and came to find me. I was in my room studying hard for an exam the next day.

"Miriam, here's a letter for you," she said with a smile. "The messenger says if you want to send an answer, he must have it tonight."

"Oh, where has it come from?" I asked, as mail usually arrived around noon.

"From Kiahsien," she replied.

"Kiahsien!" I echoed. "Whoever would write to me from there? Well, thank you for bringing it to me."

Tearing open the envelope, I turned back to my desk. A letter was always an event in those war days. The writing was unfamiliar, and I looked at the signature. What was *he* writing to me about? Quickly I began to read, then gave a gasp. I read on more slowly, my amazement growing. Dan was asking me to marry him! He felt, from the little he

79

had seen of me, that this was God's will for us. I could not believe it. Surely he had made a mistake! I was not pretty, my hair was straight and drawn back in a bun, my family had always teased me about my large mouth, my figure was hidden in a straight and unflattering wadded gown. I was shy, I could not sing, I had no gifts. In fact, I was very ordinary. It was often a wonder to me that the CIM had even accepted me.

But as I held the letter in my hand, my heart went out to him. No normal girl can receive an offer of marriage from a good man and be unaffected by it. Naturally, my heart beat faster. But was this God's will for me? How could I know? He said he wanted an answer immediately— by tomorrow—a typically masculine demand!

I pushed back my chair and dropped to my knees by the bed. But I could not pray. My mind was in a turmoil. One emotion after another shook me: excitement, doubt, hope, fear, joy. But I still had no light as to the answer I should give.

"I'll go and see *An Chiao-shih*" (Miss Standen's Chinese name), I said to myself, "and I'll be guided by her. How I wish Mother was here, instead of hundreds of miles away!"

I knocked on Miss Standen's door. "Come in," she called. "Oh, it's you, Miriam. Can I help you?"

She was as surprised as I was, but she could look at the whole thing objectively, while I was already immersed in emotional depths.

"I think we should consider it from all angles," she said, "and then ask the Lord to guide us. The most important thing is, do you love him?"

"How can I?" I queried. "I've only met him a few times. I don't really know him."

"If you do say yes, you will have to leave the CIM," she went on.

I had thought of this possibility, and could not bear it. God had so wonderfully opened the door and led me into this mission. I was happy just where I was.

"On the other hand," she went on in her sweet way, "he might leave the Lutheran Mission and join us, but that is not what usually happens."

We prayed together, and then I returned to my room and wrote my reply. The answer was "No." How could I say anything else on such a short acquaintance? I sealed the letter with a sigh, and went in search of Mary.

"Here is my letter for Kiahsien," I said, holding it out to her. "Would you mind giving it to the messenger for me, please? I doubt if my Chinese is good enough to get the idea across."

I walked slowly back to my room. How could I take my exam the next day? My world had been shaken. New thoughts crowded my mind. The idioms and characters and grammar I had learned so painstakingly fluttered beyond my grasp. What should I do?

The next morning, God had His message for me as I turned to Him in prayer, the morning of my first big exam. I read the *Daily Light* portion, and to my upset mind, four words stood out: "HE is our peace." That was what I needed—peace—and that was what He was to me that day.

Right after breakfast, I went to the quiet room alone with my pen and sheets of paper. The envelope containing the questions were handed to me: first Part A and then Part B. I committed the exam to the Lord, and wrote my answers. As He had promised, peace ruled my mind, and I was able to cope. Occasionally, the thought of the messenger hastening to Kiahsien would intrude, but Christ gave a marvelous release and power to concentrate. That evening, and many times later, I prayed for Dan. I knew what such disappointment could mean, for had I not walked that identical road of rejection myself?

Chapter Eighteen

I will contend with him that contendeth
with thee, and I will save thy children.
Isaiah 49:25b KJV

ONCE MY WRITTEN exam was over, I worked feverishly on my oral. When that lay behind me, I had a short vacation (a few days in Hiangcheng, free of study), after which I returned to the books. Day followed study-filled day, with occasional visits into the city or to the villages. Gradually, the language I was learning came more smoothly to my tongue.

I was the only trained nurse in our household of fifteen girls, so naturally all nursing jobs fell to me. As one and another became ill (the result of adjusting to a new diet and schedule), I began to lose out on language learning and gradually fell behind Isabel, my partner in study. We were neck and neck in our lessons and the competition was challenging. Fortunately, we were good friends, praying together about studies and other things, and our friendship stood the test.

In the rather restricted life we were all living, temptation came to each one of us in different ways. We discovered that Satan was always on the watch to sow discord among us, and being missionaries did not exempt us from his attacks. He also tried to shove the wedge of discouragement between the chinks of our spiritual armor, to magnify the problems and differences.

One sunny spring, after I was sitting in the garden practicing reading aloud in Chinese, I heard someone calling in the house. "Miriam, where are you? Does anyone know where Mirry is?"

"She's not here," came the answer. "She may be in the garden."

I jumped up and called, "Hello, what's the matter? Who wants me?" and walked toward the house.

"Oh, I'm so glad I found you," cried Evelyn, "Jeanie's ill and Mary asked me to find you. She's in Jeanie's room."

"Okay, thanks," I said, running upstairs.

As I slipped into my room to put my book away, I remembered that Jeanie had looked a bit pale for the last day or two. She never complained, and was a rather quiet girl. I knew she must be feeling ill.

As I entered her room, my eyes flew to the bed, and as soon as I saw her I knew she was a sick girl. Her face was white and drawn. Mary had piled some extra blankets on her, for her whole body shook and shivered in a rigor.

"Miriam, please fill two hot water bottles as quickly as possible. We've got to get her warm," Mary said.

I dashed down to the kitchen to see if there was any hot water. I found the kettle was beginning to boil for tea, so there was no need to poke the coal-dust fire into flame. I rounded up two hot water bottles, filled them, and hurried upstairs two steps at a time, hitching up my long Chinese gown.

Soon Jeanie's shivering stopped, her face grew flushed, and her eyelids became heavy. We took her temperature—one hundred and four! That was high. Already, her lips were drying and cracking with the fever.

She was still in her Chinese gown, so we undressed her, sponged her, and got her between cool sheets.

"Oh, that feels good," she whispered. "I'm so sorry to be such a nuisance."

"You're no nuisance," Mary remarked brightly. "Now tell me, how long have you been feeling ill?"

"Not too long," she replied. "I've had a headache for about two days, and today the sight of food made me feel sick. I did try to study, but had to give up. I couldn't take it any longer."

"Jeanie, you should have told us earlier how you were feeling," Mary chided her gently, "and gone to bed. I wonder how long you've had a fever. Now you must not get out of bed for anything—and I mean anything! Miriam will be here to look after you."

The next day, she was no better, her fever high and her pulse rapid. Mary suspected typhoid, but there was no hospital lab to verify it. To avoid risk of infection for others, Jeanie and I moved into one of the smaller rooms. Strict isolation was enforced, and I was thankful for the experience I had gained along this line in the Dr. Bernardo hospital.

The fever did not fall. Rigors continued to rack her body, leaving her drenched with perspiration and drained of strength. It was not easy to persuade her to drink the fluids she needed. Day and night I was with her—sponging, changing, feeding, and doing all I could. Isabel was a tremendous help. She kept my big enamel jug filled with water, and emptied the slop pail. Each evening she would fill the thermos with boiling water. The chills could strike at any time and I needed warm water to sponge her down.

When my patient dozed during the day, I would slip out for a walk along the riverbank. How green the fields looked, how sweet the air! But I was tired—physically weary and discouraged. In spite of all we were doing, I could see Jeanie getting thinner and weaker before my eyes. We were praying. Mary was tireless. But all to no avail. Was she ...? No, I dare not even think of that!

Then on Sunday morning, God gave me another message from His Word. I must have seen this verse in Isaiah many times, but that morning as my tired eyes read the words, suddenly they clicked in my mind: "I, the almighty God, am contending with him that contendeth with thee, and I will save thy children." God was on my side. He would fight with me against this illness that was taking my friend into the valley of death. "I will save," was like a strong hand reaching down, to which I could cling for assurance of deliverance. My heart lifted; God had not forgotten us. He instilled extra strength for all the nursing care. He quickened my sense to discern. He gave skill to my hands. But she was still so ill.

A telegram was sent to another station asking for help as the day and night nursing was becoming too much for me. That whole day, Jeanie lay spent. Much prayer was offered. The next day, although weak, she seemed more responsive.

At three the next morning, a dark and lonely hour, the shivering struck again. I turned up the dimmed kerosene lamp, covered her with blankets and gave her a warm drink through her chattering teeth. When the rigor eventually stopped, she needed a sponge-down. Fortunately, there was just enough water in the thermos. When she was comfortable in a dry gown and between dry sheets, I took her temperature. It was lower. With hope in my heart, I blew out the light and fell into bed.

Later that morning, I dragged myself out of the depths of sleep to find the sun shining in through the window. I rolled out of bed and padded across the room to see my patient. How thin and pale she looked in the golden light, her hair plastered to her head with sweat. I placed my fingers lightly on her pulse and was thrilled to feel a fuller, steadier, slower beat.

"She's better," I said to myself. "Praise the Lord!"

She did not stir; she just slept on. I tiptoed to Isabel's room and told her of Jeanie's night rigor and her present health-giving sleep, and then slipped back into bed myself.

That day, another nurse came and took over the night duty. I was glad to hand over some of the responsibility, but the real joy was to see the change in Jeanie. She had turned the corner and was starting on the road to recovery. This was God's power at work. He had saved her. The whole atmosphere of the house lifted as the good news ran from mouth to mouth. "Jeanie's improving. God has answered!" It was six slow weeks before she was fit enough to join us once more in our daily schedule.

Chapter Nineteen

Behold, I send an Angel before thee to keep
thee by the way, and to bring thee into
the place which I have prepared.
Exodus 23:20 NASV

HIANGCHENG WAS ONLY a stepping-stone to our permanent area of work in China. We were there to study Chinese and to become oriented to life in the interior. Each one of us was longing to know in which province we would finally be located.

In Aberdeen Park back in London we had discussed this matter of designation many times. Most of us had a hidden longing to engage in a certain kind of work, whether among the tribal people of Yunnan or the Muslims of the far Northwest. There was a glamour attached to distant places—the thrill of danger, the desire to make Christ known in areas where no one had heard before. As for me, the Lanchow hospital had captured my imagination.

Knowing of this tendency among new missionaries, Miss Bond had warned us: "The CIM leaders in Shanghai know the needs of the land much better than you do. I hope you will be prepared to go along with their suggestions. I know they spend a lot of time in prayer before designations are made."

Some of us thought rebelliously, "The Lord knows the needs even better than headquarters (HQ), and He can guide us Himself." However, we were learning to fit in with the mission's methods. For those who do, there are the added joys of obedience. It was easy to agree with it all in principle, but sometimes self insidiously suggested that in such an important and personal matter as designation, I was the best judge—guided by the Lord, of course!

As our time in Hiangcheng lengthened, we often prayed about our future work. One evening in late March I found this message: "Behold, I send an Angel before thee to keep thee ... and to bring thee into the place which I have prepared." My heart leaped as I read it. Isabel and I had been praying together specifically about the future, and in His tender love, God gave me this promise. My place was already prepared.

May passed. So did June. Then one day early in July a letter arrived from Loho saying that the Honan superintendent had received the all-important letter from Shanghai and would be visiting us soon. (Normally, the General Director or his deputy made the designations, but it was now impossible for them to travel from Shanghai.) Our first reaction was excitement, followed by sadness because this would mean the end of our time together, then followed by tension over possible disappointment.

When the big day came, I had to wait until nearly the end, as usual, because my maiden name started with a T. Some girls came out radiant, some near to tears. Deep in my heart, under the pulsing of suspense, there was peace because of the message God had given me. Then it was my turn. Old Mr. Trudinger smiled kindly, but I could tell he was weary. It had been a strenuous day for him under the strain of many interviews.

"Well, Miriam, are you prepared for a shock?" he greeted me.

"I don't know," I replied slowly, "but I am trusting God to guide us all."

"It's like this," he said. "Mr. Weller felt that the place to which you should go is Kinghsien in South Anhwei."

My heart did a flip. This was the last place I expected to go. "Oh, no, not there, Lord, please!" I prayed desperately.

"There is a tremendous need for a district nurse to be on call for our missionaries in the part which lies south of the Yangtze River, and also in the western part of Chekiang province. At the moment it is impossible to get there because Japanese troops are strung out along the river, effectively blocking the way. We suggest that you stay on here in Hiangcheng for some months, until God opens up the way for you. How do you feel about that?"

I felt in a whirl—and I felt a part of me had died. No exciting journey to a distant province, just unpack my trunks and stay put!

"It is rather a shock," I admitted at last, "and so different from what I had hoped for. But deep down I am ready to do as our leaders feel best. At least, I think I am!" I added honestly.

"Yes, I can imagine how you are feeling," he replied. "Mr. Weller had heard that you wanted to go to Lanchow, but he believes South Anhwei had a prior claim. However, we don't want to be unreasonable, and we do want to do God's will. So Mr. Weller sent special word that if you definitely feel that the Borden Memorial Hospital is where God wants you, then he will change your designation to Kansu. Suppose you wait before making a definite decision, and then write directly to him in Shanghai? Let us pray about it now."

So I wrote a letter to Shanghai, accepting the designation to South Anhwei. The responsibility was in God's hands, and I was glad to leave it there. A few days later these sentences from Oswald Chambers seemed like a spiritual hammer hitting the nail of my problem on the head: "Let God fling you out, and do not go until He does. If you select your spot, you will prove an empty pod. If God sows you, you will bring forth fruit."

Chapter Twenty

Whom have I in heaven but Thee?
And there is none upon earth that I desire besides Thee.
Psalm 73:25 KJV

THE SUMMER WAS over. My friends had scattered to faraway places, and I was waiting to help Mary Guinness during the birth of her second child. I was lonely. The big house, once overflowing with life, seemed quiet and empty—dead. I sat on the upstairs veranda dreaming dreams.

Six months had passed since the first letter had come from Dan in Kiahsien. Some weeks later another letter trickled through from him, written in Chungking, with the news that he was returning to America. But he still hoped I would change my mind, and made various suggestions that showed how much he cared. Many weeks elapsed, when another letter limped in with a Burmese stamp. Now I was longing for the next!

My emotions were like a seesaw. For days I would enter happily into all that was going on in the church, the villages, and the school. Then suddenly I would find myself thinking of what *might* be—and down I would sink in a whirl of self-pity. I would try to relegate him to the back of my mind, but when I prayed about the situation, all the uncertainty and excitement would roll over me like a flood.

Another contributing factor was the weather. The sweltering heat of a dry Honan summer exhausted me. I slept on the upstairs veranda under a mosquito net during the hot breathless nights, with a fan in my hand, trying to get cool. Cool? That was a forgotten word. The smothering blanket of sultry air affected everyone, Chinese and foreigners alike. It was inescapable.

With one thing after another, Satan was having a heyday with me. Lack of sleep, loneliness, loss of friends, listlessness—he dragged them all into the battle to reduce me to a state of spiritual imbalance. But the weapon that nearly defeated me was on the emotional level. The only thing I longed for was a home of my own and a husband. Very natural in the circumstances, especially as the happiness of Mary and Henry in each other was so evident.

But I found that the Lord knew what was happening: my floundering, my perplexity, my weakness. One September morning, I read Psalm 73. I came to verse twenty-five: "Whom have I in heaven but Thee? And there is none upon earth that I desire besides Thee." Conviction struck me like an arrow. Could I echo in my heart these words of David? Had I not been hankering for human love and companionship and neglecting the gracious tenderness of God? Gently He exposed my sin and showed me where I had gone wrong. My emotional longings were natural, but I had allowed them to take over all my thoughts. This had shattered my day-by-day walk with my Lord.

Slowly, I read the words again. "There is none upon earth that I desire besides Thee." I looked into my heart and asked the Holy Spirit to turn His searchlight on me. Could I truthfully apply these words to myself? Could I let go of all my dreams? Could I trust my future to the Lord?

Praise God, He filled my heart with a new love for Himself. Peace came in and routed the yo-yo experience of past months. Held in Christ's nail-pierced hands, I learned the secret of perfect love. What God wanted was not a clenching grasp of the things dear to me, but the open hands of obedience and trust.

> *No clenched fist—*
> > *But an open hand,*
> > *Pierced by a nail*
> > > *To cross of wood.*
>
> *Not grasping things,*
> > *But yielding life,*
> > *His one desire*
> > > *To do God's will.*
>
> *God, take my hands*
> > *And open them*
> > *To show Your love*
> > > *To those in need.*
>
> *Through suffering*
> > *And deep concern,*
> > *Unclench the fist*
> > > *Of self-desire.*

Chapter Twenty-One

Come unto Me, all ye that labor and are
heavy laden, and I will give you rest.
Matthew 11:28 KJV

CHANGES! PACKING! TRAVELING!

While it was still dark one November morning in 1941, I ate my last breakfast in Hiangcheng for many weeks. Little Ian Oswald was now about two months old, and I was transferring to another town. As the sky lightened in the east, I climbed onto my rickshaw cart, said goodbye to the Guinnesses, and set off for Linying, another walled town a day's journey away.

I was traveling alone, and enjoyed the trip very much. The sun climbed into the sky and a gaggle of wild geese, honking their way south, cut like an arrow into the blue. Predictably, the road was in a deplorable state, with ditches dug by soldiers down the middle and also across. Suddenly, one wheel of the cart crumpled, and I found myself at the bottom of a six-foot ditch! I clambered out, a bit bruised and shaken, and brushed off the worst of the mud. Apparently, the full load had been too much and some of the wheel's spokes had broken. Fortunately, the carter, Wong-ch'eng, had a couple of spares and we were soon on our way.

It was a long day. Darkness was creeping upon us and the sturdy carter only had the flickering light on his cart to guide him. Eventually, the black mass of the city wall loomed ahead, and it was with a sense of relief that we passed through the partly shut gates. Inside, the bustle and noise of people, the barking of dogs, and the laughter of children sent a warm feeling through my heart. At the *Fu Yin T'ang* (church) we received a loving welcome by the dull light of little oil lamps.

We lived very simply—Frances Williamson from America, Marjory Stewart from New Zealand, and myself from England. Study still filled most days, but we had many more opportunities to get involved with the people than we had had in Hiangcheng: no big compound wall to keep them out.

Ts'ui Sao was a middle-aged, energetic Christian woman who wanted to serve the Lord. There was nothing she loved more than to share Jesus with her neighbors. Less than a week after my arrival, she took me with her to the home of a woman whose heart the Lord had touched during some special meetings. In the dark front room, hideous gods were plastered on the wall, dusty and grimy with the smoke that curled upward from the incense pot beneath. That day, however, marked the end of their rule in that home. The idolatrous paraphernalia was torn down and burned—paper gods, incense bowl, god-shelf, and tablets. In their place, we hung a Gospel poster. This was a witness to neighbors and friends that she was now walking the Jesus way.

It was a new experience to visit country Christians for days at a time. On December 10, Frances and I left for Fancheng, twelve miles from Linying. We walked between brown fields, past many villages, to the home of Mr. and Mrs. Chao. With this home as our base, we tramped to different villages each day to visit Christians and help them in Bible study, in witness to their neighbors. Many of them were very poor, eating only two meals a day. Their staple diet was sweet potatoes or lumpy flour soup, plus a few turnips, peanuts, or hot peppers, but no meat. However, the overriding memory of those outstation trips was the oneness in Christ that we enjoyed with these humble men and women.

One day, a Mrs. Chiang asked us to go with her to her old home some miles away. Her husband was very angry that she had become a Christian, and the previous time she had gone with missionaries, he had beaten her cruelly when she returned home. However, the love of God in her heart was urging her to go again. She wanted her own folks to hear once more.

The neighbors flocked in to see the peculiar, big foreigners. "She must be very old to have such light-colored hair" (referring to me, for Frances's hair was black), and "How can they see out of those queer eyes?" were some of the comments we overheard.

Frances was a fluent speaker, and she held their interest for a long time. I told a story from a colored poster and was glad that they seemed to understand. After supper, a big crowd gathered again: inquisitive children, attentive women, curious men. One of the Christian women went out to speak to them, but when she had finished, they wanted still more!

"*T'u Chiao-shih* (Miss Toop), will you go and preach, please?" she called to me as she came back into the kitchen.

"She can't mean me," I thought to myself and turned to Frances. "Frances, I'm sure she means you," I said. "You go."

"No, Miriam, she asked for you," Frances replied. "You go."

"I can't possibly," I cried. "I've never preached ad lib before. I've always used a poster, and I can't use one tonight because it's too dark for them to see."

"I think it would be good for you," she said firmly. "You've got to take the plunge sometime. The Lord will help you and we'll pray for you. You'll see."

She was adamant; I had to go. "O Lord, help me!" I cried as I got up and walked slowly out of the warm, smoky kitchen into the crowded yard. High above us stars were sparkling in the winter sky. Children squirmed and chattered. Someone coughed and spat. Others were talking.

"Sing the Chinese chorus of Matthew 11:28," a Voice seemed to say. And I sang as best I could:

> *"All of you who are weary and have heavy burdens,*
> *Come to Me.*
> *I will surely give you peace—*
> *Only be willing to come!"*

Silence fell on the crowd and God gave me a message. Many heard for the first time that night of Jesus Christ, the great Burden-bearer, who had died on the cross so long ago in order that they might have peace of heart and peace with God. I made grammatical errors, I know, but at the same time there was the sense that God was in charge.

The next night, Frances and I shared a bed in yet another home, and shared the room with an ox and a donkey. They twitched and snuffled all night long. The family slept in a divided-off portion of the same room. Such as they had, they willingly shared with us. When we eventually returned to Fancheng, we learned that a young couple with their child had come in from one of the villages we had visited, saying they wanted to believe. This was a climax of joy.

On December 19, we walked the twelve long miles back to Linying, tired but happy. We felt inadequate at the thought of the hundreds of villages in our area, yet God had given us the exciting privilege of witnessing in a few.

Chapter Twenty-Two

Fear thou not, for I am with thee: be not dismayed, for I am
thy God: I will strengthen thee; yea, I will help thee; yea, I
will uphold thee with the right hand of My righteousness ... I
the Lord thy God will hold thy right hand.
Isaiah 41:10,13 KJV

Letters! What a part they play in our lives. It was in January 1942 that one came for me from Mr. Trudinger, the Honan superintendent, with an unexpected request. Would I get ready to move to Fowyang in the neighboring province of Anhwei? A nurse would be needed there soon to deliver a baby. As it was that much nearer to my designated area of South Anhwei, he thought I was the logical one to go. God had prepared me somewhat for this change, but even so, it was not easy to say yes. I was very happy in Linying and did not want to leave.

Other letters also found their way to our house. Some brought black news of Japanese victories in Singapore, New Guinea, Sumatra, and Java. One told of Mr. Hogben's tragic death on the Burma Road in a truck accident. (My brother John was traveling with him, but was unhurt.) One came with happy news of Evelyn's engagement to Norman Charter: the first engagement in our Hiangcheng family. Another saddened me, when I learned that Miss Gregg, who had helped me in so many ways, had finished her earthly journey and was with Christ.

On March 31, I walked out of Linying for the last time. Some of the Christian women escorted me through the gate in the huge old city wall. As we stood together in a small group before I climbed onto the rickshaw cart, they sang, "God be with you till we meet again." Tears came to my eyes. The carter then picked up his shafts and I was pulled away. Gradually, their faces receded into the distance, and I thought nostalgically of all the things we had done together: visiting in villages to share Jesus Christ, meeting for prayer in times of emergency, working together in the church, participating in each other's joys and sorrows. What a wealth of love and fellowship they had brought into my life!

What lay ahead for me? I did not know. A few days earlier, the above verses had been God's promise to me. I was inclined to dread the responsibility of nursing our missionaries with no foreign doctor to turn to, and no hospital near at hand. I would be on call for fourteen adults and seven children, living in widely separated towns. I was especially worried about the children, for summers in the interior of China seem to breed disease. I knew of one little boy of eighteen months who died from dysentery the year before, even though a missionary doctor was there at the time. I should not have been anxious, for God had promised to hold my right hand—the hand that took temperatures, rubbed backs, poured medicines, and gave injections.

It was stiflingly hot in the small upstairs bedroom under the burning gray tiles. On the bed Marion panted in labor. Beside her, Mrs. Suen, a delightful Chinese Christian nurse, and I did what we could to help.

Some weeks earlier, my midwifery bag and I had bumped up from Fowyang, my new center, on a squeaking wheelbarrow. (The barrow men never used oil on the hubs, as they believed the ear-splitting squeals frightened away the evil spirits!) On either side of the rough road, spreading fields of grain promised a good harvest, although rain was needed.

When I arrived in Taiho, with its cobblestone streets, I was glad to hop off the barrow and walk to the missionaries' home accompanied by a growing crowd of curious and noisy children. Passing through the front gate, I found an oasis of peace and cleanliness.

The first few days I was busy, getting ready for the delivery. I invaded the warm kitchen one afternoon to bake the dressings and towels in the tin oven built into the mud stove. By this time, I had almost mastered the art of controlling the heat of the coal-dust fuel. If it became too hot, my precious equipment would be scorched and useless, so I had to watch it carefully. I double-checked my black bag for clamps, scissors, thread, needles, sutures, syringes, and ampoules.

Then came the night when Dick knocked on my bedroom door to say that Marion's birth pains had started. I dressed quickly (my heart thumping) and gathered together the equipment I would need, with a quick "O Lord, please help and guide me!" Marion gave me an encouraging smile as I entered her room. The contraction came again, and I prepared for the delivery. This was her second child, so I expected a short and easy birth. Gradually, the pains grew in intensity—and I could see the baby's head coming down. "O Lord," I said in my heart, "please help me!" Then his head pushed through the vagina and soon the baby lay on the sheet.

But something was wrong! There was more blood than usual after his delivery, and she kept on bleeding. I quickly removed the baby, wrapped him in a towel, and handed him to his father. I turned back to Marion, and started rubbing (or massaging) the top of the uterus to try and stop the bleeding—but to no avail. It was not flowing quickly, but why didn't it stop? In the light of the lamp it seemed to lessen—but it kept on coming! Desperately, I kept on rubbing, hoping to stimulate the uterus to contract. Emergency treatment could be given, but it was fraught with danger, and I dared not attempt it on my own. "O God! Help me now. You are the only One who can stop the weakening flow of blood," was the cry of my heart.

Marion grew pale. Her pulse quickened. The hemorrhage was taking its toll. Dick moved around helplessly. Joy turned to concern.

"Fear not, for I am with you," came the comfort of God's promise. "I am holding your right hand." And I clung to that word. Five hours after the bleeding began, God's hand reached down and touched the weary body. The bleeding miraculously stopped. Marion slept—to wake refreshed and take up the duties of motherhood once more.

Chapter Twenty-Three

Wait on the Lord: be of good courage, and
He shall strengthen thine heart.
Psalm 27:14 KJV

THE BUSTLING MARKET town of Fowyang in North Anhwei, situated on the Sha River, was my new home. I found the church there a living organism, full of movement and growth. Each Sunday the large brick building overflowed with people. Masses of country folk, clad in every shade of blue and gray, squeezed onto the benches: men on one side of the church, women on the other, and children everywhere. The Chinese peasant is aggressive, noisy, and uninhibited; church services were unpredictable. Lusty singing trumpeted forth, but it was rarely in tune. If the morning sermon was too long, some of the old ladies would sway in sleep, especially if they had trudged in from a distant village on tiny, bound feet. One old soul fell right off her bench one Sunday, causing quite a commotion.

Perhaps because of war, drought, poverty, bombing, and sickness people's hearts were responsive to God's Spirit. Groups of new believers were springing up in many rural areas, and they regarded Fowyang as their mother church. However, they knew little of Christian doctrine or the practical aspects of living the Christian life, as the following story will indicate.

A Christian farmer came in to see Mr. Bert Kane, the senior missionary. He said he was being troubled by fire demons; during one month, forty small fires had broken out spontaneously in his home.

They would suddenly flare up in the roof, in the kindling stacked in the kitchen, or in the hay stored for the animals. (In many areas demon activity was all too real, causing demon-possession, illness, depression, madness, constant yawning, or a bottomless appetite. Poor peasants borrowed money to hire Buddhist priests to practice exorcism. But only the name of Jesus Christ compelled the evil spirits to leave.)

This man was an earnest Christian, and there seemed to be no reasonable explanation for these attacks. However, a few days later one of the Fowyang church elders happened to pass through this farmer's village and heard him berating a neighbor with the foulest of heathen curse words.

Immediately, he walked over to him. "Mr. Lin, Mr. Lin," he cried, "how can you use such filthy words? You sound just like an unbeliever!"

The man stood stunned.

"Come, Mr. Lin, let us go inside," the elder went on more gently. In the privacy of that Christian home, where a bright Gospel poster hung in the place of honor, the elder quietly said, "You are a Christian, Mr. Lin, but you still indulge in your old and sinful habit of swearing. I am not surprised that you have been troubled by demons. This kind of behavior gives a loophole to the devil. The Lord Jesus is your example, and the Scriptures say of Him, 'There was no guile found in His mouth.' You must ask the Lord's forgiveness for this sin and also ask for His power to help you make a complete break from your former ways."

To teach Christian doctrine to such as Mr. Lin, Short Term Bible Schools (STBS) had been started and were now a regular feature of the church's program. They were held during the winter months when farmers were less busy. Each STBS attracted thirty to fifty people, men and women who were willing to leave their farms for two or three weeks at a stretch. They gathered in a central spot, studied their Bibles day after day, learned the power of prayer, and enjoyed fellowship with other Christians. Mabel Williamson and Emmie Stevens gave themselves to this teaching ministry.

Another type of teaching was to help illiterate people to read. In most country congregations of fifty to sixty, often only one or two could read their Bibles. To enable new believers to become strong

Christians, Phonetic Reading Schools were planned. Ruth Nowack told interesting tales of her experiences as she held such schools in one market town after another. Quite often she cast demons out of some woman who was causing disruption in a class.

As I was hoping to work later with either Emmie or Ruth, I was eager to learn all I could of what God was doing in these areas. However, until the fall, my priority was still language study.

As I have mentioned earlier, that summer of 1942, the heat was suffocating. Temperatures ranged from ninety-six to one hundred and six degrees for weeks on end. Our tiled houses were like ovens, and even at night we had little relief. I also suffered from prickly heat. Big patches of red irritation covered parts of my body, and it "prickled" day and night. Sleep was broken and fitful. During the day I tried to study, a palm leaf fan in one hand and a towel for mopping perspiration lying on the desk.

Added to the physical discomfort and heat, other worries needled me. For one thing, letters from my parents took months to reach me: not weeks but months! I longed for news of them, and when day after day went by with no mail, tears were not far away. One letter from my brother Billy was mailed to Shanghai, redirected back to London, readdressed via Chungking, and was ten months en route! Some letters never arrived, sunk by Hitler's submarines. I walked the way of loneliness. Uncertainty gnawed at my heart.

We also began to feel the economic effect of China's battle for life against the Japanese. Wheat, millet, and sorghum were basic to the rural people's livelihood. When grain prices skyrocketed, the cost of everything rose. Money began to lose its value. Each quarter, our remittances were sent from Chungking via Chinese merchants to the neighboring province of Honan, as the fighting had dislocated the usual means of the money transmission. When notifications of the money's arrival reached Fowyang, one of our missionary men had to go personally to collect the amount designated for all our Anhwei missionaries and bring it to Fowyang. From there, another man would cycle to the next station along the river with their share until all was distributed.

Soon we found, through bitter experience, that by the end of the quarter, the buying power of our dollars had sadly depreciated. We decided to invest the money God sent us by immediately buying grain. This gave more stability to our resources. Even so, we felt the pinch. Many commodities such as sugar, kerosene, and imported goods were out of our price range, or were unobtainable. Saccharin and local honey took the place of sugar. Wheat syrup replaced jam. Vegetable oil was used instead of kerosene. Soya bean milk was used on porridge and in cooking. Crushed eggshells supplied calcium, and bean curd often substituted for meat.

There were a number of us living in Fowyang: the Kane family in a small house in one part of town, and the rest of us in units surrounding an enclosed courtyard, using a common kitchen.

One evening we gathered for discussion. Bert Kane, the missionary in charge, opened our meeting. "I've just returned from the country," he said. "Prices are soaring everywhere. We cannot continue to live as we are doing. Our money won't last out each quarter. We must cut back."

We looked at each other in dismay. We felt we were already being as economical as possible. "It's not that we don't trust the Lord to provide for us, but we need guidance in our use of what He sends us. What should be our priorities as we try to cope with the shortage of so many staples? It seems to me that we must keep the goat, our only source of milk for the children. Our Stanley and Douglas need the milk, and so does baby Lois," he added with a warm smile at Mel and Mary Beth. "That means the goat herd will have to stay. Winnie and I have been talking things over and came up with this suggestion. Would it be wise economically to try and get along without domestic help?"

"It will cut down on our time for our main work," remarked Ruth slowly. "As Emmie and I are out in the country most of the time, it will not affect us much, but Helen and Miriam will have much less time for study if they take on the cooking and cleaning."

I looked at Helen, and Helen looked at me. I was a hopeless cook and knew very little of the basics of menu planning. As for buying eggs and vegetables—bargaining in the market was definitely not my thing.

"I think we could manage," Helen said slowly. "At least we could give it a try."

"I'll look after the fire," Mel said, "as I have learned the trick of keeping it going." Helen and I breathed sighs of relief. That coal-dust fire was a nightmare because it was so unpredictable.

"Fine," said Bert. "We'll try this out for a month, and then we will meet again and see how everyone feels about it. Now let's commit our situation to the Lord."

We prayed together and praised the Lord for what He was doing in the lives of so many people living in the Fowyang area. Then we broke up and went to our rooms.

Thus began our servant-less days. Cooking, washing, and ironing took their toll of our time. Drip-dry dresses had not yet been invented, and the charcoal irons we used either spat hot sparks out of the little funnel built at the front, or went cold on us. Rendering down pork fat, baking bread, haggling in the market, conserving water, counting pennies—sometimes it was hard to see these chores as part of missionary work. It became difficult for me to fit in time for language study, which should have had top priority. Added to that, I also spent countless hours laboriously preparing messages in Chinese.

God spoke to me on a September morning, reminding me of His promise: "Wait on the Lord: be of good courage, and He shall strengthen thine heart." A new peace came into my being. I began discovering for myself His strength was mine—for everything!

PART V

Marriage
1942

Chapter Twenty-Four

O Lord, I know that the way of man is not in himself;
it is not in man that walketh to direct his steps.
Jeremiah 10:23 KJV

PLANS WERE IN the making for a conference of our Anhwei missionaries. Mr. R.E. Thompson, one of the directors based in Chungking, was scheduled to be with us, also Mr. Trudinger from Honan, and possibly Gordon Dunn from south of the Yangtze River. He was the assistant superintendent of Anhwei. We were all looking forward to this conference. It would give a much-needed opportunity for mutual discussion, social intermingling, and spiritual renewal.

On September 22, 1942, God dropped a stone into the smooth waters of my life. The ripples it caused have spread on and on in ever-widening circles. It came in the form of a letter to Bert Kane from Marvin Dunn, Gordon's younger brother. In it he said that he, as the South Anhwei representative, was planning to accompany Gordon to the conference. This was interesting in itself, but the unexpected ending to the letter said they would probably take *me* back to the South when they returned home! This was the first time such an idea had been mooted, and we guessed that a previous letter from Gordon had gone astray, which was not unusual during the war years.

None of us had ever thought it would be possible for me to reach South Anhwei (that was where I had been designated over a year before) until the war ended. The Yangtze River divided the North of the province from the South, and Japanese troops controlled it. Since Pearl

Harbor, any missionary caught in Japanese territory would be interned. Yet, apparently the missionaries in the South believed that if their two men could get through the Japanese lines coming north, it should be possible for me to return with them.

My mind was in a turmoil that evening. Suddenly a door was opening to an unknown future, an unknown area, and unknown people. True, it was only a crack, but if this was God's plan for me, then I could rely on Him to open it further. Naturally, for I am only human, there was also the big question that lives in most girls' hearts: "What about that man?" Marvin Dunn was the only bachelor in Anhwei, North or South. He had already spent eight years in China, and was now in his second term. At the same time, my Lord knew that deep down I trusted Him for my future. Marriage—or a single life—the decision was His, not mine. My hands were still unclenched.

Two days later, news came that Mr. Thompson had been recalled to Chungking, Mr. Trudinger was unable to leave Honan, and the conference was canceled. All of us were disappointed, but it hit me hardest because of my personal involvement in the effects of this decision. Obviously, I would be remaining in Fowyang. Bert sent a telegram to the Dunn brothers telling them not to come north. The door to South Anhwei was swinging shut.

Or was it? South Anhwei was the place to which the CIM leaders, after much prayer, had designated me even though the door was closed at that time. God had given peace as I accepted this. If He wanted me there now instead of some years later, could He not open the way? Japanese soldiers were no hindrance to Him.

I prayed that if this was God's time for me to go forward, He would overrule. One of the fleeces I put out was that if the Dunn brothers decided to proceed anyway and managed to cross Japanese territory, I would know that God was opening my way. A telegram had been sent; all indications were that they would remain at home. Meanwhile, I had lots to do.

A month later a letter arrived on Bert's desk from Gordon Dunn. He and Marvin had navigated Japanese-occupied territory safely and were in Shucheng, north of the Yangtze. The telegram had never reached them. Here was God's answer to my fleece. The light was turning green.

On October 30, I was busy preparing dinner in our little kitchen. The coal-dust and mud fire was behaving well, and its red heart glowed under the pots and pans. I was chopping onions with a big *ts'ai-tao* (Chinese knife) when Bert walked into the compound followed by two tall young men whom I had never seen before.

"Hi, there!" he called. "Anyone at home? I've brought some visitors to see you."

Mary Beth and little Lois appeared at their door, and Emmie opened hers. "Why, it's Gordon Dunn!" she cried.

I left my onions, hurriedly rinsed my hands in the enamel basin, and walked into the sunshine, my face flushed with heat from the stove.

"This is Miss Toop," Bert said to them. To me he said, "Let me introduce you to Gordon Dunn, your assistant superintendent, and his brother Marvin."

"How do you do?" I said. "What a surprise to see you. I'm afraid I can't shake hands as mine smell of onions."

Mary Beth invited them into the living room, and the others crowded in, full of questions. I had to dash back to my onions and the dinner when I would have given worlds to have been able to join them.

That same Friday afternoon, Gordon came over again to find out what I thought about traveling south. He did not minimize the physical hardships of the long trip (about five hundred miles), but stated them frankly. He also mentioned the immediate need for a midwife, as a baby was expected at the beginning of December and there was no nurse among the small missionary force there. He did not mention it at the time, but I learned later that it was his own baby that was expected.

Many a man would have been unwilling to take such a dangerous journey when his first child was due almost before he could get back. Not many wives would have allowed their husbands to go, either. Obviously, God's will was paramount to this couple and their devotion was a challenge to me.

Gordon was also forthright as he explained the church situation in South Anhwei. Numbers were small, interest low, and materialism rampant: not an encouraging situation.

I told him how God had led me in praying, and that I was willing to go. He set next Monday as the day. It was his use of the word "next" that confused me. I discovered, not for the first time, that even between missionaries there were language problems! If an Englishman (Gordon was Canadian) had been talking, he would have said "this Monday" and all would have been well. To me, "next Monday" referred to a week later. So I got the impression that I had a full week in which to get ready. What was my consternation when I discovered that we were leaving in two days' time! I had not even begun packing!

Those two days were a blur of chaos and activity. Because we would be climbing mountain trails part of the way, Gordon said my things—books, bedding, clothes, medical equipment—had to be packed into forty-five-pound parcels so they could be carried on each end of a carrying pole.

My trunks and footlockers were too large. So we scrounged around for cartons and boxes, and hung them one by one on the old brass hook of a Chinese rod-scale. Articles both light and heavy were flung in. When the weight quivered at the forty-five-pound notch, the box was removed and someone packed the contents more neatly. I could never have done this without help; everyone pitched in. My room was like a circus.

By Monday night, the odd assortment of boxes was ready, including my bicycle, which Gordon thought would come in useful later. I was up before daylight on Tuesday, November 4, to do the final tidying up. Then we walked to the river and boarded an old wood-burning launch. The three of us said goodbye to our friends, the boatmen loosed the ropes, and we backed into midstream. My big adventure had begun.

Chapter Twenty-Five

*Lead me, O Lord, in Thy righteousness because of mine
enemies; make Thy way straight before my face.*
Psalm 5:8 KJV

IT WAS RATHER unusual in the China of that day for a young lady to be
escorted by two men, one of them single. But under the circumstances,
it could not be helped. Of course, I fell in love with Marvin before the
end of that five-week trip. He was kind and thoughtful, he had a sense
of humor, was tall and active, was a spiritual man, and his Chinese
language was excellent. But—he had red hair! I had thought I could
never marry a man with red hair. But somehow my attitude changed.

We had many opportunities on that five-hundred-mile journey to
become better acquainted. I discovered that Gordon had left Canada
for China in 1931, and Marvin had followed him one year later. Their
father had broken sod in the Saskatchewan prairies in 1911 with teams
of oxen. But in the 1920s, their parents sold the big and prosperous farm
of six hundred and forty acres and moved their family to a small town
in Alberta. There in Three Hills, the miracle of Prairie Bible Institute
was in progress, and Mr. and Mrs. Dunn wished their four children to
be exposed to the wind of the Spirit that was blowing there. In 1927
Gordon entered Bible school, and one year later Marvin did the same.

Their home was always open to missionaries. Among these were
three giants of a former day: Dr. Isaac Page, Mr. Charles Judd, and Dr.
Robert H. Glover, all representing the China Inland Mission. It was not
a surprise that the sons' thoughts were directed to China. After some

113

months of language study in the Men's Training Home in Anking in 1931 and 1932, they had both been designated to work in the southern part of Anhwei province, along the Yangtze River basin.

Marvin Dunn, as a newly recruited missionary to China in 1932 ten years before meeting Miriam Toop, and eleven years before their wedding.

As we sailed south, our wooden boat moved quickly with the current. A cold wind blew, and my wadded winter gown was a godsend. That first night, we disembarked and slept in the home of CIM missionaries. The next morning, Marvin set off on foot alone, accompanied by a bouncy little black kid goat.

It turned out that Gordon had had a third reason for running the Japanese blockade. The first was to attend the conference, the second was to take me back, and the third to pick up a billy goat! In the South, milk was in short supply. The canned produce was unobtainable. There were no cows; milking goats was the answer. The Chinese variety produced only a cup or so of milk a day, not enough to keep the missionary children in good health. Gordon knew that in the northern part of Anhwei, Swiss goats had been introduced and mated with local animals. As a result, good milkers gave an abundance of creamy milk. Why not do the same thing in the South by taking a Swiss billy goat there?

Gordon and I traveled on by boat. In places, the river was so shallow that the bottom of the vessel scraped along its bed. However, when we reached deep water and a following wind began to blow, the sail was hoisted and we made good time. Each evening the sailors dropped anchor at some small river market, where we were supposedly safe from bandit attack. In such circumstances, the *Daily Light* verses of November 11 were a real encouragement. One week of the trip was over; the most dangerous section lay ahead. But I believed with the Psalmist that God would lead and make His way straight before us.

At Liuan we again joined up with Marvin. From here on, there was no more boat travel. Instead, I resorted to other types of transport, such as being carried in a swaying sedan chair, balancing on one side of a wheelbarrow, riding a bicycle, or walking. The scenery was beautiful, and one day I even found some violets. For the most part, the land was rugged and the villages were far apart. Wherever we went, the little billy goat went too, and when he got tired the cook boy carried him in a basket at the end of his carrying pole.

Shucheng was the last CIM center before we reached the Yangtze. We arrived there on Saturday. The Christians asked Marvin to preach the next day. His Chinese sounded very fluent to me. He wore a long Chinese gown, which made him look taller than usual. At the end of the day, we missionaries had a time of sharing and fellowship, after which we prayed, asking the Lord for His protection over us in the dangerous path ahead.

Leaving Shucheng behind, we climbed gradually into the hills. Our route snaked up hill and down dale. The roads were narrow, and paved with stone slabs. We found that the woven straw sandals, such as the coolies wore, were the most comfortable for walking. Civilization dropped behind us, and we Caucasians roused great curiosity. Our immediate destination was Ho Pu Lin, a small town where a Travel Bureau had been set up to enable merchants and travelers to cross through Japanese territory into South Anhwei. Armed protection was provided also. It was through this organization that Gordon planned to negotiate travel arrangements.

One day, as the country flattened out into a plateau, I rode ahead on my bicycle. The sun was shining, but the air was cold and invigorating. After some lonely miles, I stopped at a small roadside inn, dropped onto a backless bench, and asked for a cup of tea. The old innkeeper placed a handle-less cup on the table. From a black kettle that was bubbling on a charcoal fire, he poured boiling water on green tea leaves in the cracked teapot. That tea was delicious, fragrant, and thirst quenching.

Soon another traveler walked up, and as we sat sipping our tea, he and I fell into conversation. With no one else around, I did not mind using my stilted Chinese. But as I told him of Jesus his face was a blank, for he had never heard His name before. I tried to explain God's way of salvation as simply as I could, but the word "cross" puzzled him. How could I make it clear? On the ground near the bench was a dry piece of bamboo. I picked it up, snapped it in two, and formed a cross. His expression changed, and I knew he understood that much. Unfortunately, I did not have a tract with me, but the message had been passed on.

As the sun dropped behind the hills, we came to a small country town and found our way to the inn. The peasants had never seen a white woman before, and when news of our arrival spread, the narrow street outside the inn began to fill with a noisy crowd. They shouted and called at the entrance, straining to catch a glimpse of me. My two escorts hurriedly bolted the door and shot me upstairs to the attic. But this did not deter the mob. They pushed and hammered on the gate, which eventually gave way. As the people surged in, first Gordon then Marvin spoke to them, barring the way to my hiding place. I had never had such an experience before. I sat in the dark with a galloping pulse, listening to the throaty shouts of men and the excited squeals of children, and asked the Lord for His protection. It was not until the landlord also harangued the crowd that the uproar gradually died down and the people dispersed.

The next morning was frosty and cold. Gordon went out shopping and returned with a bundle of smoking hot *yu-t'iao* (dough strips fried in deep fat). He carried them dangling from a wisp of twisted straw: tasty, golden-brown, crisp, and hot, a perfect breakfast for a cold morning. In beautiful sunshine we set out on the last few miles to Ho Pu Lin. There was a tang in the air and a song in my heart. Soon we should be in Free China, south of the Yangtze.

Little did I know then that our first attempt to cross the river would be unsuccessful, and that we would be held up on this same side of the Yangtze for five long days. The way was not as straight before us as we had expected.

Chapter Twenty-Six

He knoweth the way that I take.
Job 23:10 KJV

THOSE FIVE DAYS were spent waiting, but there were compensations. The weather was sunny and cold. Sometimes we would take the little goat out to feed; sometimes I would study; sometimes Marvin and I would talk; sometimes I wrote letters. We also had to forage for food, as there were no shops inside the stockade. Because the tides of war tended to flow back and forth in such areas, goods meant more to the people than money, so we often had trouble persuading the farmers to sell. However, we always had enough to eat.

On November 26, 1942, two days after we had retreated from the river, a party of weary travelers arrived from the South, having taken the very route mapped out for us. We hoped this meant that the gunboats had left, but they told us they were still there. This group had decided to risk the crossing, and made it. They had also discovered that Japanese motorboats were nosing along the riverbanks, which made the venture even more hazardous. All we could do was wait.

Three days later, the leader heard that the ships had gone, and we could proceed. Six days after our first abortive attempt, we set off in a smaller convoy at noon, and managed to get safely to the river by seven-thirty that evening. It was a dark night, for clouds hid stars and moon. A drizzle of rain was falling.

Near the bank we could just discern five boats silhouetted against the moving water. In spite of orders to keep as quiet as possible, bedlam broke out. Slipping and stumbling down the bank, it was each for his own. In the confusion, it was hard to locate the boats, as they could show no lights, and any semblance of order vanished. The forty-four coolies scrambled on board with their loads, shouting and cursing as others shoved in before them. It was amazing that no one came up to investigate what all the noise was about.

The Dunns and I managed to get on the same boat, as did the cook boy and the little kid. After filling with passengers, the boats pushed off into midstream, and we hoped the billy goat would not betray us with a bleat. The creak of oars and the slap of water were the only sounds. It was strangely peaceful after that fierce melee on the shore.

The crossing took nearly an hour, for the current was swift and the river wide. When we reached the other side, the boatman told us he could not row right to the shore. We would have to wade through the last few yards. I took off my shoes and stockings, tied them around my neck, hitched up my wadded gown as high as I could, and climbed over the side. It was not the cold water that made me gasp: I began to sink down into soft mud that squelched between my toes and seeped up to my knees! We slowly slithered to dry ground. It was horrible! In the dark it was difficult to remove the mud, dry my feet, and put on shoes and stockings once again.

Most of the coolies were up and away long before we were ready to move. Once more we formed the tail of a mobile cavalcade of men: walking on narrow paths that divided the rice fields, jumping ditches and climbing among rocks, one behind the other. It was still dark, and we wondered how the guide knew which direction to take. For over four *li* we walked in absolute silence, as this area was also under Japanese control (three *li* equals one mile).

Around midnight we caught up with the rest of the convoy, which was halted at the edge of a small lake. From the disturbed looks on the men's faces and the hissing of many voices, we guessed that something had gone wrong. We soon heard that other boats, which should have been waiting to convey us to the farther side of this lake, were missing. The leader peered this way and that.

Some men ventured along the edge of the water to see if they could find them. But it was useless. We were stuck, stranded in Japanese-occupied China, with the lake before us and the Yangtze at our rear.

As they had done on a former occasion, the leaders conferred together. The guide came over to us. "You three foreigners are in special danger," he said. "It is not safe for you to remain here. If the Japanese should find you, they would keep you as prisoners. We are different. Being Chinese, we can escape detection, but that is impossible for you. We have decided to send you back across the Yangtze under escort to the place we left this morning, and you can come across tomorrow with another group."

Both Marvin and Gordon protested against this plan.

"But where can you go?" the man asked. "You cannot hide as we can. The Japanese have many soldiers along this bank also."

"Give us a little time to talk it over before you make the final decision," pleaded Gordon.

"*Hao*" (Okay), he grunted, "but don't take too long. You should be far from here before daylight comes."

The three of us stood together. God was the only one who could help us now. Naturally, Gordon was anxious to go forward, not back. The baby was due any time now, and his heart was in Tunki. We prayed, asking the Lord to guide and show His way, and we all felt we should not go back. God had brought us safely over the biggest barrier; we could trust Him for the path ahead. After all, it was known to Him.

After further consultation, the leader surprisingly agreed to go along with our decision. But was it surprising? Had not we committed our situation to the Lord who is able to work in men's hearts?

"Tell the white lady to cover her head," the guide commanded. "Even though it is dark, her hair and skin might betray you if we met anyone. You must all follow me closely."

He produced a square of blue cloth, and when I had tied it over my hair, we walked in single file to a nearby village. The coolies had long since scattered to the hills. We walked for a mile in dead silence, until we came to houses. Down the one street we walked, between shuttered and barred homes. The leader stopped and rapped softly on a solid wooden door. A whispered conversation followed, and then we were called and told to slip inside the dark building. By two o'clock in the morning we were asleep.

The next morning, we were able to examine our surroundings more closely. To my horror, lurid Japanese posters screamed their message of hate from the walls of the main room: "Down with England and America!" Had we been betrayed? Our host was a personable young man who talked quite freely. He told us he had been forced by circumstances to serve the enemy. He added that he hated doing this, but had no alternative. "You are safe with me," he said. "I am your friend. Don't pay any attention to those posters."

He continued, "There are Japanese soldiers in the vicinity, but they will not come here. I am in contact with the Wang Ching-wei troops, who are in the pay of the Japanese patrolling this region, and they will warn me of any enemy troops who may move in this direction. However, you must not go outside this house during the day." Thus God kept us in the eye of the storm, in safety and peace.

When the evening darkness fell, we said goodbye to our friendly ally, and headed back to the lake where we found the convoy gathering together.

"The boats are here," said the leader, "so we should make our target this time. The boatmen told me there is too much mud for them to get in any closer, so you will all have to wade out to them."

Once again, we struggled barefoot through fifty feet of slushy mud to the sampans. The coolies carrying heavy loads had a bad time. After crossing the lake, we disembarked and had to wait until everyone had reached land. We then tramped off with another armed escort for the base of the mountains that lay between freedom and us. Already, tension was lessening. Muttered conversation broke out here and there. Danger was falling behind us with every step we took.

At two in the morning, they let us rest before our final assault on the mountain pass. Everyone was glad to sit. An old moon climbed wearily into the sky and gave a soft glow to the dark ridges above us. The soldiers built a fire. Its flickering flames were reflected in shining black eyes, ruddy cheeks, and white teeth as they gathered around it, laughing and talking. They hung a huge cauldron above it, and when the water began to steam and bubble, they threw in handfuls of yellow cornmeal. Soon they passed around bowls of scalding porridge, satisfying and filling on a cold night.

By four o'clock, we were climbing steadily. The moon shone more bravely, and our spirits rose. As the eastern sky flamed into color, we reached the top of the pass, and stood with praising hearts looking out on range upon range of mountains in South Anhwei, with the Yangtze far behind us.

We were not yet out of danger. After a short rest, the descent began. There followed a long trek across the plain, a meal, and finally a last strenuous climb up the Mei Ling Pass. A marvelous panorama of mountain ridges lay before us, but we had no time to absorb its beauty. Everyone was eager to reach Chen Chia Lung, the southern station of the Travel Bureau. We joined the others, jumping from step to step down the stone path, soon to be safe in Free China at last, on the afternoon of December 1, 1942.

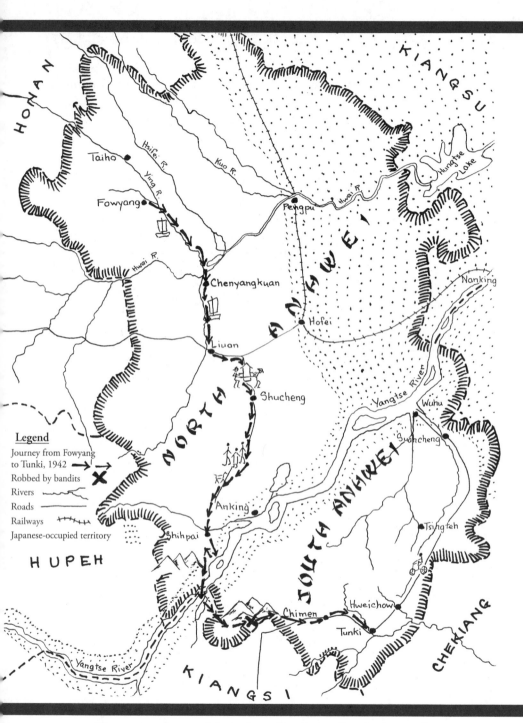

The opening chapter of the book graphically describes the drama of
this map. The large X is where Miriam Toop and Marvin Dunn
were robbed by bandits. Chapter 27 integrates the opening chapter
into the chronology of Miriam Dunn's experiences in China.

Chapter Twenty-Seven

Thou shalt remember all the way which the Lord thy
God led thee... to humble thee and to prove thee, to
know what was in thine heart.
Deuteronomy 8:2 KJV

At Chen Chia Lung, we terminated our association with the Travel Bureau. They had brought us safely through the dangerous Japanese lines into Free China. Now we were on our own.

In the inn, we three had to make some decisions. We were truly thankful to God for hearing our prayers. Our hearts were light as we thought of the future; only a few more days and we would reach our journey's end! However, all our coolies had not yet arrived, as the climb the night before had been tough. Gordon was impatient to get on the road to Tunki. Many miles of hard travel still separated him from Vera. Naturally, he wanted to reach her as soon as possible. He wanted to leave the next day.

Plans for Marvin and me depended on how soon the coolies reached us. Even if they came very soon, could they move quickly enough to suit Gordon? Or should I go ahead with him and let Marvin come more slowly with the carriers and the little goat? Could I keep up with this man who would push himself to the limit to cover the miles? Our discussion ranged back and forth. Perhaps I should accompany Gordon with a minimum of baggage, plus my medical supplies, and Marvin could bring the rest?

It was then that I recalled the chaotic day I had packed my boxes.

123

My medical gear was scattered indiscriminately through all my stuff to even up the weight of the individual cases. Because of the pressure of time, I had not made a list of their contents. It would take hours to go through them all now to pick out the relevant items. As soon as I explained this to the men, Gordon said, "That settles it. I can't wait any longer. I will go on ahead as fast as I can. You and Marvin and the coolies will follow at a slower pace, and we must trust the Lord to look after Vera. After all," he said with a characteristic lift of his left eyebrow, "I've trusted Him this long and she is safe in His hands. But I do want to get going."

The next day was gray and miserable. A chilling rain fell with dull monotony on wet stones. Leaves drooped under the weight of glistening moisture. A leaden sky mourned overhead. But nothing could stop Gordon now. He walked off down the cobbled street at a good pace.

A few hours later, the carriers dribbled in with the baggage, soaking wet. Marvin paid them off as arranged, and later was able to hire other men to carry the boxes on to Chi Men, where we hoped to catch a bus to Tunki.

Immediately after breakfast the next morning, which was cloudy and bitterly cold, Marvin and I were ready to hit the trail. Eight o'clock came and went, then nine, then ten—and the newly hired men did not show up. As so often happens, something that seems so insignificant at the time has an unforeseen bearing on the future. This delay proved to do just that. It was eleven o'clock when we finally set off. I rode the bicycle, followed by the coolies whose carrying poles jogged and creaked in unison, while Marvin brought up the rear with the cook boy and the little goat.

The rest of the day, we followed the road as it wound between and over the hills. Villages were few and far between. The land was poor and showed little signs of cultivation. Rocky outcrops protruded through the vegetation. But we glimpsed beauty: a green-carpeted grove of feathery bamboo, glimmering silver in the wind.

The hours flew by, and the coolies reminded us of the need to find a stopping place for the night. We had only managed to travel thirty *li* (ten miles) because of our late start. If we did not do better the next day, we would never make Chi Men and the motor road in time.

The following day, the road deteriorated. It was impossible to ride the bicycle very much, and our progress was slow. The carriers grumbled when we tried to press them on. I could see now why Gordon had insisted my trunks would have been too cumbersome for travel such as this.

Rugged mountains hemmed us in, shutting out the sun. The valleys were cold and dark, the villages gray and poverty stricken. This was wild and turbulent country, covering the boundaries of three provinces. Such border areas were a long way from the centers of law and order, and were often the bases from which bandits and outlaws operated.

As the afternoon closed in, the coolies clamored to stop for the night. Marvin wanted to keep going, as he knew of a safe stopping place some miles farther on, and did not relish an overnight stay in this desolate country. However, the men refused to go farther, so we agreed to spend the night at the next hamlet. It proved to be a dreary-looking place, its people sad and withdrawn; no one smiled. Even the children were quiet, showing none of the curiosity which the sight of foreigners usually evoked.

We entered the one poor inn. I was given a small inside room to myself. Marvin was in the common room with the baggage arranged along the wall, and the coolies huddled together in a small, dark adjoining room. Marvin then scoured the village for food. All he could buy were a few eggs, which we scrambled for supper. It was cold, and I was glad to snuggle down in my thick blue *p'u-kai*. Sleep came quickly, for we were all exhausted from trudging up and down the stony road.

Suddenly I awoke. Some unusual sound had disturbed me. Then I heard it more clearly—the guttural voices of excited men outside the inn. Blows rained on the outside door, accompanied by shouts to open up. Someone lifted the heavy wooden bar from the inside and a cascade of noise burst into the inn. My door was flung open, and light flickered toward me from a blazing torch held high by a uniformed man with a rifle in his other hand. "Get up," he ordered me. "Hurry, get out of your bed!"

Above the babble of sound in the common room, I heard Marvin's voice. "Put on your wadded gown," he called in English, "and do what they say."

I sat up, reached for my warm gown, and slipped it on, my fingers fumbling over the frogs that fastened it together. "Do you want my passport?" I asked in Chinese. The man paid no attention. It was quite possible that he had not understood my question.

Meanwhile, Marvin asked the leader what organization they belonged to, and by what authority they were carrying out this inspection. That seemed to infuriate them. One man stripped the watch off my wrist. Another ran his hands through my suitcase, stuffing stockings, soap, toothbrush, toothpaste, etc. into his pockets. One threw my beautiful Scots wool blanket around his shoulders, and another seized the traveling rug. By this time, I realized that these uncouth men were bandits.

When they had taken their pick, they tied one end of a rough rope around my neck and the other to one of my wrists. They talked continually among themselves in excited, raised voices, but I caught only scraps of their conversation. I did hear one mutter something about taking us into the mountains. Did this mean we were being kidnapped?

They pushed me forward to the bigger room. It was lit with the fitful flames of more torches. My eyes flew to Marvin. He was standing beside the bed, his hands tied behind him in the center of a ring of armed men with their rifles trained on him.

His suitcase had been ransacked also, and one bandit was wearing his hat. Another had donned his warm Canadian overcoat, while he himself was in the blue- and white-striped pajamas he had put on for the night.

The men were in an ugly mood, jittery and on edge. "You are spies!" one of them yelled. "The things we discovered in your luggage are those that spies carry."

At this point, some of them cocked their guns and it looked black for us. Yet peace miraculously flooded our hearts and kept us unafraid. At a signal from the leader, one man prodded Marvin from behind. Another led me forward. They tied the loose end of my rope to the one binding Marvin's hands and pushed us together into the dark room where the coolies crouched. Before the door slammed behind us, the ring of men broke up. I looked back. My boxes were ranged along the wall, just as the carriers had left them, with the carrying poles carelessly flung on top. I saw four bandits run quickly over, sling them onto their shoulders, and march out into the night. The others followed, draped in their new acquisitions, their pockets bulging with a strange assortment of articles.

After the uproar and noise, a silence that could be felt descended, broken only by the whispers and movements of the coolies behind us. Then out of the darkness came Marvin's voice with a most prosaic request. "Do you think you could untie my hands? I can't do anything with them tied behind my back like this."

I struggled to get the knots undone. When his hands were free he removed the rope from around my neck. We stumbled around trying to find the door and entered the common room, which now looked strangely empty. A small oil lamp on the table gave a feeble light. The old landlady was energetically trying to fan to a flame the gray and dusty embers in the portable charcoal stove.

"Ai-yah!" she moaned as she put the blackened kettle on the fire. "I'm so sorry. To think that this happened to you in *my* inn! What a calamity!"

The coals began to glow. As we waited for the water to boil, some implications of what had happened began to sink in. My entire precious outfit had gone in one fell swoop of a bandit's gun. All our money had been stolen, with three days of travel still before us. Marvin did not even have warm clothes, and it was bitter December weather. The bandits had taken everything.

I got up slowly and went to my room. Rather hopelessly I looked through the jumbled contents of my suitcase. Suddenly I spied my little *Daily Light.* Did God have a message for us? I took it back to the fire, where Marvin was sitting with bowed head. It was now the early hours of December 5, and I turned to that morning's reading.

The old lady had gone back to bed. The charcoal glinted with new life in the shallow iron bowl. Tea steamed in two handle-less cups on the table. The occasional spit and crackle of fire was the only sound in the room. I began to read.

Every single verse on that page was applicable to us. I felt myself choking up, and my voice faltered when I came to the words: "Thou shalt remember all the way which the Lord thy God led thee." Tears came to my eyes and I put the book down. In a hushed voice Marvin began to pray and we committed everything to the Lord. The two hours we had just passed through seemed like a bad dream, yet they had brought us an unforgettable consciousness of God's love and care. His presence was very real in that cold and shabby inn, for He had led us there.

"You'd better try to get some sleep," Marvin suggested. "We can't leave here until it gets light." He hesitated a moment, then added, "You don't know how sorry I am that this has happened."

"It wasn't your fault," I protested. "You'd better get some rest as well."

Back in my room I began to sort out the things in my case. There was pitifully little. I saw a small notebook and picked it up, idly flipping through its pages. Then I gave an incredulous gasp, for underneath my fingers three brand new ten dollar bills clung to one of the pages. Money—from nowhere—money—from God!

I ran back to the other room, waving the notes in my hand. "Look!" I cried. "Isn't this marvelous? Here is thirty dollars the brigands didn't get!"

"Where did you find them?" Marvin asked.

"In my suitcase," I replied, and told him the details.

"That is amazing," he remarked. "This will pay for our night's lodging and for food tomorrow. And I've just remembered something else."

"What's that?" I inquired.

"You remember that I wanted to try to make Shan Li last night, but the carriers said it was impossible? Well, when Gordon and I left South Anhwei to cross the Yangtze two months ago, I left my bicycle there— and also two hundred dollars, just in case we might meet trouble on the trip. We'll be able to pick that up later on today. God knew we'd need that money, and I'm sure He guided me to leave it with friends there."

"Oh, how wonderful!" I exclaimed. "Perhaps it will pay for our bus fares from Chi Men to Tunki."

"It should," Marvin replied. "Now off you go, or you'll be too tired for anything tomorrow—or actually today. This whole thing has been such a shock. Good night."

After an early breakfast of rice gruel, we set off again, into a cold and frosty morning. The landlady refused to take any money and insisted that Marvin wear an old gray sweater to help him keep warm. He looked rather odd as he walked on ahead, but amusement at his comical appearance took my mind off recent happenings. As for myself, I was traveling in style, carried in a makeshift sedan chair. Originally, the coolies had been hired to take us as far as Chi Men, and as their loads had disappeared, Marvin decided they should carry me instead.

Later in the day, we reached Shan Li, and stayed with the Christian couple with whom Marvin had left his two hundred dollars. It was there that he discovered a tiny gray louse in the seams of the old sweater. One probably meant many more, and as the bite of a louse can cause typhus, the sweater was burned.

"Miss Toop, do you happen to have an extra cover (of a wadded gown) in your suitcase?" he asked me.

"Yes, I do," I replied. "For some reason the bandits didn't take the clean one in my case. (I was wearing one over my gown, as that was the way the Chinese protected the patterned silk of the warm, winter garment.) Why?"

"Well, I was wondering if you would mind if I wore it over my pajamas. I'd like to get something to cover these large blue and white stripes."

"Not at all," I said, "but I'm afraid it won't fit you very well."

I went to find it. The next time he appeared, my blue cover gown was stretched tightly across his chest, the sleeves halfway down his arms, and the bottom part flapping around his knees, with the blue and white stripes adding a bizarre touch below!

To complete the picture, when we set out the next morning, he was wearing a fez-like cap made of a facecloth and a bit of blue material. His ears had nearly frozen the day before. We had no combs or toothbrushes, and his razor had also been taken. There had been no way to replace them. It was a scruffy pair of travelers who eventually reached Chi Men on the afternoon of December 7. Needless to say, we bought toilet articles there and felt distinctly better.

The next morning we went to the bus station, and Marvin put me on the Tunki bus. We still did not have enough money for two tickets. He rode his bicycle instead. The cook boy carried my bicycle on one end of his pole with the little goat in a basket on the other.

The old bus made rather slow progress, and at various stopping places I was glad to see a distant dot on the road gradually grow into a blue figure on a bicycle. At one stop, Marvin caught up with us and bought some hot roasted sweet potatoes from a wayside vendor. They tasted delectable on that cold day. As the bus rolled in at the Tunki stop, Marvin also arrived. He jumped off his cycle and helped my suitcase and me to the road.

Gordon looked at us in amazement when he saw us on the path. "You look as if you've met bandits," he exclaimed. "Where is your stuff?"

We poured out the most important parts of the story, and in turn learned of God's marvelous provision for Vera. Dr. John Webb, a medical missionary, had arrived in Tunki with a British Military Mission group. When he learned of her circumstances and that this was her first pregnancy, he promised to stay and help if I did not arrive in time. On December 3, little Barbara was safely delivered, ready to welcome her father home on the fourth from his long trip. A Chinese nurse looked after mother and baby until I took over on the eleventh.

Two more things must be mentioned to round out this story. The little goat must have suffered from the hardships of the trip more than we had realized, for after a few weeks, he died, leaving no progeny. Thus ended an unsuccessful experiment to improve the strain of native goats in Tunki.

The second item underlined afresh God's care for us. It was a little later that we heard of a group of Chinese travelers, following the same route we had taken from North to South Anhwei, who also fell into the hands of armed brigands. For them, however, it ended in death. That might have been our experience. Instead, we could look back and remember God's care and protection.

Chapter Twenty-Eight

Be strong… and work: for I am with
you, saith the Lord of hosts.
Haggai 2:4 KJV

LIFE BEGAN TO fall into a pattern as I settled in at Tunki. Some of my time was spent looking after Vera and the baby, some in language study, some in household duties, and some in church activities. I found the whole church setup very different from Fowyang.

The congregation was small, but the members were well educated, and many could speak English. They dressed smartly (I felt so conspicuous in my one outfit and lack of accessories!), for Tunki was a bustling and important city. The Christians were friendly, but they lacked the warm love and spiritual life of the thriving churches in the North. Materialism had crept in and was doing its deadly work.

Three couples, Marvin, and myself comprised the total CIM force in South Anhwei. Our task was to reach out to share Jesus Christ with the millions still living in the grip of idolatry. George and Grace Birch were the missionaries in charge in Tunki, and I made my home with them. Two of their children had been at the big Chefoo School in Japanese-occupied China, but were now in an internment camp. Danny and Helen were at home and eagerly looking forward to the coming of a new baby in January.

Gordon and Vera's station was Hweichow, some twenty miles east of Tunki, but they were temporarily in Tunki for Barbara's birth. John and Eleanore Crook also worked in Hweichow. Eleanore and I came out to China the same year, but from Tsingtao she had returned to Shanghai and then proceeded to Chekiang province. En route she passed through John's station, and he could not get her bright eyes and brown curls out of his heart and mind! A letter went south, later followed by John himself, and an engagement was announced. Eleanore had set her heart on a white wedding gown, but during the war the price of silk was astronomical. She and John prayed about it and a wedding dress came from heaven—literally! One of Lt. Col. Jimmy Doolittle's flyers, returning from the bombing raid over Japan, ran out of fuel over Chekiang and bailed out. He met Eleanore, and when he heard she was getting married, he gladly gave her his parachute, which provided her with a beautiful white wedding gown!

Marvin left Tunki for his home and work in Tsingteh on December 12, and life seemed empty. Soon letters began to trickle in from him, and I looked for them eagerly.

In January 1943, we had our first snowfall of the winter. Into this cold, white world little Miriam Birch was born. Everything went smoothly during the delivery, and the following days were busy—but

Lt. Col. Jimmy Doolittle, April 18, 1942 posing with his crew on the deck of the USS Hornet in front of a B-25 just prior to the bombing raid over Tokyo.

not too busy to enjoy an unexpected visit from Marvin.

On February 2, he asked me to go for a walk with him in the rain, and I happily accepted. But my joy turned to consternation when he gently told me that he felt I should know that he was corresponding with a girl in Canada. Once again, my world seemed to fall apart. It had been such fun at the beginning of our walk to dodge the raindrops, but now they symbolized the feelings of my heart. We walked on, and he told me more. This girl was a missionary candidate when he met her in Toronto, and he had been attracted to her. However, at that stage she was not prepared to commit herself.

That was the fall of 1941, and they both realized it was impossible to make hard and fast plans. So they decided to hold their relationship lightly before the Lord, write to each other, and wait for God's direction. Marvin had left Vancouver a few weeks later, on the last ship to sail from Canada for China before Pearl Harbor brought America into the war. Since then, postal services had been badly disrupted. He had received no letters.

We walked slowly home. It had not been easy for him to speak so frankly, but at least it had brought everything into the open. The future was in God's hands.

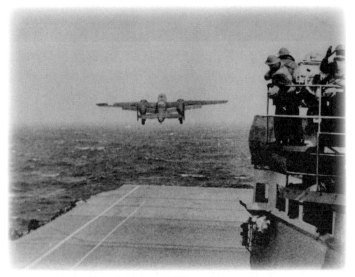

*A B-25 taking off from Hornet for
Lt. Col. Jimmy Doolittle's raid against Japan.*

I asked the Lord that night for some message that would reassure and comfort me. Nothing came, but the very next morning the *Daily Light* portion renewed my confidence. "I am with you," Jesus said, "and in Me you can face the uncertainties of life. I am your strength and song."

It was good to know that He had His hands on my life, and on Marvin's also. He gave peace, and the sense of loss and disappointment grew less. So it was with a serene face that I saw Marvin mount his bicycle and ride off down the hill to his bachelor rooms in Tsingteh.

Chapter Twenty-Nine

*He was their shepherd according to the integrity of his
heart, and guided them by the skillfulness of his hands.*
Psalm 78:72 KJV

SPRING CAME TO South Anhwei: the delicate pink of peach blossoms,
the startling yellow of rape fields in bloom, the soft glow of flame-
colored azaleas on the hills.

Rumors of Japanese troop movements began to circulate as the
two armies stirred to fresh activity after the winter freeze. One day, we
heard the distant rumble of planes, but none flew directly over Tunki.
Hweichow, however, was severely damaged, with much destruction of
property. Life grew tenser.

Meningitis struck in the area. Modern medicines were exorbitant
in price and also scarce, and people died in great numbers. Men and
women turned to the temple priests, the only help they knew. One
night, the incessant sound of rolling drums, squealing pipes, and
snapping firecrackers billowed around our hill in waves of heathen
superstition and panic. When fear of death stormed their hearts, the
veneer of Western culture split and crumbled, revealing dependence
on the ancient religions of the land.

One day, a note came from Marvin. He was still waiting for a
letter from the girl in Canada. But he felt an inner constraint to set
aside the morning of March 30 as a time of prayer and fasting. Would
I do the same in Tunki? What we both desired was the revelation
of God's will concerning our future. So that morning Marvin and I,

135

he in Hweichow (where he was staying temporarily) and I in Tunki, spent the morning in prayer about the whole matter.

For me it was a time of heart searching. What were my motives? Was Christ first in my life? What was more important to me? As I took up my pen and wrote to Marvin, I knew I had come to the place where I was willing to be single for the rest of my days if that was God's way.

Naturally, I waited eagerly for a letter from him. It came in a few days—just as my language teacher appeared at the door for my lesson. Torn between a sense of duty and a longing to know what he had written, I had to sit through an entire hour with that unopened letter scorching the pocket of my gown! When I did get a chance to read it, he had written that he felt he must wait. So—I had to wait too.

But not for long. April 7 was a day of surprises. All that morning, it rained and cold winds blew. Then the rain changed to snow. It was an ideal day for study and I buried myself in my books. In the late afternoon I heard a commotion in the living room, the excited voices of Danny and Helen, and Marvin responding. Why had he come? Surely this was no ordinary visit! Scarcely daring to believe he was there, I involuntarily sank to my knees to ask God's help before joining the others outside.

That night all barriers were swept away as Marvin told me of his love. Joy welled up and overflowed as we talked together. He told me that since his last note to me he had had a number of letters from North America, but none from his girlfriend. He then had a long talk with Vera, laying the situation before her. She told him that ever since she had first met me in the Tsingtao Language School, she had been praying that God would bring us together. Apparently, with this accumulation of guidance, not even a snowstorm could stop him from cycling the twenty miles to Tunki!

Because Marvin wanted his letter to be the first to tell his friend our news, he suggested that we keep our engagement secret for the time being. This should not be difficult, as he was leaving immediately on an evangelistic tour with Pastor Cheng to towns near Japanese-held territory. This trip was important, as he thought it might be the last time for some years that Christians in that part of China would be encouraged by the visit of a missionary. It was with bottled-up feelings that we said goodbye the next morning.

Language study filled many hours of my day. The third exam was looming and it would be ideal to get it out of the way while Marvin was away preaching. I plodded through the epistles and Genesis in Chinese, and got involved in Christian's adventures as I translated *Pilgrim's Progress. Matthew's Primer* also led me deeper into the intricacies of Chinese grammar and idiom. I breathed a sigh of relief when I finally sat for the exam in May, even though this was not the end. Three more exams still lay before me. The CIM expected its missionaries to continue slogging with the language until they were easily conversant in Chinese.

On May 18, Marvin returned from his preaching tour and we announced our engagement publicly. I had drawn a map of Anhwei province, with the word "ENGAGED" across the top. A small picture of Marvin cut in the shape of a heart was pasted in Tsingteh in the south, and a similar one of me at Fowyang in the north. I traced in the route of our journey from Fowyang to Tunki, and crossed guns indicated the site of the bandit episode. Two big red hearts pierced by an arrow were placed at Tunki, and across the center of the map were the words *"HE GUIDED THEM BY THE SKILLFULNESS OF HIS HANDS."*

What a commotion when the Birches realized the significance of the occasion! Of course, there had been guesses and surmises before, and it was so delightful to be free and open with our friends once more.

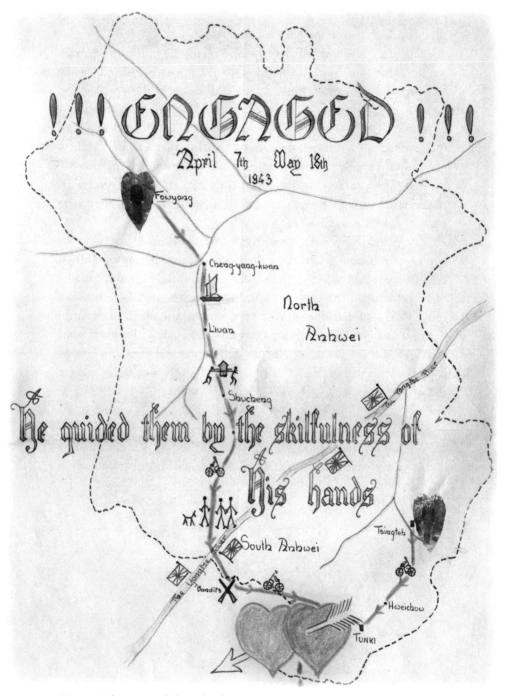

Miriam's drawings while on her honeymoon in 1943. Notice the small picture of Miriam in Fowyang, and picture of Marvin in Tsingteh, the double hearts with an arrow, the interesting symbols, and the beauty of the calligraphy.

Chapter Thirty

Heirs together of the grace of life.
I Peter 3:7 KJV

THE NEXT BIG event was our wedding—when and where? British subjects in China wishing to get married were required to have a consular wedding as well as a religious one. The nearest British consul was over 1,000 miles away. It would take us weeks of wartime travel to get there. In addition, it would be exceedingly costly and probably dangerous.

Our happiness overflowed when a letter came from the consul in reply to Marvin's letter, saying he would waive a consular wedding under the circumstances, as long as an ordained minister performed the ceremony in a church. George Birch was such a man, and he gladly agreed to marry us—right in our little CIM church on the hill, among our Chinese and Western friends.

The next question was when? Gordon Dunn was in the North again for the deferred conference: we could not be married without him! He was expected back in early June, so we planned the wedding for June 22, right after our own South Anhwei mini-conference.

What about a wedding dress? The white silk I would have loved cost too much, and our finances, after the bandit episode, were in bad shape. I did not feel it was right to invest a lot of money in a dress I would wear only once. Then Vera knocked on my door one morning, carrying a package in her hand.

"Miriam, I know you are looking around for material for a wedding dress," she said. "I also know how expensive silk or brocade is downtown. The Lord reminded me that I had this packed in my trunk. It's not the usual stuff of which bridal dresses are made, but if you'd like to have it, it's yours."

She opened the parcel and a length of white voile, daintily crisscrossed in pale pink, spilled onto the bed. "Oh, it's beautiful," I cried, "but you must have saved this for some special occasion."

"Yes, for the wedding of my new sister-in-law," she answered with a misty smile. What could I do but accept it, thanking God for the selfless giving which made it possible.

What about a ring? Marvin gave me a unique and very meaningful one. It happened like this. One of the finest Chinese Christian ladies in South Anhwei had been a single lady called Christine Kiang. She was born in the home of a high official, and according to the custom of the day, her feet had been bound when she was a small girl. However, her father was quite progressive, and believed that girls should be educated as well as boys. This was revolutionary in the 1880s. So she was sent to school, and as missionaries then ran most girls' schools, she heard the story of Jesus. But it was not until she was in her thirties that she attended a meeting at which Miss Gregg, my old friend of London training days, was speaking. The Holy Spirit moved in her heart, and she committed her life totally to Christ. Even though crippled by her bound feet, she was active as a Christian. The needs of the small churches of South Anhwei pressed on her, and she gave herself unstintingly to them. She gradually developed into a fine Bible teacher, and God used her to encourage fellow believers.

When I arrived in Tunki, Miss Kiang was dying. I never met her. She, who had been a wealthy and powerful mandarin's daughter, was living in one room in the rented house that served as the church in the small town of Tsingteh. (This was the town from which John and Betty Stam had been abducted by the Communists in 1934.) Marvin was working there at that time and he was with her when she died. In material things, she was poor, but while she was still conscious, she gave Marvin the only valuables she possessed, some pieces of Chinese gold given to her by her opulent father. She wished them to go to the CIM. When Marvin wanted to get a ring for me, he bought some of that dedicated gold, took it to a goldsmith in Tunki, and had it fashioned into a slim wedding band.

Marvin carefully typed invitations to the wedding while I worked on the marriage certificate. Vera made the cake, and everyone was involved in one way or another. Because Gordon and Mr. Thompson were delayed in getting back, we had to change the date of our wedding to July 2, 1943.

Friday dawned clear and beautiful after some days of rain. The chapel was decorated with pink hibiscus flowers and hanging Chinese lanterns. Delicate bamboo entwined the pillars and also formed an archway in the church. We had not been able to locate a veil anywhere, so I walked with uncovered face down the aisle, a gardenia (Marvin's favorite flower) in my hair, and escorted by Mr. Thompson. Chinese friends filled the church, and some took part in the ceremony. Danny was page boy and Helen made a sweet little flower girl. So God united us in Himself as man and wife—"Heirs together of the grace of life."

We spent an ideal honeymoon on Yellow Mountain, one of China's beauty spots. A Chinese poet wrote: "If one has seen Hwang Shan (Yellow Mountain), one need see no more." It is a Chinese painting come to life: high mountains of sheer rock rising into the sky; ancient pines stunted by the storms of centuries; panoramic view of the surrounding country seen from some lofty pinnacle; the "Cloudy Sea" at sunrise, spreading in endless waves as far as the eye can see; the thunderous "Thousand Foot Cataract."

Day after enchanting day, we explored the peaks and valleys, climbing hand in hand up and down the flat stone steps used by countless multitudes of pilgrims who for generations had visited the many ancient temples dotting the area. We delighted in the clear tumbling streams and relaxed in the shade of bamboo and pine. The beauty of God's handiwork thrilled us. The quaint and expressive Chinese names intrigued us: "The Peak of Faith's Beginnings," "Bridge of the Immortals," "Celestial City Peak," "Heavenly Dog looking at the Moon," and many others. All too soon we had to return to Tunki and the work God had for us there. Mounting our cycles, we were on our way.

One very beautiful thing God did for us was revealed in a radio-letter, the wartime forerunner of today's air letter forms. Mother and

Dad wrote to us from Canada, where they were engaged in deputation work for the Bible Society until they could journey on to England. (War travel restrictions were the cause of the delay.)

Mother wrote: "You little thought, Marvin, when we met here (in Vancouver) in 1941 that within two years you would be claiming our Mirry as your bride, did you? Somehow the news was not so strange to me, for right then and there I said in my heart, 'I'd like this young man to meet our lassie,' and the Lord seemed to confirm to me that you would do so… May our loving heavenly Father, who, I believe, has given you to each other, richly bless and make your united lives rich in fruitful service for Him. Ever so much love, Mother."

In His caring love, God had given my parents the opportunity to meet their future son-in-law, despite the fact that I came from England and he from Canada. In those days this just did not happen to missionaries—but in our case it did! It was another indication to us that we were in the center of God's will.

Chapter Thirty-One

*Ye are the light of the world. A city
set on a hill cannot be hid.
Matthew 5:14 KJV*

DURING THE MINI-CONFERENCE held just prior to our marriage, it was decided that Marvin and I should remain in Tunki if we could rent a small house in the city. Tunki was the economic and political center of South Anhwei, a strategic place for Christian witness. At the same time, John Crook was ill with what was later diagnosed as amoebic dysentery, though at the time I thought he had sprue. He needed special attention. Even though married, I still carried the responsibility of being the district nurse. So after our honeymoon, Marvin started enquiries about our future home, and I took on John's full nursing and dietetic care. His wife was expecting her first baby in September. She was worn out preparing the diet John needed in conjunction with the intense heat of the Yangtze valley summer.

One item John could eat was chicken, and I never in my life cleaned and prepared so many birds as I did in the next few weeks. Pulling off feathers, extricating entrails, tugging on windpipes, cutting the chickens in pieces, and then cooking them to try and tempt John's appetite was a new experience. He also needed liver, and someone had to buy this in the market each day: no refrigerators or freezers in war-torn China. Marvin often got up very early to milk the goats—not the Swiss stock we had hoped for, but the skinny native variety that gave so little milk.

In September of 1943, two months after our marriage, Marvin felt he should go back to Tsingteh to see how the Christians were faring. By this time John was feeling much better, but I still could not leave Tunki, as Eleanore's baby was nearly due. So my husband went off alone.

When the time came, Eleanore's labor was long, but Vincent arrived safely, though my patient suffered a common complication of a first birth. I had never done such stitching before, and even though I was apprehensive as I prepared the instruments, God guided my hands.

On October 13, six long weeks after he had left me, Marvin returned. I was so glad to see him! My nursing commitments had been met, and I was free.

No house was available in town at the price we could afford: $23,800 inflated Chinese dollars was the cheapest we could find. It was then decided that Marvin and I should move to Tsingteh, where God's Spirit was working. We stacked our few belongings on huge transport wheelbarrows, and Marvin and I rode our bicycles to our new home some seventy miles east and north of Tunki.

Tsingteh is a small walled town set on a hill and surrounded by fertile valleys. It was in this town that John and Betty Stam were captured by Communist guerillas in 1934 and forced to march twelve miles over the hills to Miao Sheo. They were beheaded outside that village on the morning of December 9. In the intervening years, a living church had emerged, the most virile in South Anhwei. A number of missionaries had worked there from time to time, and now that privilege was being given to us.

John and Betty Stam, murdered by Communist bandits on December 8, 1934, twelve miles outside of the city of Tsingteh (today spelled Jingde) in South Anhwei.

Marvin Dunn with a group of Chinese men in 1943, reviewing the location of the murder of John and Betty Stam twelve miles outside the city of Tsingteh, Anhwei.

It was one hundred days before it was safe to bring out the coffins of John and Betty Stam for burial. In 1934 the coffins arrived in Wuhu, Anhwei, for a postmortem medical exam, where they are now buried.

Two short days after we arrived, a week-long Bible school was held. Pastor Cheng and Marvin were the main teachers. As the Holy Spirit spoke to hearts, many evening sessions ended in weeping and the confession of hidden sins. On the last day, five believers were baptized in the river outside the city wall, giving spontaneous testimonies to God's blessing. What a thrilling introduction this was to some of the happiest days of my life!

God seemed to enclose us in an iridescent circle of joy. It was not that life was easy, but everything was gilded with the brightness of our love, our joy in being together in service for our Lord. We found we had to make mutual adjustments. I am not a tidy person; Marvin is, and sometimes I was a real trial to him. He got frustrated, and so did I. Then I felt badly, and tried to do better. Marvin is also very careful about money, especially mission money. I will never forget the look in his eyes when he found out that I was hazy about some mission accounts I was responsible for. It was a salutary lesson on an important matter.

On the other side of the coin, I could be quite emotional. Marvin's ancestors, however, were Scots, and some of the austerity and reserve for which they are noted came out in him. He did not find it easy to "let go," especially as he had been on his own for ten years as a single worker.

He was also influenced by the customs and culture of rural China. However much I pleaded, when we were out for a walk, I had to walk behind him (a la Chinese)—and we did not even hold hands in public. He knew the heathen around us in the very conservative atmosphere of inland China could easily have misunderstood such actions, but it hurt me sometimes.

Morning by morning, the water carrier brought his brimming pails to the gate. Marvin unbarred the wooden door, and old Liu would slop his way to the wide-mouthed earthenware jar standing three feet tall. Resting his heavy buckets on the rounded edge, he would carefully pour the sparkling water until it nearly brimmed over.

We would go to the city gate to buy wood and charcoal, as it was cheaper to get it from a woodcutter from the country, carrying his load into town over his shoulder, than to buy it in a store.

In the market, we bought freshly roasted peanuts, as butter and margarine were nonexistent. We would spend the evening rubbing off

Marvin Dunn making peanut butter.

the peel, and the next day Marvin would grind them into golden brown peanut butter.

We made our own bread too. There was no convenient dried yeast available, so we obtained a little lump of fermented rice at the local wine shop. Marvin taught me how to add sugar and water, put it in a sealed jar, and in the morning it would be fizzing and bubbling, ready to act as leaven in our dough. One day we took two slices of freshly baked bread to the winemaker to sample, and he thought it was very good.

It was not long before I came to know and love the Chinese Christians. They were a congenial group. Mrs. Chu was the wife of an official and a daughter of the magistrate who had been helpless to aid John and Betty Stam when the Communists captured them. She was an attractive, friendly person, who had known persecution for Christ's sake. When she became a Christian, her father-in-law was furious, burned her Bible, and made life very difficult. She continued steadfast, and her resultant maturity added much to the church.

Mr. Yen was the church secretary. He had been converted only three and a half years, but already he was a strong Christian. A bean curd maker by trade, he had to get up at four each morning to grind the soya beans that he had put to soak the night before. He utilized this time of solitude memorizing Scripture, which became his source of strength. Eventually, he won his wife to the Lord. This woman had had a terrible temper. When she began to curse and swear, everyone on the street kept out of her way. She was the terror of the neighborhood, illiterate and unkempt. But a marked change came over her when she finally became a Christian. Everybody knew something wonderful had happened to her.

Mr. Chang was a farmer living outside the town. Before Christ found him, he had been a gambler and drinker. His children were terrified of him. His home was hell on earth. But one day he was born again of the Spirit and became a new man in Christ. His wife was so impressed by his transformed life that she became an enquirer. The very father who once had made their lives so miserable was teaching his children Bible verses.

On the only birthday I spent in Tsingteh, January 11, 1944, something exciting happened in another home. Mr. Wu was also a farmer, living in a small village some miles from the town. He smoked opium, but the witness of the living church reached out even to him. He made the great decision to follow the Lord Jesus Christ, and decided to burn all his idol paraphernalia, including his ancestral tablets. From now on the eyes of heathendom would be watching to see how the demon spirits would treat this man and his family.

The Christians understood the importance of this day. A number of them went out to his farm to help him break with the power of the spirits. We walked with them through the crisp wintry air, between dry brown fields. After a time of prayer and Bible reading, Mr. Wu went to his god-shelf on the wall. From it, he removed the wine cups, incense and candle holders, and the old tablets inscribed with the names of his father, grandfather, great-grandfather, and so on. These he threw into the yard outside the front door. With an axe, he then pried the dusty god-shelf off the wall. Some of the Christians helped to peel off the rather tattered paper gods pasted above the shelf and carried them outside to the heap of idol stuff already on the ground. Mr. Wu also picked up a beautiful little china statue of the Goddess of Mercy and added it to the growing pile. His opium pipe was flung in with the rest. Finally, he tore down the mirror above the entrance of his home that had hung there for years to frighten off the evil spirits.

As we all stood in a circle in the yard, Mr. Wu seized his axe and smashed these symbols of Satan's power to pieces. He then thrust a lighted stick into the tinder dry collection. The flames leaped to life and we sang a song of praise to God for yet another soul set free. Before leaving, we gave Mr. Wu a Gospel poster to paste on his wall where once the old gods had hung. By this, his friends and neighbors would know he now walked the Jesus way.

We were feeling very happy and fulfilled in the midst of this growth and witness. God was working. Men and women were being saved. Christians were growing spiritually. There was a sweet spirit of love and caring in the community.

On February 18, 1944, Gordon arrived unexpectedly from Hweichow with shattering news. Probably because of the worsening military situation in South Anhwei, the CIM Council in Chungking had cabled him, as superintendent, saying that all missionaries in the area should evacuate. Gordon and Vera themselves were to travel north to Fowyang, which was the logical place for the superintendent of CIM to work in the province. To do this, they would have to make the long and hazardous journey to Chungking, then travel north and east to the northern part of Anhwei—a trip of four thousand miles to reach a town five hundred miles away. It would have been foolhardy for their family to attempt a crossing of the Yangtze River as we had done a year earlier.

And what about us? Our temporary designation was Hokow, in the neighboring province of Kiangsi, some two hundred miles southwest of Tsingteh.

Gordon broke the news to the Christians at the prayer meeting held that evening in Mr. Chang's home. It came as a shock to them all. Discussion flowed back and forth long into the night, for they did not want us to go. But we knew we would have to accept the mission's ruling. The next day a deputation of women arrived, pleading for us to stay, which unsettled us again. However, the decision to leave was finally made, and we had to pack hurriedly.

Gordon wanted us to get away as soon as possible. Barrows and carts were hired, some stuff was sold, and furniture was stored in Mr. Wang's house. A farewell meeting was arranged and love gifts exchanged. Early on February 23, we walked down the cobbled streets for the last time, wheeling our bicycles in the midst of a growing crowd of rather gloomy Christians.

They escorted us outside the south gate, and stood together as we cycled off along the rough road into the valley. Our hearts were heavy too. It was not easy to say goodbye to those we loved, to leave this inland city. Yet we knew that God was with them, and that He would enable them to shine brightly for Him in "the city set on a hill."

PART VI
Keeping Ahead of the Japanese
1944

Chapter Thirty-Two

*The glory of this latter house shall be greater
than of the former, saith the Lord of hosts:
and in this place will I give peace.*
Haggai 2:9 KJV

WHAT A CONTRAST we found as we came to work in North Kiangsi!
Our hearts sank as we learned of the problems and difficulties
that faced us. Yet the verse that came as a wonderful promise was the one
above. It gave us hope for the future, and with hope came determination
to serve to the best of our ability.

It was March 25, 1944, when we finally arrived in Hokow, our
place of temporary designation. We disembarked with our baggage
from a small river steamer, tired yet excited, wondering what lay ahead.
We had run the gamut of travel experiences. Truck, barrow, bicycle,
train, and boat had carried our belongings and us over the nearly two
hundred miles from Tsingteh in just over a month. China offers variety
and stimulation to travelers, if not too much in the way of comfort and
speed.

The first missionary to go to the towns along the Kwangsin River in
Kiangsi was not a Westerner but an ex-officer of the Chinese Imperial
Army. Having found Christ in his own province of Chekiang, Captain
Yu climbed the hills to take the Good News to former Buddhist disciples
he had known in the neighboring province of Kiangsi. Mainly through
his witness, the first church on the Kwangsin River was established in
Yuishan in 1877. It happened that Hudson Taylor, the founder of the

CIM, met some of these new converts. He was excited at what God was doing and also impressed by the tremendous need for more missionaries to expand the work in the area.

In his own heart at that time, God's Spirit was laying His finger on a new area of obedience. Until then, no single lady workers had lived in China's inland cities, but in different ways, God was pressuring His servant to authorize them to do so. He knew that this departure from the accepted mission procedure would be misunderstood by missionaries of other groups, but he held on to his conviction. When he finally sent the ladies in, work among Chinese women grew and flourished, boys and girls were reached in a new way—and he was deluged with criticism. In spite of this, the courageous girls continued to go forward.

Hudson Taylor could not forget the scattered converts of the Kwangsin River, nor the teeming cities in that area as yet unreached. However, it was not until 1886 that he was able to return, this time with a few single ladies, dressed in the voluminous Chinese garments of that day. He placed them in towns where Chinese women were pleading for help. As the years passed, more cities were "occupied" by ladies. Small schools were started, health clinics were opened, and God's blessing was experienced. Hudson Taylor's venture worked!

In 1900, came the holocaust of the Boxer uprising when missionaries in many parts of China were killed. Missionaries, including those in Kiangsi, temporarily fled to the coast. When the Boxers capitulated to foreign soldiers in Peking, the intrepid ladies returned to their work along the river.

In 1907, God sent a revival to the area. Hundreds came to Christ. Large churches were built and schools flourished. The mission bought land and built airy, two-story houses for the ladies, for in summer, the heat in this valley was almost unbearable. Gradually some strong-minded leaders emerged among those single lady missionaries. They became legendary, and their power in the churches almost absolute. It was not that they did not love the national Christians. Indeed, they were tireless in their service. But in those days the emerging pattern traced the missionary as the leader, rather than the servant, of the church.

In 1927, roving Communist bands brought death and destruction to the countryside. Terror and persecution fell upon the people. In

Kiangsi province alone, some seven million people died. Christians suffered cruelty and the churches stood empty.

In 1934, Mao Tse-tung, the leader of the Chinese Communist Party, called for the scattered groups of Communist guerillas in southern China to join him in Hunan. From there, the twenty-thousand-man army began the Long March to Yenan in northwest China. This meant that more peaceful conditions prevailed in Kiangsi, and Christian work began again out of the ashes.

Slowly, the church began to recover. Preaching bands could once more go in safety to country areas. Parents were willing to send their children to Christian schools. The missionaries were encouraged—and totally unprepared for the sudden destruction that fell from the sky in 1940.

At that time, Japan made a swift advance into North Kiangsi, and Japanese planes bombed and strafed indiscriminately. Cities became empty shells as people fled to the hills. When they returned, many found their homes razed to the ground and fires raging. Just as suddenly, the enemy retreated, and once again the suffering people had to rebuild their lives.

It was to people with this history of suffering and loss that God sent us. We found the Christians spiritually numb. Scarcely anyone came to services. They needed love and care and prayer. Unfortunately, Marvin soon found that he had other responsibilities that took up much of his time. Because of unsettled conditions and dwindling personnel, and also because of changes in mission policy, our leaders decided that some of the big houses and school buildings needed to be sold. For many weeks Marvin traveled up and down the river where, in the spring of 1944, only three of the eight towns where CIM ladies had formerly worked now had missionaries in residence. Those ladies were not young. Two had come to China in 1898!

Would God fulfill the promise He gave us? Not in our short stay in Shangjao, the town on the Kwangsin River that finally became our home, but it did give us hope for the future. The church building was in shambles, and so was the house. Two bombs had struck the latter while Cliff and Florence Paulson were living there in 1941. One tore off the front part of the building, and the other buried itself in the ground near the kitchen. Shortly after this, the Paulsons had to leave, and Chinese and Japanese soldiers had occupied the house intermittently since then. They had used the furniture for firewood and the walls of some rooms were black with smoke. Shutters hung crazily on the windows and the floors were deep in filth. In the chapel, only two benches remained.

At the first meeting Marvin had with the Christians, we noticed the great contrast between their attitude and that of the Christians in Tsingteh. Two men, for instance, were very upset that we had come to Shangjao at all. They and their families had been living in the missionary house, and had to find new quarters when we arrived. So they vented their frustration on the church, walking out before the end of the meeting. We found it hard to relate to this difficult situation, and even questioned the wisdom of staying on in the midst of such friction.

However, as we prayed and visited and opened our home, a nucleus of believers began to form. Some of the Chinese officers' wives in the vicinity asked me to start an English class, and soon a number of these ladies came regularly to services also. We began a Sunday school and home Bible study. After some months, Marvin was able to report to headquarters, "The chapel is getting too small."

But it was uphill work. In this war-ravaged area, the hearts of so many seemed set on material things at the expense of the spiritual. Only the Spirit of God could wean them from the love of that which to them spelled security, and into a life of Christian commitment.

Chapter Thirty-Three

Bear ye one another's burdens, and
so fulfill the law of Christ.
Galatians 6:2 ASV

GOD SOMETIMES CHOOSES very unlikely people to do the jobs He wants
done. I am not an outgoing type, and was content to be with Marvin
and follow his leadership in our contacts with the Chinese believers. I still
tried to keep up with language study, and spent hours with my books. I
was much happier doing that than planning menus and cooking meals!

It was Marvin who suggested changes when our diet became
monotonous, sometimes buying an appetizing snack from a roadside
stall. When he had time, he also bought our vegetables and pork in the
local market. He fixed the oven so that I could bake bread and cookies.
I grew to appreciate him and his thoughtfulness more and more: his
sturdy common sense supplemented my less practical ways.

Soon after settling into our Shangjao lifestyle, a steady stream of guests
began to flow our way, people who needed hospitality and love. I wondered
sometimes if God knew what He was doing in directing them to our home.

Shangjao was a communications center. People traveling west from
Chekiang and Anhwei provinces had to pass through our city, which
was the first big town they hit on the railway. A main highway also ran
through it, and the river was busy with launches and junks. Living in
our bombed and devastated house, God gave us an unexpected ministry:
to serve refugee missionaries. We learned that missionary life was not
just preaching and teaching the Word to the Chinese people around us.

Though we did not realize it then, the direction of our future missionary service had its beginnings in Shangjao.

However, our first guests were not refugees. Mr. Graham Hutchinson was the superintendent of the CIM work in Chekiang, and he came to our home in order to accompany Marvin on his initial trip to visit the churches in the cities along the Kwangsin River. He was a quiet and gracious gentleman. Marvin appreciated his wealth of experience, and also his kindly manner. His wife was a beautiful, auburn-haired woman with a lovely complexion that even the burning sun of inland China could not harm. We had moved permanently into the house shortly before their arrival, but only part of it could be occupied. Whitewash had markedly transformed the wall, and at least things were clean—or so we thought.

It was to our chagrin to be wakened in the middle of the night by a knock on our bedroom door, and be led to the guest room by Mr. Hutchinson. There, under the mosquito net, his wife was crouching on the camp bed. Above her a moving black line crawled from the ceiling down the wall, along the string that held up the net, and down over the net itself. Bedbugs! Thousands of them! It was frightful, but they understood.

We moved our guests to the dining room until morning and hoped for the best. We never did get rid of those bugs until some U.S. army personnel gave us some army issue DDT "bombs," which finally annihilated them.

On the day that our first refugees arrived from Chekiang, God impressed the above verse (Galatians 6:2) on my heart. Bearing burdens, caring and sharing, helping and listening—this is an important part of the Christian life. Ken and Maybeth Gray later told us that rumors of an advance by Japanese troops caused such panic in their city in Chekiang that hundreds of Chinese decided to flee westwards—to Kiangsi. They wanted to escape before death and destruction invaded the hilly beauty of West Chekiang. The Grays knew that if they remained on, it could mean capture and internment, so they also headed for the railway station. Every carriage was jammed with refugees; there was no room for them. But the missionaries prayed, and God worked a miracle. On the morning of June 21 at three-thirty, a freight train carrying military rice slid quietly out of the station while the passenger train was still waiting. In one of the boxcars were four missionaries and one little boy, enjoying free transportation to Shangjao! Twelve hours later they reached our home, hot and tired, yet full of praise for God's provision.

They spent a few days with us and then moved on to Hokow, where there was a big, clean house with many rooms. It was there, on September 27, 1944, that I became the district nurse again and delivered Wendy Gray into the world.

For Ken and Maybeth, this new baby came as a very precious gift from the Lord, for Wendy filled an empty place in their lives. Three years earlier, in 1941, on the day that Japanese planes bombed Pearl Harbor (December 8 in our part of the world), Ken and Maybeth were living in Japanese-occupied territory. When they heard the news, they knew they had to run. They packed a few essentials, snatched up their little daughter, Gwen, and fled on bicycles to Ninghai in Free China. Word reached them there that the Japanese authorities they had eluded were furious because they had escaped their clutches, and had vowed to kill them if they ever caught them.

Chinese Christians in Ninghai were wonderfully kind, giving them money and hiring a sedan chair for Maybeth and Gwen. They moved on to Changhsien, where the Sharmans gave them shelter. After a short respite the news became worse, and both families had to evacuate on December 30, 1941. That night, the only shelter they could find was a cold and dirty inn. Gwen became ill, probably with pneumonia. But danger encircled them. They had to keep moving. Two days later Gwen died.

Ken made the tiny coffin with his own hands, a little wooden box, crude and austere, such a cold receptacle for their little daughter's body. Then a beautiful thing happened. A Chinese Christian girl, herself a refugee, heard of their sorrow. She brought them a length of pink silk, which was to have been her wedding gown. They laid Gwen's body in this soft and glowing shroud, but danger prodded them forward again. For a day they carried the little coffin with them, then buried her one dark night in pouring rain. God took Gwen from them on their first refugee journey, and on their second, three years later, He gave them Wendy. It meant a lot to me to have a part in this moving story.

The day after the Gray party left us for Hokow, some very unexpected guests turned up. They were five Englishmen who had managed to escape from a Japanese concentration camp in Shanghai. When they arrived in our town, the police took them to the magistrate. He was in a quandary, and came over to ask us if we could give them hospitality. "They might not like our food," he said. Naturally we agreed, and for three days these men lived in our home. When they left they gave us a tin of real butter, worth its weight in gold, from their small store of provisions. We had not tasted such a delicacy since leaving the coast in 1941, and how we enjoyed it!

Soon after we had celebrated our first wedding anniversary (July 2, 1944), the Birch family arrived on our doorstep. They, too, had recently received a telegram from Chungking telling them to evacuate from Tunki and move to the Kwangsin River. Tired and hot, they appreciated a few days in our home before moving on to Hokow.

It was some weeks later, when Marvin and I also happened to be in Hokow, that their little daughters, Helen and Miriam, developed high fevers. I did what I could for the two children, but the fever persisted. When Helen took a turn for the better, we hoped the same would happen to Miriam. Instead, she continued to toss and turn, her golden curls dank with sweat.

That evening George came into our room. "Marvin," he said quietly, "you know how ill little Miriam is. Grace and I have cried to God for her healing, but there is no change. We both feel that she should be anointed with oil. Would you and Miriam come to our room and pray for her?"

"Yes, I'll gladly do that," Marvin responded. "Do you have some oil?"

"No, I'm afraid we don't," he replied. "We could only bring the bare necessities with us on the truck, and oil was not one of them."

"I'll have a look in my medicine box," I chipped in. "There's sure to be something there."

After a little hunting, I found what we needed and we went to the Birches' room. We stood together around the cot. Marvin placed a few drops on Miriam's head and prayed according to James 5:14,15, putting her in God's hands: "Is any among you sick? Let him call for the elders of the church, and let them pray over him, anointing him with oil in the name of the Lord, and the prayer of faith shall save him that is sick."

There was no immediate recession, but God did perform a miracle. Helen was soon allowed to get up, her hazel eyes looking particularly large in her white little face. The fever had been hard on her. It was not until she tried to walk that Grace noticed she could only limp around, complaining of pain in one leg. Later we realized she had had polio.

What of baby Miriam? Her fever gradually went down and she was soon trotting about as before, completely healed.

Chapter Thirty-Four

The peace of God, which passeth all understanding,
shall keep your hearts and minds through Christ Jesus.
Philippians 4:7 KJV

THAT SUMMER OF 1944 the sun poured its heat down on us in the humid Kwangsin valley. How thankful we were for our big house with its airy rooms, even though some of them were still unfit to live in. Carpenters and masons were working spasmodically, and the end seemed to be in sight.

In mid-September, I was scheduled to go to Hokow to deliver Maybeth's baby, as mentioned in the previous chapter. At the same time, Marvin had received a letter from our director in Chungking asking him to travel to Poyang, some one hundred and forty miles east of Shangjao, to sell some mission property. We decided to start off together.

At Hokow, I took up my nursing duties, and Marvin picked up a new companion, George Birch. Together they cycled from one river town to another, encouraging the believers and sharing God's Word with them. Gradually, they made their way to the mouth of the Kwangsin River, where Poyang was situated on the edge of a lake.

After a period of negotiation, a Chinese Christian doctor bought the building, and Marvin and George set a date for their return to Hokow. Suddenly Marvin fell ill. Day after day, the fever climbed: it was paratyphoid. In those days, careful nursing was the only effective treatment, and George knew that Marvin was longing for his own special nurse! So one day a telegram was delivered at the Hokow mission compound: "Marvin ill typhoid. Suggest Miriam come immediately."

This came as a shock to us all. Fortunately, Maybeth and the baby were doing well, so there was nothing to keep me from my husband. Ken Gray kindly made arrangements for me to travel to Poyang by boat. Naturally, my thoughts were never far from Marvin, and as we sailed down the busy river, I importuned God for his recovery.

But there was another matter I needed to talk to God about. He had heard our prayers for a child, and our own baby was due in three months' time. As I watched with interest the passing panorama of river life, my fingers were busy knitting a delicate white shawl.

As the needles flew back and forth, I reminded the Lord of the problems connected with the delivery of our child. No Western doctor was available, no nurse. I was over thirty, and Japanese troops were on the move. The miles slipped slowly by, and the lovely pattern of the shawl began to take shape. To me it was an allegory: God had His pattern for the future, and He would work it out.

At last we reached Poyang. (Sixty miles to the west across the lake, Kuling, my birthplace, towered into the clouds.) I staggered off the boat, glad my days of immobility were over. A smiling George met me at the wharf with the wonderful news that Marvin was over the crisis. But I realized how ill he had been when I saw his sunken eyes and thin face, now covered with prickly stubble of red beard! Daily, thereafter, he improved, so George felt that he should return to Hokow, leaving us to start on the return journey when Marvin felt able.

Then something happened that once again changed the pattern of our lives. A telegram was forwarded from Hokow to Poyang. It was from our leaders in Chungking: "Urge immediate complete evacuation." Evacuation again! We were bewildered. We had been in Shangjao just over seven months. With God's help, the little group of believers there was growing. How could we leave them now? It did not seem fair. Added to this was the more personal concern as to how the days of rough travel might affect Marvin's weakened body, and also our unborn child.

The only route to western China was to travel by truck five

hundred miles south to the U.S. Air Force (USAF) base in Kanhsien, then fly about one thousand miles west to Kunming in Yunnan. Was this a new part of God's pattern? Knowing our own helplessness, we committed ourselves to the Lord. In our little backwater, we did not realize how dangerous our position was. Japanese troops were about to cut us off from the West in a pincer movement.

The first thing to do was to get home, and this took longer as we traveled against the current. When we reached Hokow we found that the Grays, Winnie Rand, and Miss Ford had already gone. The Birches and Miss Moody were packing and selling. Everything was in a state of upheaval.

In Shangjao, we also had to sell or give away all the wedding gifts we had been enjoying. This bomb-damaged house was home to us, but soon the rooms were as empty as when we had first seen them, though considerably cleaner. Our own baggage had to be reduced to a minimum, and many precious things were left behind. I will always remember my sense of loss as Marvin burned the love letters he had written after our engagement. I was afraid he would never write to me in that way again!

Marvin contacted the British Military Mission (BMM), and they kindly arranged for us to ride, free of charge, in one of their trucks going south to Kanhsien. More refugee missionaries from Chekiang came to Shangjao, as well as the folk from Hokow. We had to say goodbye to yet another group of Chinese Christians, assuring them of our prayers.

Very early on November 23, 1944, the BMM truck pulled out of our compound, loaded with seventeen missionaries and their children, plus suitcases. Old Miss McDonald sat beside the driver, and because of my pregnancy, I sat in the cab also. The rest, some of them quite elderly, squeezed into the back, scarcely able to move except when everyone emptied out for periodic stops. Mercifully, we all kept well. Two days of traveling brought us to Ningtu, where Swiss missionaries gave us loving hospitality. As they were citizens of a neutral country, they had nothing to fear from a Japanese advance, and were remaining.

Some of the party traveled on the next day. However, as the BMM assured us another truck would soon be available, and splitting the group gave more comfort and room to all, some of us waited. On November 30, our remnant boarded the next truck and reached Kanhsien that night. The verses in *Daily Light* for that day reminded us of God's promise of peace in a tense situation.

We found that the first party had already been able to fly out. Our group consisted of the Birches, the Hutchinsons, two single ladies, and ourselves. Conflicting reports met us. "No more U.S. planes will be available to missionaries." "The air base will soon be closed." "The whole situation is very critical." "There will be a plane tomorrow."

We contacted the Americans soon after our arrival. They very kindly suggested we all move out to the air base and live in the barracks so that we could be more easily contacted when a plane arrived.

What a change to be surrounded by American GIs! We will never forget the first breakfast we ate there—three fried eggs and one piece of bacon in one serving, coffee with milk and *white* sugar, and toast with lots of jam and butter. We suffered a mild but happy case of culture shock.

However, the last two nights were rather a nightmare. Bright moonlight flooded the countryside as we prepared for bed. Suddenly, the air-raid warning wailed into the stillness, rising and falling in quivering sound. "Jap planes are coming! Get out to the trenches immediately!"

We flung on our clothes and joined the flowing stream of men. All moved quickly to where black jagged lines in the ground showed where the deep trenches of safety lay. Soon we heard a faint hum in the distance, which grew louder and louder until the planes were overhead, when we instinctively ducked. Actually, the men said we were in little danger, for the airfield was about a mile away, but we did not have too much confidence in the Japanese pilots' accuracy. The bright flash of explosions preceded the dull boom of the missiles, one after another. When the all-clear signal sounded, we returned to bed.

The last night, as we made our way back to the barracks after one air raid had ended, an emergency alarm halted us in our tracks.

"We'll never make it back to the trenches," one GI called to us. "I can hear the planes already. Come, there's a pit over here, and its shelter will be better than nothing. Hurry, there's not much time. Get down fast!"

Urgency sharpened his voice. We clambered over the rough ground and fell to the earth. Bombs whistled past us, the earth shook, the pit was foul with refuse, and fear stalked among us. "Lord, watch over us. Keep my baby," was my heart's cry. And He heard. Soon silence returned, the moon shone serenely, and we were safe. "Thank You, Lord."

It was just after midnight when we finally fell into bed. Earlier that evening a transport plane had flown in and was returning to Kunming, the capital of Yunnan, the next day. The authorities told us to be ready with our baggage at two-forty-five that morning. Within two hours, our party assembled at the gate of the barracks and was taken by truck to board the C47 waiting on the tarmac. It was December 5, 1944, the second anniversary of our encounter with the bandits, and two months before our baby was due.

Chapter Thirty-Five

We must all appear before the judgment seat of Christ; that
everyone may receive the things done in his body, according
to that he hath done, whether it be good or bad.
II Corinthians 5:10 KJV

O UR PARTY CLIMBED out of the truck at three o'clock that morning
and began walking toward the big plane. It was the first time
any of us had flown, and we were looking forward to it. Men were
busy with the final preparations for the flight. The moon still shone,
though it was low in the sky. A cold breeze bit into our bodies.

A man walked toward us in the silvery darkness. "How many are
there in your party?" he asked.

"We are eight adults and two small children," Mr. Hutchinson
replied.

"Oh, I didn't know there were so many of you." He hesitated and
then said, "I'm afraid three of you will have to wait for the next plane
out."

There was a flurry of exclamations, and his voice cut incisively
across the hubbub. "On our USAF planes we are only allowed to
carry as many passengers as we have parachutes. Excluding our crew
members, we have enough for only seven—and the children must
have one each," he explained.

How should we divide up? The officer suggested that perhaps the
women and children should go, and the men wait for the next plane,
but none of us felt this was the right thing to do. Marvin and I were

the youngest of the group, so we volunteered to stay. Everyone agreed that the Birches and Miss McDonald, who was 75, should get out of danger. Miss Loosley offered to remain. Then Graham Hutchinson walked over to us. "Elsie and I want to wait," he said to us. "We feel that Miriam should get out as soon as possible, especially as there is uncertainty as to when the next plane will come in. So we and Miss Loosley will stay and you two go on."

As we began to protest, he said teasingly, "I am your superintendent, you know, so you'd better do as I say."

We thanked them both, said goodbye to the three, and climbed into the plane. Hard bucket seats lined the interior. We settled ourselves in these while one of the crew members battened down our cases to keep them steady. We felt very small and insignificant in the empty body of the giant bird. At four-forty-five all was ready. The engines burst into life. We roared down the runway and leaped into the dark sky. Our ears hurt. It was cold. We tried to relax. We moved around and looked out the windows, but all we could see were the clouds, which gradually grew paler and rosier as the sun climbed in the east behind us.

That flight in a non-pressurized plane was not a happy experience. We both got airsick and longed for firm ground. After three hours, we sensed that the plane was heading earthwards, and were told we were landing at Chikiang to refuel. We left the sunshine, scissored through the clouds, and saw rain driving against the windows. All around us were dark and massive mountains, half hidden in angry-looking clouds.

"We're lucky we made this landing safely," growled the pilot as we got out to stretch our legs. "This is a dangerous place in which to build an air base, even a temporary one. Those mountains are too close and too high."

Soon we were airborne again, on the last lap of our flight. Rough weather dogged us—heart-swallowing drops, shuddering heaves, and a gray cloudscape. We were all feeling a bit depressed and fearful when George Birch started to sing a chorus. We all joined in, Helen's sweet treble soaring like a bird above our adult voices:

"When your fears rise mountain high
And would block your pathway,
Wait, oh, wait upon the Lord,
Believing as you pray.
Then your eagle wings will grow—
Up, up, up, up, up you'll go—
Over, hallelujah! Over,
With the mountains down below!"

Less than two hours later, the clouds melted away and far beneath us lay Yunnan: tree-covered mountains, patchwork fields, tiny houses, and ribbon-like roads. The pollution smudge of the city drew our plane like a magnet; we circled the airfield and landed in bright sunshine. As we walked down the little ladder to terra firma, our last link with Kiangsi was severed.

Bill and Vera Tyler gave us a warm, if somewhat harassed, welcome. They were doing a wonderful job at the mission home, and did not allow the mounting difficulties to get on top of them. Missionaries from all over the southern part of China had received orders from their consuls to evacuate immediately, and they were pouring into Kunming.

The day after we arrived, a convoy of trucks from Kweichow rumbled in, with twenty CIM missionaries and their children. Each day brought in still more, and soon the house was overflowing. People slept on bedding rolls on the floor, and meals were served cafeteria style. On Boxing Day, December 26, a planeload of children from the emergency Chefoo School in Loshan pushed our numbers up to seventy!

But one plane never made it. On the evening of December 13, the phone rang. Bill took it. A sympathetic American voice conveyed the news that the plane on which Graham and Elsie Hutchinson and Miss Loosley had left Kanhsien that morning had crashed into the mountains when attempting to land at Chikiang. The plane burst into flames. Everyone died instantly.

We were stunned. Just eight days earlier our pilot had managed to land our plane safely on that very field. Today our three friends had died there. For Marvin and me the news was heart searching—and humbling. If the Hutchinsons had not so self-sacrificially changed places with us, we would have been on the plane that crashed.

Elsie and Graham Hutchinson

That evening as we prayed together, we read the passage in *Daily Light,* and once more God's message came to us, this time bringing a challenge for future service. Graham and Elsie were with Christ. They had entered into His presence together. Their work on earth was done, and done well. "You too must appear before the judgment seat of Christ. They will receive their reward for the good they have done. What of you?"

So we gave ourselves again to the Lord—to go where He planned and to do what He wanted us to do.

As I climbed into bed, I said to my husband, "Marvin, if our baby is a boy, I'd like to call him Graham. What do you think?"

"I think that's a good idea," he agreed.

Chapter Thirty-Six

The Lord, He it is that doth go before thee: He
will be with thee, He will not fail thee.
Deuteronomy 31:8 KJV

"Marvin," Bill called, "can you come into the office for a moment?"
"Sure," Marvin replied. "I'll be right there."

Sitting at Bill's desk, Marvin was given the unwelcome news that we could not remain in Kunming, nor could we move to any other city in China. We had to fly over the Hump to India!

"I've just been on the phone to the British consul, and these are his orders. Every missionary coming to Kunming has to go out—to India."

"But do you think they would make an exception in our case?" Marvin asked. "Miriam has about five weeks to go. I don't know much about such things, but I have heard that any travel at this time could be dangerous for her."

"Yes, I know," Bill said, "and I specifically mentioned you folk to the consul. But he says those are his orders and you will have to go with the others."

India! Flying over the Hump in December was hazardous. Many planes did not make it. Was this really God's plan for us? No personal direction had come from Him. Yet outside forces were driving us to leave China and fly with two suitcases to an unknown land, like baby birds being thrust out of the only nest they knew. Our hearts were in Tsingteh and Shangjao. Living in Kunming, we were at least in the same country. Then we remembered that we had recently made a new commitment to the Lord, and His hands were on the wheel.

Royal Air Force (RAF) planes, flying back and forth between Calcutta and Kunming, were ferrying dozens of refugees to India. Our names were sent in with many others. We were booked to fly on December 29, 1944, and waited at the airfield, but bad weather forced the cancellation of our flight. We trailed wearily back to the CIM—and what a lovely surprise the Lord had prepared for us! My sister Peggy, serving with the Red Cross in Yunnan, burst into our room with Bill, my brother, a doctor in the same organization!

What an emotionally packed time followed. Marvin, thus, met two of his new family in Kunming. This was a few days after he had received a sad letter from his mother telling of the sudden death of his younger sister, Anna, from leukemia.

On December 30, we really did leave, and that flight was eight hours of misery. The only interesting thing was our first taste of Coca Cola, brought to us by a friendly American airman, when we touched down on Myitkyina airfield, halfway to Calcutta. The weather was extremely hot and humid, we had been airsick, and the warm, slightly fizzy brown liquid tasted strange. During the night, we landed at the immense Dum Dum airfield on the outskirts of Calcutta.

In that city, we experienced anew God's love and provision, and saw His answer to our prayers concerning the birth of our baby. Early on the morning of February 5, 1945, Marvin and I were driven by an old Indian *sais* (chauffeur), in a Baby Austin car, to the modern Lady Dufferin Hospital. At ten to seven Rosemary Anne was born. An efficient Indian nurse did all that was necessary—anesthetics were available and a lady doctor was on call. Everything was perfect.

Marvin and I looked at our refugee baby—pink and wrinkled, sleepy and sweet, blue-eyed and bald—and knew she was the most beautiful baby in the world. We called her Rosemary after my mother, and Anne for the sister Marvin would never see again on earth.

We thought back on our doubts and fears in Kiangsi, on the days of truck and plane travel, on the bombings and uncertainties. And we remembered the message God had given us on the first of January 1945, soon after we arrived in Calcutta: "The Lord, He it is that doth go before thee: He will be with thee, He will not fail thee."

Our wonderful and faithful God was silently working out His pattern in love.

Chapter Thirty-Seven

Behold, I send an Angel before thee, to keep thee in the way,
and to bring thee into the place which I have prepared.
Exodus 23:20 KJV

CALCUTTA! MANY THINGS struck us as strange and different in India's largest city. Cows, for instance, were allowed to wander at will, for the cow is a sacred animal to the Hindus. Towering palm trees with rustling fronds decorated the city squares. Downtown department stores dazzled us with their elegant displays, while in the native quarters we found an appalling contrast—apertures, three feet square, honeycombing the buildings on both sides of the road, served as shops for the Indian poor.

Modern streetcars rattled along streets crowded with lumbering bullock carts. Fourteen-wheel trucks thundered past loincloth-clad coolies who jogged effortlessly with baskets of produce balanced on their heads. Jeeps and the ubiquitous rickshaws were halted side by side by the smartly dressed police. Dominating all was the roar of planes, as B24s, Liberators, Lancasters, and Spitfires swept across the sky. Calcutta's main street, Chowringee, was a microcosm of the Allied world: friendly Americans, dark-skinned Africans, smart Chinese, kilted Scots, giant Sikhs, and phlegmatic Englishmen, all wearing their distinctive uniforms and badges.

The big question facing us was: What were we supposed to do? Before leaving Kiangsi, God had given us the above promise of His protection and guidance. Now we were in a strange land, surrounded

173

by millions and millions of Indians, unable to understand a word of the rapid and mellifluous verbalizing that impinged on our ears. What was the way He had prepared? How could we serve the Lord in Calcutta, with no knowledge of the Indian language?

While I was in the hospital, deeply happy in caring for Rosemary, Marvin went through a time of fierce testing. The sudden changes that had come into our lives, the uncertainty of the future, the loneliness of living in an unknown Oriental city, the new responsibility of a family—all seemed to descend upon him. It was much harder for him than for me, for I was entering into the joys of looking after my own child, after helping so many other mothers with theirs. A few days before Rosemary was born, Marvin had been offered a job with the Chinese staff of the British Army Intelligence Service. Accepting this would mean temporary resignation from the mission on the one hand, and a good salary and material security on the other. Was this the way God had prepared?

My dear husband is a man who walks with God. As he attended to the various duties of each succeeding day, he found that God was leading away from the secular job and into work among Chinese people. And this is how it happened.

One Sunday in March of 1945 in a Brethren Assembly, we met John and Betty McGehee, a young and dynamic American couple who had many contacts with both American GIs and Chinese families. When John decided to fly back into China, we were invited to move into their apartment with Betty and her children, so that meetings could be held as usual. The pieces of the jigsaw puzzle were fitting together and we felt release of spirit in the consciousness of God's perfect leading. Bible classes, Chinese Sunday school, preaching opportunities in Mandarin, and English classes for Chinese people more than filled the hours of our days.

But in July, the pattern changed again. John flew out from China at the end of June, as he and Betty felt they should travel back to the States on the repatriation ship *Gripsholm*. Before they sailed they took us out to tea on the second of July to celebrate our second wedding anniversary.

Where would we live now in overcrowded Calcutta, where houses were at a premium? God was testing us again. Did we really believe He could find accommodation for us? His next provision came through an Armenian businessman, Armen George, and his attractive, dark-haired wife. They generously opened their lovely home to us China refugees, feeding us with tasty Indian curries and Oriental fruits.

At the same time, Marvin was asked to help full-time in the Inter-Mission Office in Dalhousie Square, which had been set up to cope with the large numbers of missionaries still flying out of China over the Hump. With remarkable generosity, the Bengal Government provided the office accommodation. In addition, they allotted a lakeside building with large, dormitory-style rooms to the missionary refugees, who often had to wait in India for weeks before they could leave for the West. (In the East and in the West, World War II was still going on, and transportation was almost impossible to obtain.) Over three hundred missionaries faced this traumatic experience of evacuation, often arriving in India battered in mind and spirit.

The days and weeks in humid, stifling Calcutta slipped by. We gave God thanks that V-E Day dawned on the eighth of May 1945, although in our part of the world fighting was still going on. On August 10 and 11, we read in the papers that atom bombs had been dropped in Japan, and on the fifteenth came the longed-for news that in Asia, too, the war had ended. Our thoughts flew to China, to Chinese Christians we had left behind, to our missionaries and children interned for years by the Japanese, and to the future and what God planned for us.

A two-day public holiday was declared. Decorations and flags sprouted everywhere. Government buildings were brilliantly illuminated, and one night we drove around in a *gharry* (one-horse carriage) to see the sights. On August 19, we attended a Thanksgiving service in the cathedral, where thanks was given to God that the horrors of war had ceased.

A few days later, the Chinese community staged their own typical Victory March. It was fantastic: one mile long, interspersed with numerous bands playing popular tunes, children carrying glowing lanterns, adults holding banners, while the snapping of firecrackers and beating of gongs added to the cacophony of sound. Many in the procession doubtless hoped they would soon be back in China, their homeland. Naturally, we hoped we would be also.

Just at that time, Bishop and Mrs. Frank Houghton flew into Calcutta. Bishop Houghton was the General Director of the CIM, but we had never met him before. He asked us to his room for an interview. We told him frankly that we wanted to go back to China, and were willing to work anywhere, though Tsingteh held first place in our hearts. We found him very understanding, and after prayer together, the interview was over.

It was while we were on vacation in Kalimpong, near Darjeeling in the Himalayas, that the letter came from him which was to set our lives in a new groove, one that lasted for nearly eighteen years. But more of that anon…

One great thrill of that vacation must be told. We slipped out of bed before four o'clock one morning, leaving Rosemary asleep in her cot. A small taxi transported us to Tiger Hill, which we climbed in the dim light of a waning moon. It was cold, and our breath hung in clouds around us as we panted up the last stretch of the path. At the top, we turned our faces to the west, hoping we would be among the fortunate few to see the highest mountain in the world. We had met many who had made the same attempt we were making, only to be disappointed.

As we waited, the sun's rays flared out of the east and struck the snow on the massive range before us. Mt. Everest glowed pink against the deep blue of the morning sky, flamed orange, turned gold, and then sparkling white as the sun swiftly climbed higher. Our eyes feasted on the beauty God had created, and our hearts worshiped Him in the stillness of that majestic sight—range after range of mountains covered with eternal snow that shimmered with light.

We discovered in India that the way in which God led us, His children, though sometimes veiled and sometimes dark, held unexpected joys.

Miriam Toop, on the far right, as an eighteen year old, before her departure from China to London in 1931. With her twin brothers Bob and Billy, her sister Peggy and her mother Rosetta and father Joe.

Brothers Marvin and Gordon Dunn in Chinteh in the province of Anhwei.
–1932–

Photo
Memoirs

Marvin Dunn, a new recruit with the China Inland Mission prior to his departure from Canada to China in 1932.

Miriam Toop during her years in nurses training in London prior to departing for China.
—circa 1938—

Gordon and Marvin Dunn with another missionary in the 1940's, obviously dressed in heavily wadded clothes to combat the cold northern winters in China.

Marvin Dunn, in 1940, attending the Miao-Shou Conference.

Wedding Day, July 2, 1943
At Tunki in the province of Anhwei.

·Photo Memoirs·

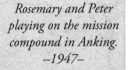

Rosemary and Peter with their parents
on the mission compound in Anhwei
—1947—

Rosemary and Peter
playing on the mission
compound in Anking.
—1947—

Rosemary, Peter,
and Jennifer with
their parents in
Anhwei, shortly after
Jennifer was born.
Dressed in their
Sunday traditional
Chinese gowns.
—1947—

Marvin, Miriam, Rosemary and Peter
during the winter in Anking.
—1948—

Peter in his Sunday best
wadded gown.
—1948—

Marvin and Miriam in the center of their students at the
language school in Anking, with Peter and Rosemary
—1947—

Grandparents Rosetta and Joseph Toop with Jennifer, Rosemary,
and Peter in England during the furlough in 1948

Joseph and Rosetta Toop,
Miriam's parents, upon
their retirement in England

Family portrait taken while on furlough in Three Hills, Alberta, Canada.
Marvin and Miriam with Rosemary, Jennifer, and Peter.
—1948—

The three amigos, Peter, Jennifer, and
Rosemary in their Chinese wadded gowns.
—Chungking, 1949—

Jennifer, in the spring of 1950, in her
traditional Chinese wadded gown.

Marvin, Miriam, Peter, Rosemary and
Jennifer taken in Hong Kong, just after
our escape from Communist China,
and shortly before the birth of David.
—1951—

When it was decided that Rosemary
would depart for Canada to go to school
in Alberta, her mom and dad gave
her a doll on the condition that she
would try not to cry. Here she is, six
years of age, holding back the tears.

Rosemary in Three Hills, Alberta adjusting to life without her family.
—1952—

Miriam with David in Kowloon overlooking Victoria Harbour, with Hong Kong island in the background, where David was born in 1952.

Marvin holding David with Jennifer and Peter looking on in 1952. Shortly after our escape from Communist China.

*Family picture taken in Hong Kong before returning to Canada for a furlough
to join Rosemary. Miriam and Marvin with David, Jennifer, and Peter.*
—1952—

*Peter holding his brother
David in Hong Kong
—1952—*

Margarate and George Dunn, Marvin's parents, Three Hills, Alberta, Canada.
—1952—

Miriam and Marvin Dunn holding David, with Peter, Jennifer, and Rosemary
in Three Hills just before Peter and Rosemary were placed in the C. I. M. home
prior to Marvin, Miriam, Jennifer and David's return to Hong Kong.
—1953—

The four Dunn children, David, Jennifer, Peter, and Rosemary together for the last time before Jennifer and David return to Hong Kong and Rosemary and Peter stay in Three Hills.
—1953—

David, Jennifer, Peter, and Rosemary four years later. Reunited at Grandma Dunn's home in Three Hills
—1957—

Peter and Rosemary in 1958 at the Detenbeck Memorial Home in Three Hills, Alberta, Canada, shortly after Marvin, Miriam, Jennifer and David returned to Malaysia.

The Dunn family in Three Hills, Alberta. Back row Peter, Miriam, Marvin, and David. In the front row are Jennifer and Rosemary.
—1965—

Brothers Marvin and Gordon Dunn in Malaysia
—circa 1965—

The Dunn family in 1965 prior to Marvin and Miriam
returning to Kuala Lumpur in Malaysia.
L-R: David, Jennifer, Peter, Miriam, Marvin and Rosemary.

The Dunn Family in
Three Hills, Alberta
Back: Rosemary, Peter, Jennifer
Front: Marvin, David, Miriam
–1957–

Marvin and Miriam Dunn, Calgary, Alberta.
–January, 1979–

PART VII

Language Schools in West and East China
1945

Chapter Thirty-Eight

My grace is sufficient for thee: for My
strength is made perfect in weakness.
II Corinthians 12:9 KJV

KALIMPONG IS A beautiful spot, high in the foothills of the Himalayas. We had spent nine months in the humidity and oppressiveness of Calcutta, and needed the stimulus of invigorating mountain air.

We stayed in "Ahava," a peaceful, well-ordered guest home, which took its name from a place of rest mentioned in Ezra. We did not realize the personal significance of this name until near the end of our vacation. On October 2, 1945, a letter from Chungking dropped into the mailbox. It was from Bishop Houghton asking us to take on the responsibility of being parents in a small Emergency Language School to be set up in Loshan, West Szechwan. You could have knocked me down with the proverbial feather! How could I, with so little experience of missionary work, still working toward a language exam, and with a baby to care for, rise to such a task? (Of course, as I thought about it later, I realized that Marvin was the important person in the thinking of our leaders. He had had over twelve years on the field, spoke Mandarin well, was an efficient organizer, and had a gift with people.)

"Well, what do you think?" Marvin asked as we read and reread what the Bishop had written.

"Oh, I'm scared!" I exclaimed. "And that part of China is completely new to us. If it were Anking, you at least would have friends among the Chinese to whom you could turn." (We knew the CIM was planning to

179

reopen the Anking Training Home in 1946.)

"That's true. But, as the Bishop says, this will be for only a few months, to help the English girls who have been waiting for years to get out to China. The only way they can get in now is via Calcutta, and Szechwan is nearer to India than Anking. However, I believe we should spend some time in prayer and fasting about this letter. I'll see Miss Clemance (the lady in charge) and ask her if we can book the Prayer Room for tomorrow morning. Shall I tell her you won't want breakfast either?"

"Yes, dear," I agreed. "We *do* need to know the Lord's mind about this step. Okay, I'll feed and bathe Rosemary early so that we can have an uninterrupted time together with the Lord."

Later that day, some inner compulsion made me turn to Ezra 8, and when I came to verse 21, I knew why. "Then (Ezra) proclaimed a fast there, at the river of Ahava, that we might humble ourselves before our God, to seek of Him a straight way for us, and for our little ones, and for all our substance." It was no coincidence that we were planning to do the very same thing in this "Ahava" in Kalimpong.

God's guidance to us was affirmative, as it had been for Ezra, and the verse He gave us was the one heading this chapter. He promised that His grace was going to be sufficient for all that lay ahead, and we were strengthened.

A few days later, we left Kalimpong in a taxi for Ghoom. There we boarded a fascinating little train that went backwards as well as forwards as it negotiated the steep decline to Siliguri. A night on another train plunged us once more into that muggy sponge—Calcutta!

In the early hours of October 20, 1945, Armen George kindly drove us to the Great Eastern Hotel where we boarded the airport bus for the Chungking plane. He and his wife were always so gracious.

That same afternoon, after a rough flight, we swooped down on the island airstrip in Chungking. It was like coming home: the Chinese faces, the familiar blue of Chinese gowns, the smells, the sturdy peasants and their energetic movements, such a contrast to the more lethargic Indian people. After being ferried in a flat-bottomed boat to the riverbank, we climbed the four hundred stone steps that led from the river to the city and thence to the CIM wartime headquarters.

Eleven busy days later, the alarm woke us at four-thirty, and we caught the bus going north and west to Changtu. Rain was drizzling down, but this apparently was typical Szechwan weather. The next day, however, the sun shone and we reveled in the beauty around us: terraced rice fields climbing the hillsides, a spreading tree shading a wayside shrine, stone roads winding off the highway to numerous temples and villages. We were tired when we reached Changtu that afternoon. Bus travel on gravel roads was not exactly a holiday—the wooden seats were narrow and the springs old.

On November 2, Marvin was very busy. He and Arnold Lea had negotiated in Chungking with the U.S. Army who generously gave us from their surplus equipment much of the furniture we needed in the new Language School. We picked up desks, chairs, beds, and cupboards in Changtu. These were loaded on a boat to the accompaniment of shouting coolies, inquisitive children, and much sweating on the part of all! We had been advised that a good stove would be a real investment, but were staggered at the cost—forty thousand dollars! It took us a long time to get accustomed to the inflationary prices.

A trail of eight rickshaws trotted down to the riverbank on the afternoon of the third. In these were John and Jean Lockhart, with baby Margaret, traveling back to their home in Loshan along with our baggage and us. Somehow, we managed to squeeze into the remaining space on the boat, which carried the furniture. At dawn we were awakened by the shouts of boatmen as the sail was raised and oars were manned. Life was primitive and public as we shared the boat's facilities with the crew. But it was a beautiful day and we enjoyed the opportunity to relax with the Lockharts and learn more about Loshan. (Incidentally, Jean Lockhart had been with me in the Hiang Cheng Language School, so it was delightful to meet again.)

We spent three days on the river. The first day passed without incident, but not the second. We had been told that brigands lurked in the area. When we stopped at Pengshan the first night, we asked the magistrate for protection. He detailed four armed men to travel with us. Later the next day, we entered the municipality of Meishan, and these men left, but four new soldiers clambered up the gangplank to take their places. So far, so good.

It was soon after we left Meishan that firing broke out and shots tore across the bow of our boat. Brigands! A group of armed men shouted to the boatmen to head for the bank, and we tried to make ourselves as inconspicuous as possible. Our guards jumped into the shallow water with guns loaded, and in typical Chinese fashion, began to bargain! After a short parley, some money changed hands and we were waved on our way. How thankful we were that a solution was arrived at so easily.

Travel that day held another exciting episode. In places, the fast-flowing water boiled and churned between steep banks. From time to time, stone bridges, supported by four or five narrow arches, spanned the river and great skill was needed to guide the vessel safely through them. One wrong move could result in our being flung into the wild water or dashed against the stone bastions. In order to steer the boat, its momentum had to be faster than that of the river itself. As we sped rapidly toward a bridge, the captain first had to decide which archway to aim for, then the rowers were called to put all their strength into the oars. Tense silence fell, except for the grunting of the men, the roar of the torrent, and the swift action of the oars. As we knifed through the water, we knew that our lives, humanly speaking, depended on the skill of our captain and his men.

The next day we docked at Loshan, one of the cheapest living areas in all of China. Flowing past the ancient city gates was the River Min, down which we had traveled. Green hills fanned out behind; far to the west towered the distant mountains of Sikang. Loshan means "Happy Mountain," and we prayed that each member of our future household would be happy here.

Meanwhile, there was much to be done in preparation for their soon arrival. The furniture we had brought needed scrubbing, and more furniture had to be made and curtains sewn. Marvin believed a volleyball court was necessary, so this was attended to. We were pleasantly surprised to find that electricity was available, but some of the rooms needed rewiring. John Lockhart was a great help in engaging workmen, introducing teachers and ferreting out more domestic help.

The Lockharts and Margery Sykes lived on one side of the huge house, while Joan Ipgrave joined our side to help the students in their studies of Chinese. Margery's work in the church would later give opportunity for the new workers to spend weekends with her in country outstations, thus helping round out their orientation to China and the work to which God had called them.

God graciously gave us gifted and helpful personnel to initiate us into the work He had given. His grace was more than enough.

Chapter Thirty-Nine

We look not at the things which are seen,
but at the things which are not seen.
II Corinthians 4:18 KJV

WHILE STILL IN Calcutta, we had met some of the young people who were to join us in Loshan. One returning missionary came out from England with six new girls, some of whom had been waiting almost since the beginning of the war to come to China. They had had more than their share of danger during the destructive air raids on London, but God had kept the vision of China's need before them. This first group of recruits to sail from my home country after the war was called the "Victory Seven." One of them remained in India to teach temporarily at the Chefoo School located then in Kalimpong, and the other five flew into Chungking.

But only four of them reached Language School. On the evening of November 12, 1945, there was a knock at our door and a telegram was handed in. "Motor accident. Weston killed," we read. As we looked into each other's faces, shock was mirrored there. The little book telling Beryl Weston's life story is prefaced thus:

"Beryl Weston holds a unique place in the membership roll of the China Inland Mission as the only member of it whose missionary service ended within a few days of reaching the field."

We had met her briefly in Calcutta, and were looking forward to getting to know her better. It was easy to ask "Why?" especially when the need was so great for workers. Then the Lord showed us, as we read the evening portion of *Daily Light* that we must not look at the seeming tragedy, but trust Him and His eternal plan.

Later we heard the details. An American officer, formerly a Baptist missionary, was traveling by jeep from Chungking to Chengtu and had offered to take three girls and their luggage along with him. Unknown to him, the tires of the jeep were in poor condition. Within the course of the afternoon, two of them had blown out. There was only one spare tire. Repairing the last puncture held them up a long time. It was getting dark when, for the third time, the uneven wobble of the jeep told them that yet another tire had gone! Rain was falling and there was no inn in sight. They decided to spend the night in the vehicle and fix the tire in the morning.

Early the following morning, they repaired the tire and set out again, expecting to reach their destination within an hour. The road twisted and turned down the mountain toward the great plain in which Chengtu is situated. Then it happened! One wheel went over the edge of the road and the jeep catapulted into the gully below. Beryl, sitting in front, was thrown under the vehicle and killed instantly. The driver and Edith and Dorothy were unhurt, though badly shaken. Under the shadow of this solemn and inexplicable experience, the first post-war Language School began.

Within a few days, the four girls were settled and studies started in earnest. A single male student, in the person of Gordon Harman, also joined us. In February, three more girls arrived—Mary and Ellen from England, and Ella from Australia. This brought our total to eight—four Anglicans, three Baptists, and one Presbyterian.

God did make us a happy family at "Happy Mountain," in spite of the sad beginning. That does not mean that all went smoothly! Language learning was a testing time, and it was easy to become discouraged or overconfident, defeated or insensitive to others' problems. One girl did not *hear* the new sounds clearly; another could not *make* the sounds; some found Chinese idiom impossible; and another kept mixing up the radicals. Tensions eased when they could laugh at themselves as well as at each other.

We had great fun on the volleyball court, letting off steam and getting rid of language frustrations. Each had to learn that teamwork was important, passing the ball to another rather than keeping the spectacular smash for oneself. Some learned faster than others, but gradually our game improved. We worked together and prayed together, learned together and grew together. We found that when Christ is the center of each life, LOVE is there.

Chapter Forty

I will instruct thee and teach thee in
the way which thou shalt go.
Psalm 32:8 KJV

AS THE WEEKS and months slipped by, the time for designations
drew near. Mr. Arnold Lea, the Szechwan superintendent, came
in April to do this. Not only the new workers were praying about
their future; we were as well. As we talked things over with Arnold,
it seemed certain that we would be moving back to eastern China.
However, he suggested that at first we should all move up to summer
bungalows on Mt. Omei instead of breaking up the school in May or
June of 1946, as had been originally scheduled. There, study could
be continued in cooler air, and in the fall our "family" could move to
their stations.

Was this the right thing to do? Marvin and I had our reservations.
It would undoubtedly be physically refreshing for the young people to
go up to the mountain. On the other hand, they would be even more
isolated and cut off from the Chinese people. We felt they needed to
use the language they were learning.

This was mentioned to Arnold, but no conclusion was reached.
It was encouraging to find in our evening reading on April 11, that
the outcome was not ours but God's. "I will instruct thee … in the
way." So when a letter eventually came from Chungking confirming
the move, we knew this was of the Lord. We were learning in different
situations that God could guide us through our leaders. This gave us

185

a growing confidence in the principles Hudson Taylor had laid down many years before. It was exciting to live on the growing edge of faith.

June 4 was a momentous day, the last day of study in Loshan. To celebrate, we all went to a restaurant for a Chinese dinner. Szechwan is renowned for its succulent dishes laced with red peppers. We needed glasses and glasses of clear green tea to dilute the hot spices.

Gordon left us then, but small, curly-haired Lilian Hamer came to take his place. Two years earlier, she had applied to the CIM. When they told her there was no chance of sailing then, she joined the Red Cross and reached China earlier than any of the others. Her determination and courage commended her to the China Council who accepted her as a new worker. Upon being released from the Red Cross, she made the long and rugged journey from Yunnan to Loshan for the months of study on Mt. Omei. (Many years later she was martyred in North Thailand.)

It was mid-June when we piled into an open truck with all our supplies. We were dumped at the bottom of a flight of stone steps that led into the clouds. Thirty-four coolies were hired to carry our things to the small summer cottages that we had managed to rent. Soon we were settled in and studies commenced, but with a more relaxed routine than in Loshan itself.

Mt. Omei is one of China's sacred mountains. From where we lived near its base, we could see, facing west on a clear day, the Golden Peak of the holy mountain itself. Even so, it was a long day's climb away. As we looked towards the east, a perpendicular drop revealed the vast plain where Loshan lay within its gray walls beside the river. The ancient Pilgrim Way, its stones grooved in places by the feet of countless worshipers, snaked up past numerous temples and slid down into deep valleys on its search for the summit. The temples offered shade, refreshment, and lodging to the traveler. At times, through fissures in the rocks, glimpses of the haze-covered valley could be seen far below.

At the peak itself, each Buddhist pilgrim hoped to see Buddha's Glory. This happens only when the sun shines from a cloudless sky onto thick mist filling the valley. As the worshiper stands gazing earthwards, suddenly a circle of yellow light is seen, rimmed with a luminous rainbow. In the middle of the circle, the shadow of the man himself appears a thousand feet below. Many pilgrims in the past would throw themselves off the cliff into the halo believing they would fall straight into the arms of Buddha. This practice is now discouraged.

We never tired of the constant change of colors in sky and mountain, the prodigality of trees, flowers, and gorgeous butterflies. It was here on Mt. Omei that we celebrated our third wedding anniversary. The surroundings brought back memories of our honeymoon on another of China's sacred mountains, Hwang Shan.

Summer studies officially ended August 9, and holidays began. Marvin organized a long-planned hike to the Golden Peak. I, however, was disappointed that I could not join them, although I was not a bit disappointed over the reason. In September, we were expecting our second child, and I knew it would be foolish to attempt such a climb just then. So Rosemary and I waved Daddy goodbye one morning as he and most of the girls began to climb the Pilgrim Way.

A few days after their return, a day of prayer and fasting was set aside with special thanksgiving for all God's goodness to each one of us. As Marvin and I looked back to our apprehension of nearly a year ago, we were humbled to see how God had undertaken for us.

The letters the girls sent us after they left confirmed that it was His doing. Here is what Mary wrote:

"Ella and I often find ourselves praising the Lord for our first home in China, and the happy months at Loshan. We realize it is that intangible thing called "atmosphere" that determines our opinion of a place, that this is, to a large extent, controlled by those who plan and guide our lives. So we know it was the love of God which was shed abroad through your lives, and your prayerfulness, that made our Language School such a happy place in the deepest sense of the word … So please realize that we have given Him all the glory, and retain thankful memories of our houseparents. Love to Rosemary."

Chapter Forty-One

When ye pray, believe.
Mark 11:24 KJV

EVER SINCE MR. Lea's visit, our young people had been concentrating their prayers on the stations to which they had been told they would go when the summer ended. However, Marvin and I were still in the dark about our designation. One day, I wandered out on the hills to be alone with God. In my hand was a little book, and I wanted to read it in the beautiful outdoors.

"The Word of God tells us, 'When ye pray, BELIEVE'...(Mark 11:24). Believe against and over every barrier and difficulty. Believe and praise, no matter how deep the rut your mind and spirit are in."

There was more, but this was the challenge. The Lord caused me to pray for Marvin and myself, and to praise Him for His direction for our lives, even though I did not know where that would be. I returned to our cottage with a deeper trust in my heart.

We moved back to Loshan where everyone began packing. Before the end of August, Edith, Ellen, and May sailed away to Ipin. A few days later, Mary and Ella left for Chengtu. Joan and Lilian were staying in Loshan, while Dorothy was going to deliver our baby in our home.

Just before that event, a letter came from Mr. Sinton in Shanghai. The letter brought news of our designation.

"As we thought and prayed over the matter of designation, it seemed to us as if the place for you would be Tunki. That would be going back to your old stamping ground, and although it is a barren spot, yet a witness must be borne there and you are familiar with the place; may we look to the Lord to give fruit to the seed that has been sown during past days."

So it was to be Tunki after all, and we planned accordingly.

On September 17, 1946, at two-thirty in the morning, I began to walk the floor. Marvin had planned to be with me when our baby was born—but as the pains increased in intensity, his face became whiter and whiter. Exit Marvin! Lilian came in to help Dorothy, and at breakfast time, Peter Graham was born, all nine pounds of him. (Graham after Mr. Hutchinson.)* Rosemary was very intrigued with her baby brother. As she sat on the bed looking at him later, she suddenly leaned forward, grabbed his tiny hands, and tried to make him do the actions of the chorus, "Two Little Eyes," while she sang to him. This was what Joan had taught her, and she was sure she should do the same with him!

Marvin spent his spare time packing. Two and a half weeks later, he left on a wooden boat for Ipin, with four hundred and forty *catties* of luggage (1 *catty* = 1¼ pounds). He was crammed in with twenty other passengers and their goods. From Ipin he went by launch to Chungking, sleeping each night on a wharf, as there was no cabin space. This trip took five days, and we knew it would have been impossible with children.

The only alternative was for me to travel by bus. Fortunately, John and Jean Lockhart and their daughter Margaret were leaving for furlough, and Dorothy Jones was headed for Chungking en route to Kweichow. All of us, plus many other passengers, chickens, and bundles, piled into an antiquated vehicle. Dorothy looked after Rosemary, while I held Peter, who was less than four weeks old. The bus was rickety, the roads were dusty, and the seats on the bus were not made for long-legged foreigners! Fortunately, Peter was a good baby (as long as he had a full tummy). He did not seem to mind bumping along on my knees when my arms grew too tired to hold him.

---

* *Thirty-seven years later a son Thomas was born to Peter and LeAnna Dunn. He was named Thomas Graham Dunn in honor of the Hutchinsons. Peter and LeAnna also founded a company called P. Graham Dunn, also in the Hutchinsons' honor.*

Stopping for meals at wayside food stalls was quite a pantomime. Village children scrambled and pushed to see the three foreign children, and adults also rushed to see the fun. John would order the food. When it arrived, we not only had to feed ourselves but also Rosemary and Margaret—and the bus driver was always in a hurry! We pushed hot noodles into the children's mouths while feeding ourselves at the same time. I always arranged to breast-feed Peter in the bus to save time. Chinese mothers do this, so it aroused no comment.

At night, we slept in inns using our own bedding, washbasins, towels, and facecloths, for eye infections were rife. On October 17, it was dark and pouring with rain when we pulled into the Chungking bus depot. Marvin was there to meet us. It was wonderful to see him.

In Chungking a surprising letter came from Shanghai. Our designation had been changed—not to Tunki but to Anking. Ray and Helen Frame were heading up the Language School there. The winds of change were blowing, and old traditions toppling. The former men's Anking Language School was going coed! Thirteen new workers had already arrived, but it looked as though the numbers were going to rise to forty or fifty before the term was over. This was more than two people could handle, so we were asked to help temporarily.

River steamers going to Shanghai from Chungking were booked up for weeks ahead. There was still a stream of people moving back to their homes in the East, even though the war had ended a year earlier. Added to this, the National Assembly was being convened in Nanking and delegates from the West were jamming the booking offices. The situation seemed hopeless, but God… One of the finest steamers on the Yangtze had a keen Scottish Christian as captain. We were truly grateful to God when we were able to get two berths on this ship. Marvin spent one whole morning buying our two second-class tickets. The cost? $148,700 each! It sounded criminal, and only served to emphasize the inflationary spiral of China's currency.

We embarked that evening, amid pushing, clamoring coolies and hundreds of determined passengers. Our four-berth cabin was tiny, six feet long and nine feet wide, and two Chinese businessmen occupied the other berths. I had never shared a cabin with three men before! However, they were very polite and spent most of their time on deck. It was more embarrassing later when, on the third day, all the toilets broke down and refused to function for the rest of the trip.

Captain Hamish realized that life was pretty grim in the cabin, and the decks terribly crowded. He gave us permission to use the bridge any time we wished. On November 4, 1946, he sent us a special invitation to spend the day up there, as we were to pass through the famous Yangtze Gorges. Sightseers used to travel one thousand miles upriver from Shanghai just to see this spectacular display. On either side, towering, precipitous cliffs squeezed the river into a narrow, boiling, churning mass of water. Danger leaps out of those rapids, and many large sailing boats have been smashed to matchwood in this stretch of the river. But our captain guided us safely through.

Boats going upstream are hauled by long lines of toiling men bent almost double as they creep along paths carved out of the rock at the base of the cliffs. Slowly, slowly the cargo-laden junks move against the current into free water beyond. For centuries the Yangtze River men negotiated the rapids in this way, until the advent of steam introduced new power for those who could afford it.

When we reached Anking on November 7, the river was almost a mile wide, its waters calm and lazy. Normally, steamers went straight through to Nanking, but as the Anking pagoda came into view, our nice captain actually turned his ship around in midstream and the engines kept us stationary against the downward pull of the current. He shouted through a megaphone for a sampan. Soon a little boat splashed out from shore. After it had been tied up to our lowered gangway, the four of us climbed down to it with our entire luggage. We were rowed safely to the wharf. Behind us the steamer turned again, gave a hoot from its funnel, and disappeared downstream.

Marvin was returning to a very familiar city and to people he knew. But it was with some apprehension in my heart that I walked along the rickety gangplank to the shore. As the rickshaw trundled through the old city gate and along cobbled streets to our new home, I wondered what this new life held for me. That time of renewed commitment on Mt. Omei seemed far away as we bumped along the ill-lit road. When away from the familiar, it seemed harder for me to believe. But my fears took wings when we finally arrived at the Language School compound and received a friendly welcome from the Frames.

Chapter Forty-Two

In quietness and in confidence shall be your strength.
Isaiah 30:15 KJV

PETER WAS HUNGRY! He lay yelling in his cot, beating the air with his fists and trying to kick off the layers of blankets. Marvin and I, exhausted after our long trip downriver, were enjoying a marvelous sleep when the noise began. Would he go to sleep again? Marvin rolled over and tried to close his ears.

"Mummy," called a little voice. "Peter's woken up. Can I get up now?"

"No, Rosemary. You stay in bed. It's cold this morning. I'm coming."

I threw on a warm gown and stumbled around trying to find the light switch. In the adjoining room, the yells became more sustained. "Oh, Peter, why did you wake up so early?" I said as I pulled back the blankets and picked up my warm and wet baby boy. "Stop crying or you'll wake other people up too."

Thus began our first full day in Anking. I soon found that life was going to be very different from Loshan. Our household was larger, and would soon more than triple in size. The walled mission compound was huge, as it included a large area for volleyball courts. The two-story gray brick buildings had suffered badly during the war, and the Frames had spent much time and effort getting them into decent condition again.

We found that besides the Frames and ourselves there were two

193

other staff members—tall and attractive Ruth Nowack (Helen's sister) whom I had met earlier in Fowyang, and Miss McQueen, a diminutive Scottish lady who had come to China in 1911, the same year as my parents. Already thirteen new workers were studying hard at the Chinese language, with more expected before the year's end. The pressure was beginning to build.

That day, we had our first staff meeting, the precursor of many more. Where did we, as individuals, fit into God's plan for this work? What responsibilities were to be ours? Light was given as we talked and prayed.

Ray was the superintendent, and also a language expert, having taken linguistic training on furlough. This training was to revolutionize language learning in our mission. His lectures were aimed at training ears to hear the Chinese sounds, and mouths, tongues, and throats to make them.

Ruth would assist him in this area. She loved the Chinese people and spoke the language fluently. God had given her a wonderful gift of identification with the peasants who form the backbone of China. She had much to share with the eager young missionaries who were keen to learn all they could about the land and the people to whom God had brought them.

Helen was not too interested in housekeeping, so she volunteered to look after the laundry. This proved to be a big job. Ray had made a wooden washing machine, crude but workable by hand, which was a great help. Soon after their arrival, each girl would have to be fitted for a Chinese wadded silk gown with at least two cotton cover gowns. Helen offered to supervise this also.

Miss McQueen would be "mother in Israel" to the girls and would also help in other ways. She had spent many years in Kiangsi, and her outlook on Chinese things leaned to the conservative. For instance, she insisted that all the proprieties which were in force in inland China cities be observed in the Language School, even though customs were changing. One old-style Chinese practice was that single men and women of good repute should not sit on the same bench. Not realizing this, Ray had ordered a dozen long benches for the dining room because they were much cheaper than individual chairs. Now he had to add a number of small stools for the young men to sit on. The words of Philippians 2:3 needed to be applied in our relationships with one another on staff: "With humility of mind let each of you regard one another as more important than himself."

Marvin was responsible for the business matters, such as meeting ships, dealing with coolies, keeping accounts, and so on, while to me fell the lot of managing the kitchen.

"Dear Lord, how can I do this? You know that cooking and housekeeping are not my thing. And how will I manage when the big crowds come?"

Gently, He reminded me from Isaiah 30:15 to put my confidence in Him—not to worry and fret about the future, but to be quiet in order to know His strength. This verse had been underlined in my Bible one day in Loshan, as I was thinking of the new life and responsibilities ahead. How often I needed that reminder!

Housekeeping was quite a complication, I found. Steaming hot rice was a poor substitute for potatoes for most of our young people. Yams were available in the market, and while we ourselves enjoyed them, I soon found that many of our family had never eaten them before coming to China. Added to that, the combination of a sweet vegetable with any kind of meat was anathema to the English. They longed for Irish potatoes. Our choice of fruit was also limited. Golden persimmons tasted delectable to us, but never having eaten them, some new workers were dubious about them. We served Chinese-style meals two or three times a week to gradually introduce the young people to the kind of food they would be given in Chinese homes, and to accustom them to the use of chopsticks. These meals were generally popular, but some rebelled at the gobs of tasty fat pork floating in soy sauce!

We were just getting to know the different fellows and girls, when more descended upon us. By the end of 1946, the buildings were bulging with forty young people. They came to us from England and the States, from Canada, Norway, and Sweden, and from Australia and New Zealand. They underlined again the fact that the China Inland Mission was an international organization. Most of our young people were full members of the CIM, others being associates.

All were thrilled to be in China at last. Many had waited for years. I discovered that I was younger than some of the latest arrivals.

As we prepared for their coming, I remembered how I had appreciated the verse I had been given when I had arrived in Tsingtao in 1940. Would these young folk, just beginning their missionary careers, like the same approach? I discussed this with the other staff members and they agreed that I should print Scripture verses for each new missionary, to greet them in their rooms. This occupied most of my spare time. For some, this was the only note they received on arrival, while others found many letters from home piled on their desks. Many thanked me later, saying how the verses had related to some special need or desire in their hearts.

Life was exhilarating, with young people from so many different nationalities, denominations, and backgrounds living together. At times it tended to create frustration and misunderstanding. Farmers, theologians, nurses, teachers, secretaries, university graduates, a lawyer, an engineer, a dietician—all added their quota to our corporate living. At mealtimes, the Americans discovered that what they called "cookies" were "biscuits" to the British, and what they called "biscuits" were "scones" to those from England. "Jelly" had different connotations also; to those from the States, jelly was what you spread on bread and butter, while to the British, it was a dessert to be eaten with custard! So the dining room was sometimes noisy, especially on Saturdays, when the tensions of the week began to loosen. Miss McQueen did her best to keep voices down, but did not always succeed.

One group of new arrivals brought a huge shipment of heavy cardboard cartons for us. U.S. Army surplus supplies were on sale in Shanghai, and a thoughtful person at CIM headquarters decided some should be bought for the Language School. As Marvin and I pried open the cartons, our excitement grew. Before our unbelieving eyes appeared dozens of six-pound tins of peaches, figs, and prunes; dozens of packets of M&Ms (or Smarties); sauerkraut (a new food to me); cheese in six-pound tins; also ice cream powder (something we had not heard of); packets of Hershey chocolate; tins of milk powder. This was God's miracle of provision. It made a tremendous difference to my job of planning meals. From then on, we could serve more varied and interesting dishes. How humbling it was to see how unexpectedly God had rebutted my fears!

The local market did give us fresh vegetables, such as spinach, cabbage, and turnips. Occasionally, hunters would come to the gate with freshly killed deer, and the cook would call me to buy some meat. Tasty fish from the Yangtze River also appeared on our tables, along with the inevitable pork. The English reveled in the abundance of food after being on rations for so long. They were electrified one day when we told them we had just bought one thousand eggs! In England each person had been only allowed two eggs a month.

Marvin sometimes had a headache with the accounts, but he

Rosemary and Peter with their amah in Anking –1947–

grew with the job. Every student had a separate page in his huge ledger. Each month we had to figure out the cost of board, and this was deducted from the personal accounts. Every two weeks our employees had to be paid: teachers, cook, laundry women, amahs, and coolies. Each time, they usually received more money, for inflation was on the increase. Whereas in 1937 one hundred dollars of Chinese currency could purchase two cows, in 1947 it could only buy two boxes of matches! In fact, one day Marvin returned from the bank, followed by a rickshaw loaded high with bundles of paper money. He was a multimillionaire!

In many ways, our big family was fairly helpless. They could not yet communicate with the Chinese people around them, so someone had to do this for them. Unfortunately, Anking was a very conservative city, and it was not wise for large groups of foreigners (foreign devils, they called us) to walk in the streets and nose around in the stores. How then could our students buy the odds and ends they began to need? Marvin had a brain wave. He set up Operation Street Order. A girl and a fellow were delegated to organize the students' side. Every two weeks Marvin and his Chinese assistant would buy what they needed. Orders poured in for shoelaces, peanuts, oranges, batteries, envelopes, kerosene, stoves; repairing of watches, pens, glasses, stamps for home letters (one week the stamp order alone cost over fourteen million dollars!). One girl included the following item at the end of her order: "One man, tall, dark, and handsome." This did not stump my husband. He searched around for a mail-order catalog, cut out a picture of a black-haired male, and put it in a large envelope marked "Personal and private." She and her friends enjoyed the joke.

Early in the term, I realized that I would need help in looking after Rosemary. The compound was large, she could run anywhere, and my housekeeping duties kept me tied to the house. Also, I had to nurse Peter every four hours. We prayed that the Lord would show us what to do. As we waited in quietness before Him, we were confident He would guide. Soon we heard of Hsien-ying, who wanted a job. She was a cheerful, active teenager, her black hair cut in bangs and a long bob. She loved our little girl and kept a careful eye on her, also on the Frames' little boy, Raymond. It was not easy for us. Inevitably, the closeness to our firstborn loosened a little. We comforted ourselves that it would be only for a few months. Then we would have her to ourselves again.

Even though our compound was large, after living for weeks inside its high brick walls, some of the young folk began to feel confined. They longed to explore the world outside. The city streets were too restrictive, so different members of staff organized hikes into the country on Saturday afternoons. Most of the groups, which Marvin and I led, ranged far and wide. Everywhere, we saw graves, small mounds of earth grouped together in a lucky spot. (According to Buddhist belief, graves can only be located in "auspicious" areas decided on by a geomancer. These were a constant reminder of those who had already passed into a Christless eternity. Sometimes we would see unburied coffins, draped in straw, waiting for an auspicious day for the funeral.)

Each hike gave us new insights into Chinese rural living. We saw farmers plowing their waterlogged rice fields with wooden plows pulled by water buffalos. Nearby, a boy, perched on a buffalo's back, was watching a grazing herd. Men passed us carrying smelly human fertilizer in big wooden buckets to their fields, sometimes preceded by a donkey similarly laden. Women, chattering as they washed clothes in some small pond, would glance in surprise at this group of striding foreigners.

A couple of miles from the city, an ancient, seven-tiered pagoda beckoned enticingly, and one day we walked in that direction. It was in excellent condition. Each tier was decorated with a stone balcony, and a slender spire topped the entire structure. The courtyard was paved in smooth stone and beautifully decorated with flowering shrubs. As we entered the dim hall at its base, the strong smell of incense inevitably greeted us. Ranged around the walls, hideous idols gazed down with unseeing eyes. Shaven priests in flowing gray robes tended the altar. For the first time, this aspect of heathenism hit our young people as a reality. Some of them could not forget it.

Climbing the stone steps to the top, we gazed out over the greening countryside. To the south lay the wide-flowing Yangtze. To the west, the gray bulk of its high wall delineated our city. In between stretched fields, mounds of graves, and clumps of straw-roofed houses. Farther in the distance we could see Dragon Mountain, a hiding place for bandits and Communist bands. Danger was not far away, but we were held in God's hands.

As we walked down the steps and wended our way home, there were many new sights to think over, much to write home about, and much to pray for.

Chapter Forty-Three

Under the Blood, the precious Blood,
Under the healing, cleansing flood,
Saviour, keep us from day to day,
Under the precious Blood.

BEFORE OUR ARRIVAL in Anking, Ray Frame had taught this chorus to the students. Sometimes we sang it at morning prayers, and through it we became more aware of the power of Jesus' Blood. The words reminded us of the need to stay close to the Lord as we faced the challenge of each new day.

Satan's forces are strong in pagan lands, and missionaries are among his targets. If he can sow dissension, mistrust, or misunderstanding among Christ's followers, that is to his advantage. New missionaries, after the initial excitement has passed, are often faced with problems they never expected. One girl, for instance, a university graduate, thought she would have no difficulty with the language. She enjoyed study and had done well at home. But when she began to learn Chinese, she floundered. Not only did she feel humiliated, but she also sank into depression and pessimism.

Learning Chinese is not easy. Ray and Ruth worked patiently with those who had problems. Good progress was usually made by the young people who followed the new techniques, but not by all. It was fatally easy for one who was slow to compare herself with one who was quick, and thus become discouraged. It was not uncommon, after an especially difficult lesson, to hear Ray's voice lifted in the above chorus, turning the thoughts of the students to the Lord and His power in a hard situation.

For me, this chorus became a "rope" of deliverance one night. I had a horrible dream, perhaps after a visit to the pagoda. The power of Satan seemed to grip me as I felt my body swinging in ever-lengthening curves, dipping lower and lower to a horror of darkness that gaped below me. Fear jolted my heart into thudding activity. Then I woke up, breathless. What was happening to me? I stretched out my hand. Yes, Marvin was beside me, and all was quiet. But I dared not sleep again in case that fearful dream enveloped me.

"O Lord," I whispered aloud, "help me. I'm afraid."

Suddenly the well-loved words came to me, and falteringly I repeated them quietly to myself. The conviction grew in my heart that "under the Blood" I was safe. Satan could not reach me there.

"Lord, I've claimed the protection of Your precious Blood in a new way tonight. Please be with me as I sleep."

Peace flooded in, and turning over, I slept dreamlessly until dawn. However, that same dream returned more than once, and each time I turned to Christ for help.

Another occasion when the singing of this chorus brought peace was when reports reached us of Communist activity not far away. Marauding bands, bringing destruction in their wake, infested five out of the six counties surrounding us. Only the county in which Anking was situated had relative peace. In the neighboring province of Honan, five missionaries were murdered. It was humbling to us all that the power of the Blood of Jesus, of which we sang, protected us at this time.

Chapter Forty-Four

Then I went down to the potter's house,
and behold, he was making a work on the wheels.
Jeremiah 18:3 ASV

THIS VERSE CAME alive to us in the summer of 1947. In March and April, two groups of young people left us for points west, sailing up the Yangtze River to Chungking. Marvin had to spend many hours at the river and in booking offices in the city. At each departure a stream of rickshaws rolled out of our compound gates, piled high with people and their hand luggage, while a truck conveyed dozens of trunks to the riverside. In April and May, eleven new workers joined us—eleven personalities to learn to know and love.

In normal times, a term at the Language School lasted eight or nine months. Toward the end of these terms, most of the students wrote their first section exam, and could carry on a limited conversation in Chinese. However, since some of our family had only been in Anking for a few weeks, and the rest less than five months, our leaders in Shanghai decided in the spring of 1947 that the whole group should move upriver to Kuling, another of China's beautiful mountain summer resorts.

How grateful Marvin and I were for the experience we had had the year before in moving a much smaller group to Mt. Omei for the summer. Once again, the Lord had carefully prepared us. But this year, instead of eight students there were forty-four, with all their belongings. Teachers and servants, children and staff swelled the total to seventy. Whereas in 1946 the trip took only a day by truck, this year we would be involved in a two-day trip upriver in a launch, embarking at Anking, disembarking at Kiukiang, traveling by truck to the foot of the mountain, then either climbing the thousands of steps to the top or traveling by sedan chair. This gave Marvin some frustrating experiences in logistics. He needed (and God gave him) endless patience and wisdom in planning such a move. He could not have done it alone, and the indefatigable help of Karl Mayer in Kiukiang was invaluable. (Karl received his reward later, when one of our Swiss girls became his wife.)

We all reveled in the beauties and freedom of Kuling. Studies were carried on much as before, but the schedule was less rigid than when on the plain. On the fourth of July (our American friends wanted to celebrate this day), we hiked to Tiger's Tooth for a supper picnic and watched a silver moon rise over Poyang Lake to the east. Two days earlier, Marvin and I had quietly celebrated our fourth anniversary (in Kiangsi). One Saturday, we organized an all-day hike to Lion's Leap, the highest peak in the range. Mist and fog enveloped us on the ascent, but at the top, the clouds parted and we feasted on the beauty of the scene spread before us. Jagged rocks and perpendicular granite cliffs framed a vista of tiny bright green rice fields, glinting in the sun, spreading from the mountain's foot to the misty horizon.

On the main street that ran through Kuling, there were many stores selling china and pottery. They glowed with color: bowls of every shape and size, vases dainty and ponderous, teapots slim and bulging, lidded tea-mugs, china spoons, plates crawling with dragons or sprayed with flowers, cups, saucers. Far on the plain below was the town of Kingtehchen, famous for the exquisite china produced from local clay. It was from these pottery works that Generalissimo Chiang Kai Shek ordered a delicate dinnerware service for Princess Elizabeth's wedding gift. It was there also that China's gift of appreciation to General Marshall was produced: china in the decorative 10,000-flower pattern. We heard that each plate cost about $500,000 in Chinese currency!

Perhaps it was this emphasis in Kuling that drew our thoughts to the story of the potter in Jeremiah. We also saw a parallel as we listened on Saturday and Sunday evenings, when different members of our big family gave their testimonies. One girl told how some years earlier, in spite of academic success, life had become empty and meaningless. In desperation, she drove off in her car one day, determined to commit suicide. A punctured tire effectively stopped her and gave God time to speak. He gave her a new joy and a new direction—to China. An engineer described the thrill of seeing the drawings of his first bridge become a gleaming reality, only to be disillusioned by the discovery of rust, the beginning of deterioration, on one part of the new structure. God used this to jolt him out of materialism and to measure his life by a different and eternal standard. A girl vividly described her childhood, including her own flaming temper. Then God took over, changed her inside out, and guided her to China.

In August, our General Director and his wife arrived in Kuling to designate these "vessels" to different parts of the land. A large map of China was hung on the wall, and as each one came out from the interview, he or she was given a tiny flag printed with his or her name to pin on the map. When all had been designated, there were clumps of colored flags scattered all over the country.

By September, all had left the mountain, traveling to Yunnan, Kweichow, and Szechwan in the West; to Kansu and Shensi in the North; to Honan, Anhwei, and Kiangsi in the central part; to Chekiang and Kiangsu in the East. Our prayers followed the vessels made in the hand of the Potter as they moved out to places of His positioning.

For us, a short vacation followed, although the house seemed empty and silent with the young life drained from it. All summer, we enjoyed our children in a new way. Rosemary and Peter thrived in the cool air and sunshine. Their hair grew blonder, and their cheeks became rosy. Marvin designed a little canvas chair in which we carried Peter on some of the shorter hikes. He learned to walk, crowing with delight.

All too soon, we had to return to Anking. Cases and bundles swung again at the ends of the coolies' carrying poles as they jogged down, down, down the mountain to the steamer. One coolie carried a very precious load, Rosemary in one basket and a rather apprehensive Peter in the other. I, too, was carried down (but in a sedan chair), for we were expecting another child, due in five months' time.

Peter emulating the Chinese porter in Anking, 1948.

*Peter and Rosemary being carried in the two baskets
by a Chinese coolie in Anking, circa 1947.*

Chapter Forty-Five

Ourselves your servants for Jesus' sake.
II Corinthians 4:5 KJV

Look, there's the pagoda," someone called. Our eyes turned downstream, and in the distance we saw Anking's ancient landmark silhouetted against the sky. Soon all was pandemonium as we and the Frames climbed off the launch and onto the wharf. Immediately we became the focus of a jabbering throng of coolies and rickshaw pullers.

"Whew, it's hot here," I said to Marvin as I held Peter with one sticky hand and Rosemary with the other. "I'd forgotten how humid it could be on the plain."

"Yes, I know," he replied, "but we'll soon be home. These coolies are rather difficult to deal with, but it shouldn't be long now."

Soon we were trundling through the gloom under the huge gateway of the city wall that was several feet thick. Above the gate, a dark-tiled double roof rested on tall red pillars, its corners sweeping up towards the sky. On the congested streets, our rickshaw pullers shouted warnings to pedestrians in their way. Children grinned at us as we passed. Two old men in long gowns, leaning on canes, moved cautiously to one side. Street vendors displayed their wares. Familiar smells rose from the open gutters. Large characters above the shops proclaimed the owner's name and business. Yes, we would soon be home.

That fall, thirty-six young people arrived by ship from Shanghai in groups of varying size. One of the American girls was dressed in slacks. We raised our eyebrows! And when she shinnied up a persimmon tree to

207

pluck the last golden fruit from a high bough, we looked at each other, aghast. Shut away in inland China, we had not realized how the mores of our Western world were changing. Poor Miss McQueen was shocked. But as we came to know them, we found these same girls had hearts of gold and loved the Lord deeply.

For this last term in the Language School, God gave us this verse as our motto: "Ourselves your servants for Jesus' sake." Once more, Christ was asking us to help these young people in their adjustments to each other, to the language, to the food, and to life in China. We enjoyed it, and it kept us young. We knew we were in God's place for us, and the students realized it also. One day, I overheard one of them say as I passed by, "You know, Mrs. Dunn is a thoroughly happy woman." Of course I was. God had given me a wonderful husband, two sweet children, and joy in His service.

This term, Norah Conway replaced Ruth Nowack, who had returned to her teaching work among village Christians in North Anhwei. Norah was born during the Boxer uprising in 1900. She had been called the "Miracle Baby," because when her parents were hiding from the Boxers and in danger of death she never made a sound that would betray them to the enemy. We were also glad to welcome John and Eleanore Crook (whom we had last seen in Tunki), with their two children. They had come to help the Anking church and it brought back memories to see them again.

It was in January 1948 of that term that I was introduced to a lovely American custom. The girls invited me to a party one Saturday afternoon. When I went to the sitting room, the first thing I saw was a white stork holding a flowered parasol upside down in his beak. Pink and blue bows added to the décor. All the girls were there waiting. I was mystified and a little nervous, wondering what was going to happen. The American girls were in charge and, after serving cookies and tea, one of them said, "Can you guess why we are here?"

"Not really," I replied.

"It's a baby shower," she said.

"A baby shower? What's that?" I asked.

"Well, it's a shower for your new baby," she explained.

I looked around a bit helplessly. "What do you mean? The only shower I know is when it rains."

There was a shout of laughter from the group. "It's a special party for *you*," they said. "We do it all the time in America."

Then someone lifted down the parasol, which was piled with presents, and I had to open each one. Towels, material, soap, powder, and envelopes containing cards and money spilled out. I was overwhelmed. I knew some of them had dug into their trunks to produce some of these gifts. Love overflowed in that room, prompted by thoughts and concerns for the new little life soon to join us.

A few weeks later, just before midnight on February 4, 1948, Jennifer Ruth was born in the American Mission Hospital not far away. She was not like our other babies, with her long black hair and big dark eyes in a little heart-shaped face. We thought she was sweet, but the Chinese nurses were rather disappointed. "She looks just like our babies," they remarked. "We were expecting a yellow-haired one."

A few days later, she and I were given a tumultuous welcome in typical Chinese fashion when we returned home. Strings of red firecrackers exploded and snapped as Marvin brought us in, and everyone (girls, men, teachers, and servants) crowded around to see the new baby.

A little later, fifteen more young people arrived, among them our first contingent from Switzerland. Once again, we benefited from the different contributions each group brought to the whole. Deep theological discussions took place. Music played by expert fingers charmed us. Lifelong friendships were made. Social evenings of fun and fellowship added zest to life once a month.

This term, Peter was more in evidence. He and Rosemary looked so cute in their Chinese wadded outfits, hers a long gown like the "aunties," and his a floral jacket and trousers. Peter was still vociferous at mealtimes, but once the pangs of hunger were stayed, his sunny nature reasserted itself. At the end of the meal, he would waddle from one table to another to collect the table napkins from the students. His fat little cheeks bounced up and down with his efforts, and his eyes were serious as he performed his self-appointed task. The "aunties" were his willing slaves and we were afraid he would be badly spoiled.

Chapter Forty-Six

The steps of a good man are ordered by the Lord:
and He delighteth in his way.
Psalm 37:23 KJV

I N JUNE 1948, we were booked to sail to America from Shanghai on the S.S. *General Gordon.* Miss McQueen kindly took over the housekeeping and we packed whenever we had a spare minute. This was my first furlough and Marvin's second, and we wondered what it held for us. The Lord's message was, "Your steps are planned by Me. Not only that, but it delights Me to see you walking where I lead." So, after corporate prayer for safe travel, we said goodbye to our large family and boarded the crowded downriver launch. A number of Chinese friends were at the wharf to wave us off. The propeller churned up the turbid waters of the Yangtze, and we were away.

Furlough would hold many "firsts" for both of us. I would meet Marvin's family, live on the prairies, and see Prairie Bible Institute. There would be deputation meetings, and traveling with three small children. What would the grandparents think of them? Some misgivings entered my heart. My old enemy, fear, began to do battle.

But the Lord was faithful and He gave us many delights. Family reunions began even before we left China's shores. In Wuhu, downriver from Anking, we spent a few days with Gordon and Vera and their two girls. In Shanghai, we found my brother Bill and his wife, having just arrived as new workers of the CIM on their way to Language School in Anking.

This was my first visit to Shanghai since childhood, and it was exciting to meet the veteran leaders who had spent many years at this hub of the

*Gordon and Vera Dunn and with their daughters
Marguerite and Barbara in China, circa 1947.*

mission. The large compound, with its many huge buildings, was a concrete example of God's wonderful provision. The offices hummed with activity. The small hospital on the top floor was well equipped. The prayer hall was used daily, for this was the CIM international headquarters.

Our first port of call was Yokahama, which still showed signs of war bombings. The next was Honolulu, an island beautiful with flowers and color. From there, we steamed across the Pacific. We reached San Francisco, sailing under the famous Golden Gate Bridge, where I had my first glimpse of the United States.

The next day, we celebrated our fifth wedding anniversary (on the Pacific Ocean) before disembarking at Los Angeles. On July 4, we were plunged into some of the hectic celebrations of Independence Day and visited the Rose Bowl. The Los Angeles roads impressed and scared us, with huge cars weaving in all directions at tremendous speed. It was a relief to travel by train up the West Coast to Vancouver, the lovely Canadian city that sits proudly between the mountains and the sea. Another train carried us through the grandeur and beauty of the Rockies. We finally arrived at the small prairie town of Three Hills, Alberta.

I need not have been afraid. Marvin's mother was a saint. His father had not fully recovered from a recent stroke, and I never knew him as a well man. Marvin's sister Margaret and her husband also lived in the town, and it was good to meet them after all the letters that had passed between us.

We settled into part of Marvin's old home, where I was initiated into the intricacies of cooking and baking in an antique wood-burning stove. That really floored me. I had expected such conditions in China, but not in Canada! Marvin was very patient with me when I got exasperated and felt I could not take it anymore—when, for instance, the oven just would *not* get hot enough in time for my rising bread. And the water—no one in the town had running water then, and all we used had to be pumped from a cistern in the basement. The children thought that kitchen pump was very intriguing, but it was only another frustration for me. And the outhouse—in the cold of a prairie fall—brrrr!

I had never imagined life in Three Hills would be like this. But Mother Dunn did all she could, and how we loved it when she presented us with a batch of hot bran muffins for breakfast. I am afraid my in-laws also had some adjustments to make with this new English girl invading their home with her strange accent and different ideas about things. But God drew us together in His own sweet way.

In October 1948, we set off on our travels again, right across Canada to Toronto, then south to New York, an incredible city with rushing cars and towering skyscrapers. Here we boarded the gigantic *Queen Mary* and found our cabin was down in the bowels of the ship. A series of three different elevators shot us up to the decks. Marvin stayed on his bunk most of the trip with seasickness, but at least he could keep an eye on Jennifer. My hands were full with the other two. There were always kind people who gave me help when I needed it, and we three thoroughly enjoyed ourselves.

Returning to Newington Green, London, married and with three children, was certainly different from the way I had left it eight and a half years earlier. My parents met us there, and we all moved down to Kent for four months. The countryside was beautiful, but the house was cold! All three children became fat and rosy. My sister Peggy, her husband, and little Kate visited us in a happy reunion. On Christmas Day, Marvin stayed at home and cooked the turkey while the rest of us reveled in the Christmas service in the little Anglican church nearby. God is good, and the "steps" He ordered were beautiful. We contacted as many praying friends as we could, and Marvin appreciated the opportunity of going up to London to see the pageantry of royalty.

All too soon, we had to pack again. The church that had fully supported Marvin since 1940 wanted us to take part in their Spring Missionary Conference. So once more, we crossed the gray Atlantic. I was introduced to the missionary-minded people at the First Baptist Church in Wayne, Michigan, and was overwhelmed by their love and generosity. More American "showers" filled our trunks with bed linens, towels, clothes for the children, shirts, dresses, and underwear. We were quite exhausted at the tempo of the Conference, and rotation of meetings in seven other like-minded churches in the area.

Back in Three Hills, Marvin was often out in deputation work. Rosemary was now a tall, slim four-year-old with fair hair and blue eyes. Dolls, pretty dresses, and curls were very important to her. Occasionally, other thoughts came to the surface. She came into the kitchen one day, dragging a piece of wood for the stove.

"Mummy, does Jesus see me when I am helping you?" she asked.

"Yes, darling, and at other times too," I replied.

"Oh! Can He see right into my heart, through my dress? But how?"

I answered as best I could, trusting the Spirit to help her understand.

Peter was a sturdy nearly three-year-old, curious about everything. He needed discipline every so often, but he was such a loving little boy. Once he came into the kitchen and stood near the table, looking up at me.

"What do you want, Peter boy?" I asked.

"I just want to see my mummy," he said seriously, and then ran off to play again. My heart turned over. What a rebuke this was to me. Did I love my Saviour like that? Ready to leave something that interested me in order to spend a little time with Him?

Baby Jennifer, with her large dark eyes and tanned little face, was so different from the other two. Travel was hard on her, and I rather dreaded the thought of taking her into inland China in a few months' time. She was more fragile than the others, and did not adjust as easily.

Mother Dunn's life was a constant blessing to me. The Dunns lived frugally in order to give more to the Lord for missions, and I could understand my husband better after living with his folks that summer. Mother Dunn was always busy. Her home was spotless. She loved Prairie, and her life revolved around its activities.

I also met Mr. Maxwell. I liked his honest and forthright ways. His preaching could cut to the heart, though some of his histrionics went against my more subdued English grain. He was an amazing man, and I am glad that God arranged our steps to rest awhile in Three Hills. The big Spring Conference was a revelation to me of how deep and strong was God's work through that Bible school, and how wide were the ripples caused by its teaching. Hundreds of missionaries had first heard God's call in this place, and left for lands across the sea, my own husband among them.

It was there, too, that God spoke to me again, and I renewed my vows to Him. Traveling, looking after the children, cooking, cleaning—these things had upset the delicate adjustment of my soul to God. Physical weakness and the wear and tear of life made it difficult to keep my quiet time each morning, and I had lost out spiritually. Now I could praise God for His grace and mercy, and for a renewed relationship. Life was zestful again, walking with Him.

It was during our furlough that Communism began to spread over China like a red sea. Conditions were chaotic, and we wondered if we would be able to return. Our hearts were there, and if the Lord said, "Go," we were ready. Some wondered if it was right to take our three children into such a situation. Civil war was raging; brigandage was rife. Shanghai fell in May. Gordon and Vera, the Frames, the new workers, and our headquarters staff all slid behind the Bamboo Curtain.

In the providence of God, an emergency Western office had been opened in Chungking just a few weeks earlier with Arnold Lea in charge. Strangely enough, at this very time, young people in the homelands were offering to serve the Lord in China with the CIM. Our leaders needed to know the will of God. A special call to prayer about this matter was printed in the CIM magazine, *China's Millions.*

Western China was still free of Communism, and God's Spirit was working. More men and women were needed to grasp the opportunities. Gradually, the conviction grew that new missionaries *should* be accepted. Candidate Schools were held in the different home countries. Mission leaders in Europe, Australia, Switzerland, and Scandinavia applied for passports and China visas for the new recruits. Miraculously, even the cagey U.S. State Department cooperated. Forty-nine young people were all set to sail for China!

How did this tie in with us? Marvin and I had received a letter from Arnold asking us if we would be prepared to take charge of a new Language School to be situated somewhere in West China. The Frames were bottled up in Shanghai with the previous group of new workers, and there was no one else with the same experience that we had gained in both Loshan and Anking. He asked if we would pray over the proposition and let him know. As we did so, the Lord encouraged us with the message: "Our sufficiency is of God." We wrote back in the affirmative.

Just a month after celebrating our sixth anniversary in Three Hills, a telegram changed the momentum of our lives. "Urgent you sail San Francisco for Hong Kong August 28. Can you make it?"

We cabled back, "Yes," and then went into a furor of shopping, labeling, and packing. Traveling via Vancouver and Seattle, we eventually arrived in San Francisco and boarded the same S.S. *General Gordon* on which we had sailed from Shanghai the year before.

Furlough was over. God had gone before us, protected us, and provided for us in so many unexpected ways. Now we were returning. Our ship sailed west under the stately Golden Gate Bridge, out into the choppy seas of the mighty Pacific. A new term of service lay before us, as unknown as was the path through the tossing waves, but we were setting out with One who would always stay beside us, One who loved us and our little trio with a constant, abiding love.

L. E. Maxwell Family in Three Hills, Alberta, Canada.

PART VIII

Under Communism in Chungking
1949-1951

Chapter Forty-Seven

Our sufficiency is from God.
II Corinthians 3:5 ASV

WHY, IF IT isn't the Dunns!" exclaimed a surprised voice, as we stood at the entrance to the CIM compound in Chungking, West China. "However did you get here?"

"Flew in on the *St. Paul*," Marvin explained. "Didn't you get the telegram from Hong Kong?"

"No, nothing has come through. But come along in. We are so glad to see you, and even though the house is full, we'll soon find a room for you."

The house was indeed overflowing with guests. Sixteen missionaries were waiting to fly out to Hong Kong on the same plane that had brought us in. However, we were taken upstairs, where a sleepy Peter and Jennifer were gently lowered onto a bed. Then Marvin hurried off to retrieve the baggage we had left at the airport.

It was September 17, 1949. Early that morning, we had boarded the transport plane belonging to the Lutheran Mission, appropriately named *St. Paul*, which was now the only means by which missionaries could be ferried in and out of China. We passengers were strapped into seats lining each side and facing each other. A pile of trunks, suitcases, wooden crates, and bedding rolls filled the central area. The plane taxied to position and with a raucous burst of speed seemed to swallow the runway as it fled below us. We soared over the beautiful panorama of Hong Kong. Soon we were high above China, winging our way west to the Nationalist capital of Chungking, set in a gradually diminishing circle of freedom. The red flags of Communism flaunted their challenge over much of the land, and where the flags flew, missionaries could not enter.

Peter watching a street cobbler hard at work in Chungking.

The next day, Arnold Lea explained the situation to us.

"Many people think we are crazy to bring new workers into Chungking at this time. Missionaries with many years' experience in China are getting out as fast as they can, believing they see the writing on the wall. We might have been doing the same if God had not given us the vision of many doors that are still open, and the need for more workers to enter them.

"He has overwhelmed us with tremendous encouragement. Many well-trained and exceptional young people have pleaded to join us. Governments have cooperated amazingly. Already the group from Australia and New Zealand has sailed for Hong Kong. Joan and Max Orr are eager to help on the language teaching side. Hazel Page will fly up from Yunnan any day now to give basic linguistic training.

We have been able to rent enough bungalows to house everyone—at a pinch. God is in this venture!"

He was obviously moved, yet also intensely practical. We discussed teachers, wages, servants, housing, financial arrangements, and study materials. He also underlined the darkness of the political picture. Communist armies were marching inexorably westwards and Chungking was an obvious target. He believed God would hold back the red avalanche until the forty-nine young people reached us. After that, only God knew the answer.

Two days later, we were taken by CIM truck to the hill country northeast of Chungking, where our future home was situated. We crossed the Yangtze on the ferry, then followed the bumpy motor road some ten miles. The road snaked its way between the hills to a point where foot travel was the only means of ascending the steep slopes. It was a lovely autumn day. When we finally reached the bungalow area, our eyes feasted on the beauty around us: majestic mountains stabbing the far horizon, a nearer ridge sprawling like a giant tentacle to the plain, where terraced rice fields curved themselves to the contours of the hills. How gracious of the Lord to arrange this setting for the Western Language School.

However, when we turned our attention to the bungalows, our hearts sank. As summer cottages, they were cool and breezy, but what would they be like in the depths of winter? Made of wood and plaster, many windows minus glass, no electricity, no means of heating, they would be cold and damp on sunless days. How could we fit forty-nine students, six staff, and nine Chinese teachers into the available space so that they could have *some* degree of comfort? It looked pretty hopeless. Yet God had promised to be our sufficiency. The onus was on Him. Surely we could trust Him for such things as housing when He had so marvelously guided in other ways.

The next day, we woke to a different world. The clouds came down, and the beautiful view disappeared. The sun was blotted out. The dampness penetrated. As we tramped the slippery paths beneath the pines, climbing up and down uneven stone steps, God's plan of action gradually emerged. The CIM cluster of summer bungalows should be the center of our scattered setup, and for ease of communication, each house was given a name, culled from the CIM annals: leaders, martyrs, and linguists. Taylor House was the most suitable for dining-cum-meeting hall, with its one large central room and smaller ones that could be used as an office, common room, classroom, and pantry. Forming the west arm of the courtyard was a three-room building, which we named Hoste House, where we were to live. Facing us were the kitchen and servants' rooms. In the space between was a well, and also a huge old grapevine, its gnarled branches supported on a wooden trellis. To the south and east of the kitchen was Baller House, for the teachers and for classrooms. Just around the corner to the south and west of Hoste was Gibb House, which could house twelve girls.

Along a little path on the side of the hill towards the west was Fleming House, where another ten students could be accommodated. Down the hill to the south was Fraser House. It was here we planned for our nine single men to live, eight of them crowded into two rooms, while we hoped one would not mind spreading his *p'u-kai* on boards resting on a big stone bathtub. We were renting these two bungalows from the Methodist Mission.

But this was not all! North of our home base were two bungalows. The farther one, on top of a hill, we named King House. We thought we could manage to squeeze fourteen girls in there. A little south of it lay Cassells House where Joan and Max Orr would live with the remaining girls. Since these two cottages were more separated from the Taylor House complex, we thought it advisable that someone able to speak Chinese should be on hand. It was decided that another small bungalow, which lay in the valley between the King/Cassells setup and the Taylor House base, should be set aside for more classrooms. Sheltered by whispering pines, it was ideal for study. We labeled it Grainger House.

Soon furniture procured in the city for this venture began to arrive by truck. Beds, chairs, tables, and benches were dumped on the different verandas by sweating coolies. Marvin scouted around and found men to put glass panes in the windows. Wooden shutters were a rather dark and drafty alternative.

The Orrs and Hazel Page arrived and proceeded with the study preparations. Faith Leeuwenburg became our sixth member of staff, and a very important one. She was planner of menus, maker of cakes, friend, and counselor. She had traveled with us all the way from San Francisco, but had not been permitted to travel on to her former work in North China. Nine young Chinese men, some of whom were Christians, were engaged to act as teachers.

On October 12, 1949, our first group of students arrived—eight Australians and four New Zealanders, plus their modest allotment of heavy baggage (two hundred pounds each). They settled into their drafty rooms, which soon began to look gay with pictures and drapes. On the twenty-eighth, sixteen from England and the Continent swelled our numbers, and included our first married couple. Conversation in the dining room grew more animated. Two girls from South Africa joined the family. On November 7, the last contingent arrived—eighteen from North America. Our large household was complete.

By this time, I was tired, both physically and emotionally. As I saw the Canadian girls making their way along the slippery path to Taylor House, resentment festered in my heart. Already we had welcomed dozens of young people, and the load was getting heavy. Now here were more—more needing help to get acquainted with the others, to be introduced to things Chinese, to fit into already cramped quarters. God was asking too much. Why couldn't I have my husband and family to myself? Why should I have to share them and my time and my love with all these strangers?

So my greeting was only lukewarm. Ugly self-pity was filling my heart. Rather ungraciously, I showed them to their rooms and briefly introduced them to roommates from other lands.

"Let them get on with it," I said to myself. "Why should I stay? I have lots of things to do." With no more ado I fled to the kitchen.

But God rebuked me the next morning. He used 2 Corinthians 3:5, making it very personal. "Your sufficiency is in Me," He said. "All you need for physical, spiritual, *and* emotional problems. Call on Me and you will find abundance of power." This did change my attitude, but it was not until some time later, during a Day of Prayer, that I plucked up courage to confess my wrong attitude and to publicly ask forgiveness for that failure.

I felt even more remorse when I learned that the North American group had been able to bring only their hand luggage with them; their trunks had been delayed at Hong Kong. The very ones who needed extra love and understanding on arrival had been denied it by my selfishness. This was a salutary lesson to me to keep on God's wavelength.

It was inevitable that this year's group would be called the "Forty-Niners." The year was 1949, and they numbered forty-nine in all. One of them composed a little ditty, which was sung to the tune *Clementine.*

> *"On the hilltop, near the Yangtze,*
> > *Learning Chinese all their time,*
> *Live the famous 'Forty-Niners,'*
> > *Who have come from every clime.*

> *"There are Swedish, Swiss, and English,*
> > *North American kids too,*
> *Anzacs and South African folk,*
> > *And some others, just a few."*

On Sunday, November 13, the Western Language School was officially opened. A number of visitors from the city climbed the hill for the occasion. At the north end of the dining room hung a banner of blue silk, on which had been pasted the precious name JESUS, in old-English capitals cut out of silver paper. Arnold Lea stood beneath it, facing the rows of people who filled the room. He gave a resume of the vision the leadership had been given that summer, the difficulties that had been faced and overcome, the wonderful provision God had made, and the marvelous fitting together of the jigsaw puzzle. Prayer and praise rose from awed young hearts as the picture unfolded.

Chapter Forty-Eight

In the fear of the Lord is strong confidence:
and His children shall have a place of refuge.
Proverbs 14:26 ASV

THE NEWS IN the Chinese papers was not good. Communist forces were pressing forward; Nationalist soldiers were faltering. Rumors of Chungking's early "liberation" (Communist term for capturing a town or area) were on many lips. We were alone on the hills, across the river from the city. From the human angle it seemed an impossibly dangerous situation. Red troops moving up from Kweichow would reach our hills before attempting an attack on Chungking itself. Anything could happen. But God had obviously planned our circumstances, and our confidence was in Him.

Soon after we had settled in, people from the village below us began fleeing into the hills with small bundles of belongings. This was a sign that the tides of war were advancing. But the Lord comforted us with His Word. The day after our opening service, when the visitors who had celebrated God's goodness with us had returned to the CIM headquarters in the city, the whole page of *Daily Light* for the morning of November 14 was full of wonderfully appropriate promises. (I have picked only one of them to head this chapter.) We could not but be uplifted, and on November 18 and 20 there were similarly encouraging messages from the Lord.

We committed ourselves afresh to our God and made our preparations. We needed to store up some food for the days when ordinary buying and selling would be impossible. Local vendors from Hwang Ko Ya, the nearest village, brought five-gallon tins full of golden *t'ang-hsi*, a sweet syrup made from grain, and also tins of pure honey. Farmers sold us fresh vegetables. Sacks of flour for homemade bread and cookies were laid in, also rice and kegs of dark brown sugar (no white sugar was available). Bundles and bundles of wood for the stove were piled behind the kitchen, carried up by muscular hill men. As the situation became more tense, our Christian cook bought over one hundred pounds of pork and an extra supply of eight hundred eggs.

We also stocked up on peanuts, and hour after hour two servants worked the hand mill to make large quantities of peanut butter. Holding a horizontal handle attached to a long wooden bar, they pushed and pulled to rotate the top stone of the mill. One of them poured the roasted nuts into a small hole in this stone. Soon the rhythmic turning caused a cascade of rich, thick peanut butter to flow out, coating the sides of the lower stone and oozing down into a narrow trough circling its base. From there it flowed, wholesome and tasty, into the big tins below, to be stowed in the bulging pantry until needed.

Storm clouds were gathering, but life went on. Letters from home were delayed, and anxiety was building up. To help take the students' minds off their problems, Marvin decided to build a volleyball court. During our first survey of the area, he had noticed an overgrown tennis court not far from Fraser House, a miracle in itself on those steep slopes. We cleared it of bushes and fallen branches, rolled it, and drew whitewash lines for two courts. Each day when classes were over, shouts and laughter echoed and re-echoed from the surrounding hills as young life expended its pent-up energy and tension on the courts.

The North American students were still living out of their hand baggage. Often we scanned the skies, praying that the *St. Paul* would get through once more. Then on the evening of November 21, there was great excitement on the hill. Grunting coolies, laden with trunks and boxes, began to appear on the paths leading to the various houses. The CIM truck had arrived from the city, loaded high with the American and Canadian luggage. The *St. Paul* had flown in from

Hong Kong the day before with this precious cargo. Once again, God had answered our prayers.

Many hours of each day were spent in language study. One problem, however, was the paucity of study materials. We had received only part of the order of primers from Shanghai, and the sets of special flash cards, so helpful in learning the complicated Chinese characters, were incomplete. Hazel Page took each group of new missionaries, soon after their arrival, on their two-week course in basic linguistics: first those from Australia; two weeks later the English and Continentals; two weeks after that the largest group of all, those from North America. After the different groups had passed through her hands, Max and Joan Orr took over, and with the Chinese teachers' help, introduced them to Western Mandarin. It was amazing to see how everything dovetailed together. We didn't plan it this way. God did. On November 28, Hazel left us for the headquarters in Chungking, having accomplished all she had been asked to do.

After supper each night, our whole group prayed for our big mission family in other parts of China. One evening as prayers ended, someone suggested that we sing number three hundred and sixty two in *The Keswick Hymnal*. Verse three especially fitted our situation perfectly.

"Grant us Thy peace, Lord, through the coming night,
Turn Thou for us its darkness into light,
From harm and danger keep Thy children free,
For dark and light are both alike to Thee."

When they left the bright, warm dining room, most of our "Forty-Niners" plunged into misty darkness with only flashlights to light their way home. Some must have been afraid, and some were homesick, catapulted from the security of the West into this completely different lifestyle. A few, doubtless, had problems adjusting to roommates. Some were slow in absorbing linguistic patterns. Others found the climate impossible. But to all, this verse was a reminder in the dark days and nights that the Lord Jesus Christ could give His peace in every situation.

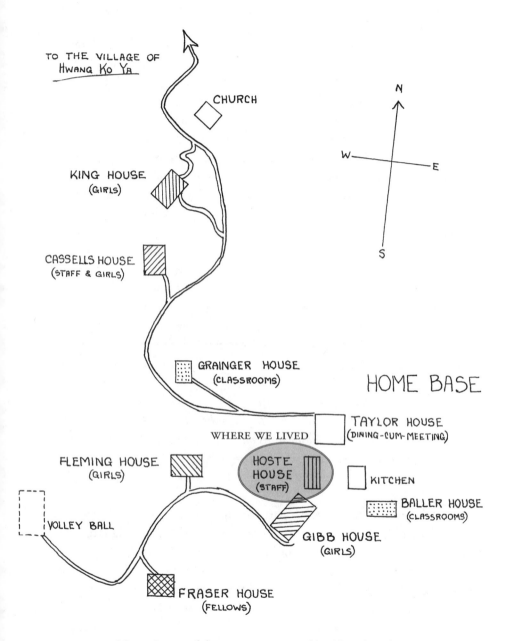

TO THE VILLAGE OF
HWANG KO YA

CHURCH

N

W———E

S

KING HOUSE
(GIRLS)

CASSELLS HOUSE
(STAFF & GIRLS)

GRAINGER HOUSE
(CLASSROOMS)

HOME BASE

TAYLOR HOUSE
(DINING-CUM-MEETING)

WHERE WE LIVED

FLEMING HOUSE
(GIRLS)

HOSTE
HOUSE
(STAFF)

KITCHEN

BALLER HOUSE
(CLASSROOMS)

VOLLEY BALL

GIBB HOUSE
(GIRLS)

FRASER HOUSE
(FELLOWS)

Miriam's map of the mission compound in Chungking brings
life to their being caught in the cross fire and the whizzing of
bullets between the Communists and the Nationalists

Chapter Forty-Nine

Jesus loves me, this I know,
For the Bible tells me so;
Little ones to Him belong,
They are weak, but He is strong.

IT WAS THE evening of November 28, 1949. Prayers were over and the "Forty-Niners" had gone their various ways. Our children were fast asleep, their cheeks flushed in healthy slumber. After a last look at them, we walked along the veranda to Faith's room, and she invited us in. It seemed certain that "liberation" would not be long delayed. We needed to chat and pray together.

"We will soon have to get more money," Marvin remarked, "and it should be silver. With Mr. Wang's help we've been able to procure quite a bit, but if trouble comes, our present supply won't last long. I've talked it over with him, and we two will set off for the city before it's light tomorrow and make it back here by afternoon."

The Nationalist paper money was almost worthless by this time, and tradespeople were demanding the old silver dollars in payment for goods. They were not easy to obtain and it took time to find them.

"Do you feel you should?" Faith asked. "Everyone is so panicky now and you might be held up for hours trying to cross the river."

"Yes, I know," Marvin replied, "but we have such a large family to care for here that the money we do have could soon go. After we have bought the silver, we may leave it in the city, and pick it up when conditions calm down a little. I think we'll be off to bed, as I must make

229

an early start in the morning."

At nine o'clock the next day, classes started as usual. By that time we hoped that Marvin and Mr. Wang were in the city. It was during the first study period that we began to hear the mutter of distant gunfire to the southeast. It persisted—louder, sharper, and more sustained. Max decided to cancel classes for the time being so that everyone could return to their individual houses. Students scurried along the paths with study books under their arms, excited, fearful, wondering.

Faith came into our room, each of us glad to have company. Sudden loud commands and the sound of running feet drew us to the window. With a leaping of the heart we saw that a few Nationalist soldiers had scrambled onto the little knoll behind the kitchen, where they hastily set up a machine gun. Soon it was chattering in the cool, crisp air, sending a hail of bullets into the valley below.

The answering shots of advancing soldiers came closer. Faith and I closed the wooden shutters and placed the three children in the safest place we could think of, under a table, covered with blankets and quilts in case of flying bullets. Our lath and plaster bungalows were not built to withstand modern weapons.

Many thoughts raced through our minds. I longed for Marvin, but he was far away. Desperate prayers rose from our hearts. Was this really happening to us? My heart was thudding, and I was afraid. We tried to pray aloud, but our mouths were dry and words would not come. Outside, the gunfire grew more menacing.

Suddenly, muffled by the blankets, a sweet little voice began to sing, "Jesus loves me, this I know." It was Peter, singing in the dark. Faith and I looked at each other and smiled, and the tension dissolved.

"Jesus loves *us*," I exclaimed to Faith, "so we don't need to be afraid! Oh, Peter boy, thank God for that song!"

"Listen," cried Faith, "that Nationalist gun is silent." We peeked through the shutters. The hillock was bare. But the opposing guns were still firing steadily, and getting closer.

An uncanny silence fell. Then our startled eyes saw the Chinese teachers coming around a corner, walking slowly backwards, their hands above their heads. Behind them were gun-toting soldiers dressed in battle green, a red star blazing from each cap.

An officer with a revolver darted into the kitchen. As he emerged, something impelled me forward. I opened the door of our room and walked across the courtyard to him. It wasn't until later that I realized that I was not afraid.

"Who are you?" he demanded. "Where are the Nationalist soldiers? Are they hiding in these houses?"

"No," I replied. "Come with me and see. Only foreigners live here."

I led him to the dining room of Taylor House; we went inside and looked in all the rooms. Of course, they were empty.

"We must go on," he said, "and find the *Kuo-min-tang* (Nationalist) men. You will be safe here. We will not harm you." With a call to his men, they moved swiftly past Taylor and took the path to Cassells and King.

I went back to Faith. We lifted the children out from their refuge, hugging and kissing them. They didn't know what all the fuss was about, but we ourselves were trembling from the shock of the past hour, even though God's peace had filled our hearts.

"Look, Mummy, there's lots of soldiers walking through the courtyard," called Rosemary, running to the window. "They've got guns."

"Come back," I called to her. "We'll just let them go by. I don't want them to see you." I knew that the sight of a fair-haired white child could draw some of the men to our room, and we didn't want that to happen. They, too, tramped on down the path, hurrying to join their comrades.

When they had all trooped past, Faith and I went to the Gibb House to let the girls there know that the worst was over. Our compound had been "liberated," and the soldiers were well disciplined. It was not until later that we heard of what happened at the Cassells and King Houses.

At the former, Max Orr heard a voice speaking. He looked through his broken windowpane and saw a soldier's face peering in. The red star on his cap alerted Max to the situation. The man demanded entrance to search for Nationalists. Max was able to eventually convince him there were only foreigners inside. The soldiers left, heading for the King House, with Max and Joan trailing them at a discreet distance.

That morning, before breakfast, May Roy had done some personal washing and hung it out in the breeze. Soon after the students' return to the King House from classes, a group of Nationalist soldiers set up a machine gun on the veranda, for this was a strategic position from which to cover the advance of the enemy. Marjorie said later, "We sat inside, reminding each other that the peace of God *does* pass understanding. We couldn't understand the peace that He gave us that day in the midst of battle."

For a while bullets from their gun zipped between May's wash hanging on the line, then silence fell. One girl ventured outside onto the veranda—and almost ran into the bayonet of a Communist soldier! He seemed just as surprised as she was. However, he followed her into the house and began asking questions. With blank faces the girls could only say, "*Ngo pu-tang!* (I don't understand!)," a sentence they had recently learned in their red primers. At last, even he saw the humor of the situation; a grin spread over his strained face as he echoed their words, "*Ngo pu-tang!*"

By this time, the Orrs had arrived and explained that this bungalow housed only foreigners; there were no soldiers in hiding. As they stood on the veranda, this group of military men also realized that this house presented a great vantage point. They, too, set up a gun. From here it was also easy to see down into the valley on the other side, to which some of their enemy had fled. When they saw any sign of movement, they whirled the gun around and sprayed the paddy fields with bullets. Fortunately, they did not stay long, and marched off taking their gun with them. After they left, the girls peeped through the shutters and saw more soldiers running across the veranda, down the steps to the chapel, and on down the hill into the trees.

Lunchtime approached. Things seemed to have settled down. Three of the men students decided to move up to Cassells and King so the girls there could come down to eat. However, they had made their way only as far as Grainger when a hail of bullets tore through the trees, splintering trunks and ripping off leaves. They threw themselves to the ground and kept as still as possible, hoping the shooting would stop. Any movement they made called forth more shots. Over an hour passed before it was safe to move on, and thus enable the girls to descend. Then sporadic firing broke out again, but finally all pockets of resistance were silenced and a column of the victorious Communist Liberation Army marched forward past the Taylor House on a lower path.

Fleming and Fraser, our southern outposts, also had exciting tales to tell of God's deliverance. Several Nationalist soldiers and a wounded coolie slipped into Fraser House for water during the fighting, but they must have been observed. Bullets hit the house, narrowly missing two of our men, who were kneeling to give assistance to the wounded man. Bullets also slammed into Fleming House, ricocheting off the pillars. One smashed through a window and buried itself in the wall, just over Lois's bed; she had left the room just minutes before.

Needless to say, as the hours passed, my thoughts were focused on Marvin. He was on one side of the "curtain" and we on the other. Between us now lay portions of two armies, blasting away with guns as they pursued their objectives. To hope for his return would seem to lead him into danger; to face further separation was unthinkable.

God's solution to this impasse would have been laughable if it hadn't been true. Around two in the afternoon we noticed groups of Communist soldiers coming back from their advanced lines to some place in the valley from which they had emerged that morning. The servants told us that the men were returning to eat their noon meal, since the Nationalists had been cleared from the area. At the same time, apparently, the other army followed the same tactics, and retired to eat their rice.

Just at this very time, Marvin and Mr. Wang began their climb from the river to the village, and then on up our hill. Everything was abnormally quiet; the village was empty. It was not until they had crossed the valley and were making the last ascent to the bungalows that they saw several dead soldiers on the path and realized they were in no-man's land.

When I saw them hurrying along the trail under the trees, I could scarcely believe my eyes. Dashing down the steps, I grabbed Marvin's hands.

"Oh, darling, how wonderful to see you! Come inside. Quick!" I exclaimed, for he still adhered rigidly to the rule that we must not embrace in public. Once inside we clung to each other, all tensions and fears of the past few hours behind us. Rapidly, I clued him in on the situation up to that point. He decided to go up to Cassells to see Max, and then to the girls at King House. Later he completed the circle to see how things were at Fleming and Fraser. At each place, he left the message that if things remained peaceful, supper would be served earlier than usual that evening.

That was a memorable meal, though I can't remember what we ate! The air buzzed with excited voices as one and another around the tables told of their experiences.

Our time of prayer together was very meaningful as we thanked our heavenly Father for His care and protection that day. In spite of the fighting and death all around us, not one of us had suffered bodily harm. One army had fled, and another had taken over, but we were free to move about on our hillside. God's love and the promises of His Word had come alive in a new way.

We sang our vesper hymn from full hearts and with renewed confidence.

> "Grant us Thy peace, Lord, through the coming night,
> Turn Thou for us its darkness into light,
> From harm and danger keep Thy children free,
> For dark and light are both alike to Thee."

Chapter Fifty

Thou hast been… a refuge from the storm, a
shadow from the heat, when the blast of the
terrible ones is as a storm against the wall.
Isaiah 25:4 KJV

THE NIGHT OF November 29, 1949, was punctuated with the sounds of shooting. Some Liberation Army soldiers took up their positions on the ridge below the King House and fired across the valley to the lower hill ridge overlooking Chungking. In the night air, sounds carried clearly, and the girls inside could hear the men of the two armies shouting at each other. As they peered through the shutters, they could see arcs of orange flame as bullets were fired into the darkness. After a while, however, the defenders on the Chungking range withdrew. The Communists stopped shooting and peace came at last.

The next day, we took stock. Several Nationalist soldiers had been left, dead or wounded, on our hills. One had fallen among the grave mounds. His body lay there for several days until a peasant came along with a shovel and quickly covered him with earth. The nurses bandaged two badly wounded men, not far from the King House. Max went with them to act as interpreter. When he saw how desperately ill they were, he took the opportunity to tell them, very simply, the Gospel message. In spite of the girls' loving ministrations, both soldiers died soon after. They were so young, killed by bullets from their own people: the tragedy of civil war.

We tried to get back into ordinary routine, but it was not easy.

Naturally, we wondered about letters from home. We also prayed that relatives in the homelands would not be unduly worried. If only they could know that we were safe and secure, protected by the Lord from severe injury and loss.

After prayers that night, we sang our vesper chorus and departed for our rooms. All was quiet; everyone went to bed early. In the middle of the night, there was a tremendous explosion, followed in a few minutes by another.

"Whatever was that?" I gasped, sitting up in bed. "It sounded awfully close. Can you feel the bed shaking?"

But Marvin had already leaped to the floor and was dragging his clothes on over his pajamas. I fumbled around for matches to light the oil lamp.

"Why are you dressing? Where are you going?" I asked.

"It seemed to come from the direction of the King House," he replied. "I'd better go and see if they are all right." Saying this, he grabbed the flashlight and ran off into the night.

I got up to see the children. They were still sound asleep, rosy and relaxed and sweet to look upon. I informed Faith where Marvin had gone, then went back to bed, but not to sleep. It seemed a long, long time before he returned.

"How was everything?" I asked him as he slowly undressed. "Are the girls all right?"

"Yes," he said. "They were all up by the time I got there, but nothing seems to have suffered except the windows. The explosion blew out every one of those new panes of glass!"

"Oh, no!" I exclaimed, "and it's just a few days since the last ones were put in. What was that awful noise, anyway?"

"I'm afraid the *Kuo-min-tang* (Nationalist Army) must have fired an ammunition dump to prevent it from falling into the hands of their enemies. We could see the light of a huge fire in the sky in the direction of the river," Marvin replied. "Ferne said it felt as if the whole mountain shook when it all blew up. By the way, did the children awaken?"

"Do you know, they never stirred," I answered. "How they could sleep through all that uproar is more than I can fathom. Well, we'd better follow their example and go back to sleep. There's not much of the night left. But first, we should thank the Lord for His care over us all once again."

Marvin blew out the light and got into bed. Lying there in the dark, he prayed quietly to the One whose love surrounded us, and committed us and all our scattered family to His care.

The next morning the verse in Isaiah 25:4 came in my daily reading: God's gentle message that He was on guard both day and night. That was also the day that the city of Chungking was officially "liberated," without the firing of a shot.

A few days later Margaret happened to glance north from the Taylor House veranda.

"Look!" she called. "Look at the soldiers marching up the Kweichow road."

We crowded outside, and in the distance we could see a long column of marching men, endlessly moving up and over the pass, disappearing down the other side. Red flags fluttered at intervals, mute reminders of the new power controlling China.

It was not until a few days later, when communications were again established with our friends in the city, that we learned of further miracles. There is no other way to describe it.

Hazel Page, who had left us the day before our "liberation" experience to fly to Yunnan, found that the only local airline office had closed down. However, on the morning of November 29, a long-distance phone call came to the CIM home from a radio station thirty miles out of Chungking. It gave the amazing news that the *St. Paul* was already on its way from Hong Kong and wanted to know if it was safe to land on the island airport at Chungking! Learning that the city was still in Nationalist hands, the pilot decided to come in. Hazel hurriedly gathered her things together and was taken to the airfield. She and the men who had driven her down watched the plane as it approached from the southwest. Larger and larger grew the silver speck until it dropped down unerringly on its target. Mist lay over the river, and if that mist had been too thick, the *St. Paul* would have had to cancel its landing and return to the coast, for the control tower was as deserted as the rest of the airport. But God's plans for His children were not to be thwarted. Bundles and bundles of freight were delivered to the waiting men, then

Hazel was allowed to climb into the empty plane. Across the river came the sound of distant shooting, and as she waved goodbye, she did not know that those guns were firing on the hills that she had just left.

After she had gone, the men examined the packages disgorged by the *St. Paul.* Some of them were large and bulky, wrapped in coarse sacking. Others were small and compact. All were addressed to the Language School. There were no porters available, so four of our city missionaries, and as many servants as could be mustered, lugged the entire load up the many steps, through the city streets, and into the CIM compound. There it was discovered that the small packets contained the last set of flash cards needed for language study, and the unwieldy parcels held forty-nine wrinkled quilts, donated by a friend in Australia for the new workers! These had been in transit since early August, and it was now late November. But as the airfreight had been paid to get them in from Hong Kong, they had been placed on the *St. Paul* for its very last flight into Chungking. God had not only kept us in times of danger, but His love planned this final touch in readiness for the long, cold nights of winter that lay ahead.

Chapter Fifty-One

*Commit thy way unto the Lord; trust also
in Him, and He shall bring it to pass.
Psalm 37:5 KJV*

WITHIN A FEW weeks of our arrival on the hills outside
Chungking, our circumstances had radically changed,
though the long-term implications were not then apparent. The
hard facts were that a Communist regime, opposed to the Christian
message, was in control. Our forty-nine students were scattered in
nine houses on lonely hills. Our whole "campus" was across the river
and six miles from the city, with no quick means of communication.
The Psalms, with their promises of guidance and protection, became
very precious to us as the weeks flew by. God often spoke to us
through them. In Psalm 37 we rediscovered the message to commit
our way to Him. Step by step, He would lead. We carried on with
the ordinary, everyday matters, and left the final outcome in His
hands.

For instance, the gaping windows of King and Cassells needed
glass once more. This was gradually attended to. It was not only our
windows that had been blown out, but every house in the vicinity
had been affected by that huge detonation; glass panes were in short
supply. Winter came upon us, and we shivered under the onslaught
of penetrating mist and howling wind. The only way to keep warm
was to pile on the clothes, and the best insulation was a Chinese
wadded gown. The village tailors had a heyday making up the

239

glowing Szechwan silks into gowns for our girls. On Sundays the cotton covers were discarded, and they appeared in all their glory: deep blues, rich maroons, soft greens, and midnight black.

Max and Joan conscientiously guided the classes. On sunny days, the sounds of students, constantly repeating Chinese words and phrases after their teachers, came from many unexpected places. They were lured from the cold classrooms to bask in the golden warmth of the outdoors. Unfortunately, this didn't happen very often. It was exciting to note the progress of our young people. They spent hours over their books, but all their class time was not serious. Gales of laughter could be heard when someone goofed. One man said he had come out to China to be a robber, when he meant to say he had come to preach the Gospel. One little slip and the whole meaning was changed.

Saturdays were study free. An energetic few might hike to a distant ridge to see the view. Others would stay home and write letters, clean house, or relax with a book. Some would saunter down the worn steps to the village. There were always things of interest to see there.

All the shops presented an open front to the cobbled street. It was easy to see their wares: rolls of materials and gleams of shining silk, baskets of beans and bins of rice, pottery bowls and china cups. Since they had so recently left the affluent West, the abject poverty of the Chinese peasants hit our young people right between the eyes. But they responded in delight to the cheeky grins on children's faces, and the raised thumb over clenched fingers, which indicated approval of the white-skinned foreigner. The students' inability to communicate with these people was a constant source of frustration, though they found that a smile went a long way in overcoming barriers.

Our young people all had to learn to adjust to a new lifestyle for health reasons, for economy, and to become closer to the Chinese people. For instance, however thirsty they might be after a long hike, there was only boiled water or tea to drink. Old-fashioned kerosene lamps took the place of electricity. Thermos flasks could be filled with boiling water for a hot drink at night, and also to take the chill off washing water on cold mornings. Wet laundry could be hung outside on dry days, but when rain was pouring down, a charcoal brazier helped the drying process indoors. (Sheets and underwear carried a permanent smoky odor!) The list is endless, but they made it, with God's help. Added to all the physical discomforts of life in inland China was the feeling of being cut off from loved ones, which can be traumatic. Following the military takeover, letters from home were infrequent, and many never got through.

By the goodness of God, the authorities left us to our own devices, so we had time to speculate on the changes that might eventually prevail under Communism. Each one needed to reassure oneself of those bedrock foundations of faith and trust in God. We knew that missionary work in China could never be as it had been before. What could *we* give in coming days? What was God teaching *us*? Our Sunday morning worship services in the little chapel at the top of the hill were very meaningful, isolated as we were from the outside world and also from the people of the land. Sometimes speakers would make the long trip up from the city, and different messages met the needs of different ones. God spoke to us personally, and also drew us closer to one another. Friendships were forged that have endured through the years.

Each Saturday and Sunday evening, the "Forty-Niners" were given the opportunity of recounting the way God had led him or her to volunteer for service with the CIM. These times were intensely interesting. One girl had been a ballet dancer; another had been a leader of a tough gang in the United States before God found her; another had been miraculously healed after the doctors gave up all hope; one fellow had renounced important research to obey God's call to China. As they shared not only God's past dealings with them, but also some of the struggles and battles of the present situation, the Lord gave love for, and a deeper understanding of, each other. We all had faults, but as we shared together, we accepted one another.

The cold, dull winter passed, and spring brought new radiance into our lives. Rose-pink *la-mei* (a Chinese spring flower) sprang from dead brown twigs. Delicate white tea flowers gleamed from the bushes. The brilliant green of new rice spilled from terraced hills and valleys. A froth of dainty blossoms hid the poverty of peasant homes. Golden sunshine enticed us to roam the many paths that laced the greening slopes. Nature's transformation was a constant source of wonder, and praise to the Lord of creation rose spontaneously from our hearts. He enhanced with beauty the way we had committed to Him.

Chapter Fifty-Two

I will save thy children.
Isaiah 49:25 KJV

SCRATCH, SCRATCH, SCRATCH—the sound floated in through the open window. At the same time, I could hear Rosemary and Peter chattering to each other, with an occasional cheep from Jennifer.

"Peter, that's my pile of leaves. You can't put them in your basket. That's stealing!" came Rosemary's voice, raised in shrill protest. "Peter! I'll tell Mummy if you don't stop."

The gentle voice of the amah (Chinese nurse) broke in, and peace was restored. Evidently she had found a solution.

I went out on the veranda and looked up the side of the hill in the direction of the voices. Under the pine trees, Rosemary and Peter were assiduously raking the pine needles, just as they had seen the Chinese hill children doing on fine days. Bamboo baskets on their backs dribbled a shower of dust and twigs onto their cover gowns. Jennifer was perched on the amah's back, her soft curls nestling against her little stand-up collar. All were absorbed in the business of gathering fuel for the kitchen fire, which was much more fun than playing with dolls.

Sundays were different. The drab cover gowns of their Chinese outfits were removed, revealing the pretty wadded gowns, which kept them snug and warm even on windy days. Jennifer's was scarlet, with shoes to match. (With the added bulk she sometimes found it a bit difficult to navigate.) Peter's gown was green. He was very proud

Peter in Chungking preparing to pick up leaves in the spring of 1950.

of it, even if on wet days the bottom got rather muddy as he climbed up and down the veranda steps. He was so busily intent on his own affairs that he quite forgot the effect of mud on his pretty green gown. Rosemary's was navy in color, dotted with red and green flowers, and she chose purple shoes. The gay colors satisfied her feminine heart.

On Sunday mornings, some of the students took turns in telling the children a Bible story. Often in the afternoons, the members of staff would be invited to the different houses for tea. (Every guest had to take his own cup with him on such occasions!) The children enjoyed these visits, and the young people enjoyed the children. Sometimes a walk with Rosemary and Peter would comfort someone who was feeling lonely, or ease the tension of a difficult day.

On Saturdays the children knew the "aunties" and "uncles" were not studying, and therefore were fair game for visitors. What could be more exciting than an opportunity to poke inside mysterious drawers, help the uncles dust their rooms (especially those pictures on their desks of pretty ladies), or nibble on peanut candy bought in the village store?

Peter loved chocolate pudding and hated spinach. However, the rule was, "No pudding until the vegetables are finished." He would sit beside his daddy chewing, chewing, chewing—his eyes fixed longingly on that delicious brown pudding nearby. "All gone!" he would exclaim triumphantly, then grab the pudding and demolish it in a few seconds.

One day after such an episode, one of the uncles noticed Peter hurry out of the dining room and disappear around the corner. He followed, and was in time to see our son disgorge lumps of chewed-up spinach from inside his fat little cheeks, and spit them into the bushes! Somehow Marvin got wind of what was happening, and thereafter Peter had to open his mouth wide to prove his spinach was gone before that delectable dessert could be his. The children provided much innocent pleasure for us all.

During the spring, all three children came down with whooping cough, one after the other. There was little we could do for them. It hurt to hear that awful whoop increase in volume and know we could not help. However, they gradually recovered and fortunately no adults contracted it.

During the summer, Peter became desperately ill with diarrhea. In a few hours his rosy cheeks became the color of chalk, and he tossed in discomfort and fever. He had a bad night, and the next morning his little body was burning hot. When I spoke to him, he did not seem to recognize me.

"Peter! It's Mummy," I cried, but his eyes stared blankly up at me. My heart dropped. I began to sing some of the choruses he loved, but there was no response.

"Oh, Marvin, he's really ill," I said. "What are we going to do? There's no doctor near us, and I doubt that he can take anything by mouth. I wonder if any of the nurses have some injections that would help." We inquired around, but no one had anything that would help.

In this moment of need, God brought to my mind the verse that He had given me years ago when I was nursing Jeanie in Hiangcheng. I turned the leaves of my Bible. I knew it was somewhere in Isaiah, and found it in chapter 49. As I read it over, the words "I will save thy children," came through with power. This applied directly to our child, and in faith we claimed the promise of God.

I sponged our little son, changed his clothes, and continued my vigil beside him. During the afternoon, the fever subsided, his movements quieted, and he closed his eyes in natural sleep. Once again, in our extremity God had reached down and answered our prayers. Peter was given back to us, and was soon climbing the hills and playing with his sisters as before.

Chapter Fifty-Three

When thou passest through the waters, I
will be with thee: and through the rivers,
they shall not overthrow thee.
Isaiah 43:2 ASV

A S THE DAYS and weeks passed, we were indeed grateful to the Lord
that we were able to carry on as usual. The Communist authorities
were fully occupied trying to enforce control over the whole area. They
did this through indoctrination classes set up in the city and in every
scattered hamlet.

In 1950, all foreigners living in Chungking, including ourselves,
were ordered to register at the Foreign Affairs Bureau (FAB). Batch after
batch of our young people went down to the city to see the officials,
armed with answers to the questionnaires that the office had drawn up.
Usually Marvin or Max accompanied them to act as interpreter, but
sometimes missionaries already living in the city would do this.

In great detail, each of the "Forty-Niners" and each member of staff
was required to give information of his or her life up to this point.
Suspicion began to grow among the officials when they realized that
we had all flown into West China just before the Bamboo Curtain
fell. Questions rapped out: "Were you not aware of the fact that our
Liberation Army was sweeping across the country?" "Did you think that
Chungking could hold out against our forces?" "Who sent you?" "Who
is supporting you?" "Why did you come?" They believed that we were
secret agents of our different governments, and that it was they who had

instigated our activities, granting passports and money to get us into the land before Communism took over.

Such questions, though, provided a wonderful opportunity for direct testimony to these uniformed men and women who had been taught there was no God. Every reply was taken down in black and white, to be entered in the "Forty-Niner File" in the FAB office. We realized it was only logical for them to look upon us as spies. Had a chartered plane just before the takeover not flown us in?

During these days, God's promise of His presence with us *in* the waters and rivers of trouble became real. Tests came to different members of our family. Sickness was one. Leslie had to enter the hospital in the city for an operation on his back. Maurine was also unwell and had to undergo surgery. The loss of study time that resulted was not easy for them to accept, but God enabled.

Another test was the loss of possessions. A petty thief began to visit the King and Cassells Houses during the supper hour. Pens, watches, cameras, and clothes disappeared from the girls' rooms. What should we do? With the pro-peasant political atmosphere, it seemed unwise to report to the police unless we were certain of the culprit.

One evening, when everyone else was in the dining room, Marvin ensconced himself behind a curtain in one of the houses. He did not have long to wait. There was a slight squeaking noise at the entrance as the hasp holding the padlock was removed. The door swung open and a young fellow walked in, shining his flashlight. As he walked past the curtain, Marvin's arm shot out and held him with a vicelike grip. He tried to explain that he had only entered to keep an eye on things while the ladies were away, but Marvin paid no attention to this and hustled him out of the house and down the path to the Taylor House. After talking things over with Mr. Wang, they took the boy off between them to inform his father. The old man was very irate with his son, and swore it would not happen again. The culprit refused to confess where he had hidden the stolen loot.

Strangely enough, Ruth and May in the King House were also tested along this line. One morning they overslept. Their alarm clock had failed to ring. It was missing from its usual place. They leaped out of bed. Their wadded gowns were gone—also a large duffle bag full of necessities. This was a big loss, for all the young people had comparatively little at the best of times. The whole school made this a matter of prayer, and God took over. Through an amazing sequence of events, the stolen things were found by a couple of Chinese laborers in an unused coal mine some miles away. They informed a relative, who told an English architect living two miles from us, who in turn sent a note to Marvin. After negotiations with the police, everything was returned intact. And the "over and above" of God's working resulted in recovery of even the petty goods stolen by the teenage thief. The police had made some investigations about him and found them hidden in a box under the stairs of his home. The old father was really angry this time! This in itself was a miracle in such circumstances, and a great encouragement to our faith. We found that God was not limited, even by a Communist regime.

Tests also came in language learning. During some classes, tears were very near the surface. Battles were fought against discouragement and envy. Some sailed through exams, while others studied long and faithfully, yet barely made the grade. And behind every situation was the tension of the uncertain future. Some wondered at the feasibility of continuing language study when in so many areas missionary work was being curtailed.

But God gave grace. He walked the hills with us. One day each month was set aside for prayer. Praise to the Lord for His marvelous works mingled with our intercessions. On such days, many of us skipped meals in order to spend time alone with God. A holy hush seemed to hang over our hills. Under the trees, overlooking the valleys, gazing up to the mountains, reading the Word, the spiritual life of each was deepened and strengthened. One girl remarked, "In the past, days of prayer have been days of boredom, but these on the hills are the highlights of each month." As the testings, frustrations, and fears were brought to the Lord, strength was given. Differences between national groups and between individuals were healed. It was thrilling to be a part of God's working in one another's lives.

We experienced in a real way His presence and His help as we passed through the waters of testing.

Celebrating Jennifer's and Rosemary's birthdays in Chungking, 1950.

Rosemary, Jennifer, and Peter in Chungking, 1950.

Chapter Fifty-Four

As the mountains are round about Jerusalem,
so the Lord is round about His people.
Psalm 125:2 ASV

FAITH AND I took an evening walk. Above us, the stars began to sparkle in the darkening sky. Around us, all was silent, though from one of the valleys rose the insistent, rhythmic throbbing of Communist drums. Those drums! They were getting to me. Day and night their beat could be heard. Did the drummers never sleep?

We stopped on the path and looked at the beauty of the heavens. Faith spoke softly, "Miriam, I'm glad I know the Lord, aren't you? I don't think I could bear the pressures if it were not for Him."

"Yes," I agreed. "Things are getting much tighter, but the Lord is with us."

"I'm glad, too, that we are on the hills," she continued, "and not in the city. I love that verse in the Psalms that compares God's protection to the mountains round about Jerusalem. I came across it today and underlined it in my Bible. It's such a comfort to know He is here."

We walked on, stumbling over an occasional stone. We talked of the pressures building up around us, and how in God's wonderful timing nothing had hindered the school term from coming to a successful end on May 31, 1950. We recalled the excitement of that day, the feast for the teachers, then the closing exercises in the beautifully decorated dining room. Mary and David had made speeches of thanks and appreciation to the nine teachers in Chinese, followed by a short message from Mr. Lea.

But to me, the most moving item on the program had been the singing, in Chinese, of the anthem "God So Loved the World" by a group of girls from England, America, Australia, and Sweden.

In June we had hoped that travel permits would be granted to allow our young people to move on to the different parts of China to which they had been designated during May. Our hopes were raised when word came up the hill that permits had been issued to allow the Leas and Hazeltons to travel to Shanghai, though it was a sad day when the students sang goodbye to Arnold, as he went down the flagstone steps for the last time. We missed his wise advice and cheery visits. But the weeks slipped by, and in spite of much prayer, no permission was given. Studies had started again, although at a slower pace than before. We could sense that around us ominous clouds foreshadowed a coming storm.

Faith and I found our way back to the Hoste House. The dim light of the kerosene lamp in our bedroom told me that Marvin was already preparing for bed.

"Good night, Faith. It's lovely to have you here," I whispered, then turned away after a quick kiss and entered our room.

Some of the tension on the hill began to build up after a telegram had been sent to us from Shanghai by Mr. Sinton, our acting General Director. On May 26, he had cabled:

PRAY. PROBABLY FACING DARKEST PERIOD IN MISSION'S HISTORY. WHAT SAITH THE ANSWER OF GOD? (Romans 11:4).

This was later followed by a news report from Peking condemning missionaries who cooperated with the Chinese church. It said that pressure would be put on all churches where missionaries were still working, although the missionaries themselves would not be harmed.

At the same time, the Spirit of God was accomplishing wonderful things in China. In the CIM churches alone, nearly two thousand people were baptized in the first few months of 1950, with many more converted. This, in spite of the fact that Communism dominated the land. Our leaders decided not to leave China yet, though it became increasingly clear that no new missionaries would be given visas to enter, and all those going on furlough knew they could never return.

The Chinese Communists hated America, and this gradually began to get through to the Americans in our group. Inflammatory posters, violently anti-USA, appeared on walls everywhere: in the city, in the village, down by the ferry, in the schools and universities. The children in Hwang Ko Ya were not as friendly as they had been. This attitude on the part of the people they had come to win for Christ was not easy for our "Forty-Niners" to accept; there was uneasiness and fear regarding the future. The arrest and imprisonment in Chungking of an American Methodist missionary and a Canadian Presbyterian did not help matters, and tension deepened.

This came close to us when our servants were forced to spend hours each week in indoctrination classes. As the brainwashing increased, there was a change for the worse in the attitude of these men and women who served us. They became belligerent and demanding. From the hill people we heard tales of midnight arrests in the village; men were taken from their beds by soldiers. Stories circulated of the disappearance of landlords in our vicinity. Grim accounts of executions carried out on the bank of the river added to the darkness of those days. And always, there were the drums, the dances, and the songs by which this new ideology was gaining control of the minds of the people.

One of the hardest things we had to face was to sense the gap that was developing between the Chinese people and us. We could no longer visit in their houses, drinking scalding tea from handle-less cups, for indoctrination classes had broadcast the seeds of suspicion and distrust. The godless ideology of Communism gradually changed the outlook and attitudes of all: the teacher, the storekeeper, the ferryman, the farmer, the wood carrier, the ordinary man and woman.

There were bright threads in the tapestry also. The long days of summer gave opportunity to explore the hills and valleys around us. Cool streams enticed some swimmers. Tennis was played with vigor, and Ruth (from Australia, of course) was the undisputed champion! Two "Forty-Niners" babies were born in the Chungking hospital and added a new dimension to our corporate life when they came up the hill. We, as a staff, quietly noted the young couples that began to pair off together for walks.

A few of the group had the priceless privilege of moving down for a few days to the city or its outskirts to live with Chinese Christians and take part in their work. But later, even these movements were curtailed, and we were confined to the hills.

God then gave some of our girls an opportunity to share Jesus with the Chinese children who roamed our hills. All day long these youngsters worked hard, raking leaves and gathering fuel. Though dressed in rags, with tousled hair and dirty faces, they were a cheerful crew. On Sunday afternoons, they came shyly to the shady meeting place, some carrying babies on their backs. As they became familiar with the songs the girls taught them, they shouted the words happily, although not always in tune.

That summer, another venture was undertaken. Where the main flagstone road started its descent to Kweichow after the climb from the village of Hwang Ko Ya, there was always a breeze, even on the hottest day. An enterprising fellow had set up a roadside stall at the pass, and many a traveler or tired coolie rested there. Some carried sacks of rice, and others were laden with salt, pigs, vegetables, or oil. Marvin decided to take one of our fellows with him one day to this place to give out some tracts. They found most of the men approachable, and glad to chat as they sipped their hot green tea. The next day, they returned with a small table, spread out some Gospel portions for sale, and talked of Christ to those who would listen. Not a big outreach, but a door that Marvin pushed open when others were being closed.

On July 2, 1950, Marvin and I slipped away beside a small stream. There we had a picnic supper, celebrating our seventh wedding anniversary.

Dark places, bright places. In them all, the Lord was round about us, as He had promised.

Chapter Fifty-Five

If any man suffer as a Christian, let him not be
ashamed: but let him glorify God on this behalf.
I Peter 4:16 KJV

I STOOD ON the side of the hill, looking towards the west. Behind, lay a gray sky silhouetting stately pines. Around me, the sound of the wind in the leaves resembled the murmur of the sea, soothing to ear and heart. Before me, spread a pastel painting in soft and lovely hues, fit colors for the Master Artist. It drew my heart out in adoration of Him, and in longing for that day when I should see Him face to face.

Below, lay the valley, scarcely visible in the enshrouding mist. On the horizon was the faint line of Szechwan hills, a pagoda sharply etched on one peak. Swirling everywhere were billows of gray haze. As the sun slowly sank to its rest, its rays changed the gray sky to delicate aqua.

The sun itself was invisible in the shrouded sky, but I could see its effects in the exquisite shades of the mists at my feet. Then a golden color in the west, marking the sun's demise, changed to a soft pink. Slowly, the mist-filled valley also reflected the rosy radiance. Completely invisible now were the objects I knew existed in the valley beneath me: the green rice fields, the squalid grass-roofed huts, the busy little village on the main stone road to Chungking, the army trucks, the sentries. Through that lovely veil, I could hear the muted shouts of men, the laughter of children, and the roar of engines. These sounds reminded me that down below were people for whom Christ died, people whose minds were being brainwashed to deny the very existence of God.

For those living in the valley, there was no beauty—only damp, clinging mist. As I thought of them, this seemed typical of their everyday life, surrounded by fear and suspicion. But looking down from above, I saw how the glory of the sun was shed abroad in a strangely beautiful way by the mists, not in spite of them. Though the glory was not brilliant, it was lovely and arresting.

This seemed to me a parable. Will not the glory of God still be seen in China, not in spite of the difficulties, but because of them? Could I not pray to this end?

The sun set. The colors vanished. Darkness came swiftly, as it does in the East. I turned slowly and walked back to the warmth and love of our home. A request rose from my heart. "Dear Lord, I pray that in these days of turmoil and suffering, Your name will be glorified in Your Chinese children, even as the mists in the valley reflected the beauty of the sunset."

Chapter Fifty-Six

For ye shall not go out with haste, nor go by flight:
for the Lord will go before you; and the
God of Israel will be your rearward.
Isaiah 52:12 KJV

THE LAST MONTHS of 1950 found us still on the hills. In spite of much prayer, no travel permits had been issued to any of our young people. One or two moved down to the city to help in the CIM office. For the rest, another winter of confinement among the pine trees loomed ahead.

It was during this time that another young man joined our ranks. Marvin was glad of his presence, as he had already spent two years in China and had a working knowledge of the language. Joan and Max Orr had left us some months earlier to welcome baby Jocelyn into their home, and had remained in the city. So David Day's arrival meant another man who could help in an emergency.

For this second winter, we had time to make better provision against the damp cold. Charcoal braziers gave cozy warmth to many rooms. We also made some changes in order to spark closer participation and sharing. Another house was rented, and we attempted to divide into two establishments to give a more family-like atmosphere. Because prospects of using the language seemed to be diminishing, there was little incentive to study. However, many did discipline themselves to continue. If God had not been very real to us, the outlook would have been grim.

In December, the Lord showed our leadership in Shanghai that His time to leave China had arrived. Pressure was increasing on the

Chinese church. If missionaries left, the pressure might be lessened. In many cities, Communist officials accused missionaries of being the tools of imperialism. The missionaries became an unwilling embarrassment to their Chinese colleagues. One morning, a Chinese Christian leader approached our directors to ask that all missionaries in a certain province be withdrawn. At the same time, letters came from many inland cities telling of the seriousness of the situation. As a result, the tremendous decision was made: to leave China after eighty-six years.

At first, a letter went out only to those working with the Chinese church to suggest they begin the process of leaving the country. As we were not in this category, we carried on as usual. In January, a telegram came from Arnold Lea authorizing the withdrawal of the "Forty-Niners" also. The backward somersault in policy changed our whole situation. We had been so sure that God had led us in. Now He was leading us out! This meant a complete switch in direction.

From different parts of China, we heard that the wheels of officialdom turned very slowly. It was proving much harder to get out than it had been to get in. As Chungking was the most westerly city where steamers traveling east could be boarded, all missionaries from Yunnan and Szechwan would need to pass through here on their way out. Also, the water in the river was low at this time of the year, which meant that only small ships could navigate the rapids. Travel accommodations were at a premium.

Fifty young people, three staff, and five children were on the hills. In the city itself, there were many more missionaries working in churches, Bible schools, and universities. Marvin went to the Foreign Affairs Bureau (FAB) in Chungking City to inquire about procuring exit permits. We could not leave the country without them.

Some of the regulations seemed designed to make things difficult. The more we examined them, the more impossible they appeared, and the promise God gave us in Isaiah 52:12 was amazingly relevant. Not only was He going to go before us in guidance, but He would also protect us from behind. Let me explain.

Each adult was required to fill out application forms in duplicate and hand them in, along with three photos, to the FAB in the city. The authorities took their time before giving permission for the next step. The traveler had to publish his name in the local paper, stating his desire to leave the country. This advertisement had to appear for three consecutive days and was expensive. On the fourth day, the applicant returned to the authorities, taking with him the three issues of the paper as proof of compliance with instructions. If there were no accusations against him, he was given permission to make preparations for leaving. All his personal effects had to be listed, in Chinese. After this, he could put his name down for a boat ticket at the shipping office. Then he had to find a Chinese businessman or shopkeeper who would act as a legal and financial guarantor, a man willing to pay any demands made after the missionary departed. The guarantor also had to fill in an official paper for the police file. This man had to be approved by the authorities, and only then could the missionary buy the ticket for which he had applied, bring down his luggage for inspection and sealing, and board the ship!

How could we do this for fifty-three people? We thought of the innumerable trips to the city that would be involved, of the mammoth task of translating the fifty baggage lists into Chinese, the money spent on advertising, and the hopeless search for guarantors for so many of us. Certainly, the first part of our verse was true; we would not go out in haste!

Marvin went down to consult with the officials in the FAB. A young woman was in charge, dressed in a drab, ill-fitting wadded uniform. Her dark eyes regarded Marvin steadily from an unsmiling face as she heard what he had to say. This was not the first time he had had contact with Lucy, as we called her, and it would not be the last. She was severe, she was a Communist, but she had an innate sense of justice. With her, as in all our contacts with the new officialdom, we missed the courteous, friendly treatment of former days.

She suggested that our big family be divided into small groups, and the names of each group published at one time. Also, the number of guarantors was cut down to two or three per group, instead of the original "one man-one guarantor" ratio. All the other regulations would stand as stated.

When Marvin returned to the hill with this news, he asked all to pray that we might be guided aright in forming the groups. It was obvious that those who were unwell, or who were nervously exhausted, should leave as soon as possible. Then it seemed wise to get the Americans out next, as there was a much stronger anti-USA feeling now because China was involved in the Korean War. After that, we chose various names, keeping to the end a small group whom we felt could take the greater strain of seeing others leave while unable to get out themselves.

The matter of guarantors was also brought to the Lord. Who else could move in men's hearts to make them willing to be scapegoats for the despised and nonproductive missionaries? Concerning this matter, we were reminded again of the verse God had given. He was vitally interested not only in our exit but also in our "rearward." Surely this meant that He would care for the men who offered to be our guarantors, and NO ILL would come to them. It was really exciting to experience such real communication with the Lord in all the details of the exit that faced us.

There were also those lists of belongings—to be written in Chinese! The "Forty-Niners" could not do this. Marvin could not do it. We needed Chinese help. God brought just the man to us. Mr. Chen had held a minor government post with the Nationalists, which usually spelled trouble under the new regime. One day, he was arrested and thrown into prison while his case was being investigated. Along with other prisoners, he spent hours in indoctrination classes. The teaching of Mao filled his mind, and he endeavored to rearrange the thought habits of a lifetime.

One day, a different sound filtered into the common cell where he was confined. Someone was singing a happy-sounding song. The prisoners looked at each other in amazement. Who could sing in such circumstances? They learned that the singer was a Christian, and not even the jailers could keep him quiet. As Mr. Chen heard the lilting choruses day after day, his heart was touched. This man had something that he wished he had. But where could he find it?

Mr. Chen was not aware of God, nor had he ever read the Bible. How could he know the promise: "Seek, and ye shall find"? But God knew about Mr. Chen. One day he was released from prison. He made inquiries and found his way to a Christian church. There he was born again and became a new man in Christ. He needed work, though, as he had a wife and children to support. Someone suggested his name to Marvin. His skills were just what we needed, for he was an excellent writer. He moved up to the hills, and spent his days writing out the long lists demanded by the FAB. One by one our hurdles were being overcome.

Chapter Fifty-Seven

*The angel of the Lord encampeth round about
them that fear Him and delivereth them.
Psalm 34:7 KJV*

M IRIAM, DO YOU hear that noise?" Marvin whispered in my ear.
"Yes, it sounds like people walking around outside," I replied.
"I wonder what's up?"

"What's the time?" Marvin asked, and I turned the flashlight onto
the clock beside the bed.

"Why, it's one in the morning!" I exclaimed in surprise. "Oh, look,
there's a light flickering outside. I can see it."

Marvin jumped out of bed and put on his thick winter coat. It was
chilly at that hour of the morning. Before he could get to the door,
someone called his name in Chinese. "*Teng Hsien-sheng*!" A blow fell
on our door, and as Marvin opened it, three or four Chinese peasants,
carrying lanterns, walked unceremoniously into the room.

"Who are you, and why have you come at this hour?" Marvin asked.
"It's not very polite to walk into a private bedroom."

"We are members of the Peasants Association. We have come here
from a meeting where we have been discussing the matter of these
houses. They belong to us now, according to Land Reform policy, and
we want the deeds. Where are they?"

"I think they are in Shanghai, or they may be down in the city,"
Marvin replied.

"Our Association has agreed that the deeds be handed over to us," the leader said brusquely. With these words the delegation stalked out into the night.

During the conversation, I had lain in bed, with the blankets pulled up to my chin. My heart was thumping. Here was yet another matter which would weigh on Marvin's mind. He looked calm enough as he locked the door and climbed back between the sheets, but I knew this had shaken him too. What would be the next problem? It was a long time before we went back to sleep.

Stresses abounded, but thus far, no actual danger. We had been forbidden to give out any more tracts at the gap. Sunday classes for the neighboring hill children had been stopped. The Christian cook and his wife had left for their home in Honan, and the new cook was not so cooperative. Indoctrination classes were poisoning the servants against us, and it seemed best to dismiss them. This in turn brought another difficulty—exorbitant demands for severance pay. Marvin made more than one trip to the city to consult Lucy. Her advice was helpful but impersonal. However, one day she said, "If you have any trouble on the hill, let me know immediately."

A few days later, members of the Peasants Association and some of our disgruntled servants marched into the Taylor House around nine in the morning demanding *Teng Hsien-sheng*. "You are to come with us to the People's Court today," they shouted. "You have to answer to accusations being made against you." They hustled him off, bunching around him as they headed down the trail. He was gone. When would he be back?

They marched him down the hill path for about three miles to the site of a kangaroo court. A wooden platform hung with red flags. Peasant officials stood on a stage. A group of frightened prisoners sat on backless benches, with farmers and workers crowded on other seats behind them. Marvin was taken to the front and given a place beside the other accused men.

One by one, the men were dragged to the platform where they were forced to kneel as the accusations against them were read aloud. An official then harangued the crowd who became more abusive as the day wore on, responding to the mood of their leaders.

"Guilty or not guilty?" would come the cry.

"Guilty!" yelled the mob, and a sentence would be passed on the cowering man—loss of land, imprisonment, house arrest, or death.

Marvin sat on the bench, his head between his hands, waiting. The sun climbed high, but there was no letup of tension. No food or drink either. The number of prisoners dwindled and the court proceedings dragged on. Slowly the sun began to sink and shadows lengthened. The prisoners' benches were now empty. Marvin's turn had come.

"*Teng Hsien-sheng,* come over here," called one of the officials. Marvin got up and walked slowly toward the officials and was led to a small room nearby.

That morning, as soon as Marvin had been taken off in one direction, David Day ran off in another, heading for the city. His feet flew down the rough steps, through the village, and onto the riverbank. He sat on the ferry, panting. It was moving too slowly for him. Once the boat docked, he darted up the steps leading to the city and burst into the FAB office. Hastily he explained the situation to Lucy, who was as unflappable as ever. She listened quietly.

"There has been a misunderstanding," she said. "I'll send one of our men over. You can return to the hill."

Before doing this, David went to the CIM home in the city to report on what had happened, and then hurried back to us. When we heard his news, my heart was cheered, and a heavy weight seemed to roll away. "The angel of the Lord"—God had promised that His angel was round about those who feared Him. Surely He was guarding my loved one this day. The waiting, however, was not easy, and I couldn't set my mind to anything. After awhile, in spite of Lucy's message, my imagination leaped from one alternative to another. Finally, to keep occupied, I continued knitting a pullover I had already started for Marvin. It was a very intricate pattern, and concentrating on this helped me through that awful day—this and the prayers of the "Forty-Niners."

It began to get dark. Where was he, this man whose life was twined with mine? Weary footsteps climbed the last bit of the path, and there he was. Free, tired, and hungry! A shout of joy went up as the news flashed from one to another, "He's home! He's home!"

He told us his story with its dramatic ending. Just as he was being taken into the side room for questioning, a man on a horse rode into the circle.

"I have come from the FAB in Chungking," he said to the peasants. "This man is a foreigner, and as such you have no jurisdiction over him. Let him go."

Turning to Marvin, he said, "You may return to the hill. Go!" It was as simple as that! Marvin needed no second bidding. He turned around and walked back along the path, down which he had passed many hours before.

God had delivered him from the malicious peasants, but there was more to come. Even as he was eating his supper, a husky young water carrier, who had recently been dismissed from our employ, came storming into the courtyard.

"Come with me to the police station in Hwang Ko Ya," he said belligerently to my husband. "I am going to report you to them for stealing my watch."

Marvin tried to reason with him, but it was hopeless. To avoid a fracas, he felt it was wiser to go down to the police. So once again that day, he left us, tired though he was, accompanied by yet another angry accuser. This time, his absence was of short duration. The police decided to refer the entire matter to the FAB. When Marvin went down to the city the next day, Lucy made short work of the young man's accusations. She knew he was lying, hoping to make a quick dollar out of the foreigner's dilemma.

That night our hearts welled up in praise to the Lord for His angel of deliverance, who worked overtime that day.

Chapter Fifty-Eight

I will lift up mine eyes unto the mountains: from whence
shall my help come? My help cometh from the Lord.
Psalm 121:1,2 ASV

WHEN I WAS a child in far-off Tientsin, my parents had insisted that we memorize Scripture verses from both the Old and New Testaments. In the Psalms, they chose the Shepherd's Psalm (23), the Traveler's Psalm (121), and Psalms 1 and 91. All of them were tucked away in my memory, and came into my conscious thinking from time to time. We lived among the hills. To the east and west were distant mountains. The heathen built sacred pagodas on the high places because they wanted to placate the evil spirits whom they believed lived there. But those same mountains reminded me that the only One who could help us during those last months in China was God, the Almighty.

It was in January 1951 that we submitted our first list of eight "Forty-Niners'" names to the FAB. Two weeks later, the next list was taken down, and so on, until all the names except ours had been handed in. Then came an uncertain waiting period.

The first group started packing, but most of the others still studied diligently, hoping to get their second exam behind them. The door in China was closing, but we had heard of the opportunities among the millions of Chinese in the free lands of Southeast Asia. Thus, dreams of service in China were changing to prayers for guidance concerning the future.

It was thrilling to see God work in the matter of guarantors. A dry-cleaner, a milkman, and several businessmen and seminary students—these and others dared to affix their names to official documents so that our young people could receive permission to leave. We proved again that it was no vain thing to turn to God for help.

Some of the servants were dismissed in February and the rest in March. Our men students got sore muscles hauling water up the one hundred and seventy steps from a bubbling spring to the big storage *kangs* (glazed earthenware jars) near the houses. David Stewart, our former nuclear researcher, helped in the kitchen. The girls took turns doing the bigger items of household laundry.

It was nearly three months after the names of the first group were handed in that permission was finally given for them to leave. On Easter Sunday, April 8, they boarded the ship and sailed down the Yangtze from Chungking, after seventeen months in China. Eagerly, we waited for news indicating when the next party could start moving. Imagine the shock when Alfie came up from a visit to the city on April 20 with the news that permission to advertise in the paper had been granted—not to the second group suggested by us, but to the ones who had planned on staying to the bitter end!

There was no accounting for the vagaries of the FAB. We could not question their arbitrary ruling. Because of this, two couples engaged in April had to face the uncertainty of prolonged separation, as their names were in different groups. The American girls, who had hoped to go soon, wondered how they could carry on indefinitely. But it was out of our hands. We again had to commit everything to the Lord.

For everyone, packing became the order of the day. If the FAB did this once, they could do it again. We had to be prepared. Lists were made for Mr. Chen to translate. Musty trunks were set out in the sun to air. Their former label of Chungking was painted out and the new destination, Hong Kong, painted in. Photographs and books were mailed to the coast, as printed material of any kind invited trouble when inspected by ignorant Chinese guards.

The Peasants Association did not forget us during this time. Periodically, the distant barking of dogs signaled another midnight visit. Marvin and I would lie in bed listening as the dogs closer to us took up the cry. After awhile, we would see a light moving outside and hear men's rough voices as they tramped through the courtyard. It didn't get any easier. Marvin wrote to Shanghai, as they requested, but nothing happened. His answer to their query was always the same, "No, the deeds have not come yet." The men would listen with hostility in their eyes, but they did not dare to use force again. Muttering among themselves, they would leave the room. The renewed distant barking assured us they had really returned to their homes. We never did receive those deeds.

On May 28, 1951, God protected us in a different way. That day, we began our summer timetable with breakfast at seven rather than the usual seven-thirty meal. It was pouring rain as the young people slopped their way along slippery paths to the Taylor House. During the meal and following prayer, the winds howled and blew with increasing velocity, punctuated with the occasional snap of breaking branches or the thud of falling trees. When we surveyed the damage later, we found uprooted and broken trees lay in all directions, like matchsticks. One sprawled right across a path used by the girls. If breakfast had been at the usual time, someone could have been hurt. At the Cassells', a thirty-foot trunk fell from twenty-five feet up, smack onto the roof just above the room where baby Kathleen lay sleeping, but she was unharmed. We heard later that in our area of hills alone, 280 trees were destroyed. Even in a small decision such as the time of a meal, God cared.

On June 12, joy reigned over the hills. David and Phyllis were to be married. Soon after David had joined our group in 1950, we thought he was attracted to a certain blue-eyed, dark-haired girl, so when they announced their engagement, everyone was happy. Because of David's ability with the Chinese language, their names had not yet been handed to the FAB, as Marvin felt he needed another man around in case of emergency.

Preparations were made for their wedding in our little church. It was decorated with blue and pink hydrangeas. Sheaves of gay gladiola added splashes of color. Friends, including the British Consul, came up from the city. The bride was beautiful, the bridegroom happy, and music filled the flower-decked sanctuary as Mr. Ellison united them as man and wife before God.

Following the wedding meal, disaster struck. Many of the guests began to feel unwell. Some were so ill with diarrhea and vomiting that they could not return to the city that night. Chinese in the village said, "Those foreigners must have served a lot of wine at the wedding feast. So many of the guests were vomiting on the way home!"

We finally tracked down the cause. A tin of tainted chicken was unknowingly mixed in with the fresh meat in the chicken salad. By the mercy of God, this distribution helped to weaken the effect of the bad meat so no one was in serious danger. However, we had been giving tins of chicken to various groups traveling downriver. Had this one been eaten by one of those small groups, someone would probably have died.

A week later, most of the remaining American "Forty-Niners" climbed aboard the *Kwei Men* for Hankow. It took them seven days to reach Hong Kong. Following them, were two smaller parties, and on July 11 the biggest group of all, eighteen adults and a baby, left the hill. At times, the exit had seemed excruciatingly slow, but now only four of the "Forty-Niners" remained with us. Our days in China were fast drawing to a close.

Chapter Fifty-Nine

He led forth His own people like sheep…
He led them safely so that they feared not.
Psalm 78:52,53 ASV

WE LAY ON our Chinese bedrolls on the only deck space we had been able to commandeer. Above us was the beauty of a star-studded sky. Around us, the humid, pulsing darkness of the tropics. Before us, the bright lights of Chungking, shining like diamonds on a black velvet backdrop. Sounds fought for recognition above the hum of human voices on deck: the gentle swish of the moving river, the loud hooting of a busy tugboat, the quavering falsetto of a hidden singer, the monotonous syncopated rhythm of a drum—those ubiquitous drums of Red China that beat faster and faster to suck men, women, and children into the whirlpool of Communist ideology.

It was August 5, 1951, a hot, stifling Sunday. Early that morning, we and a number of other missionaries had gone down to the riverside to board our ship. Sitting on rocks and logs that lined the steps leading down the steep bank to the gangway, we waited under umbrellas for our numbers to be called. It was afternoon before we climbed on board. The police had bought our tickets for us—they were fifth class, deck passage only. People were swarming everywhere. Normally, the steamer carried three hundred passengers; for this trip, six hundred tickets had been sold. This did not include the children, and there were dozens of them milling around.

The men scouted around to find a place for us to sleep. Eventually, through the natural kindness of the Chinese man-in-the-street, we were able to spread out our *p'u-kais* (bedrolls). Children whimpered, our neighbors conversed loudly together, but we lay there experiencing the poignancy of farewell.

Some weeks earlier, on June 13, Marvin had felt it would be safe for us to submit our names to the FAB, asking permission to leave the country. By that time, the "Forty-Niners" were on the move, even though there had been one or two refusals that puzzled us. Something else had happened that seemed to indicate that it was time for us to go. One afternoon, some officials appeared on the Taylor House veranda. Mr. Chen was in Marvin's office busy at his writing, but in his courteous way, he went out to see if he could help them. Instead, when they identified him, they marched him off to the city, and as far as we know, to prison, for he never came back to us. Was it because he was helping the foreigners, the Christians? We do not know.

On July 17, only five weeks after our application went in (the shortest period of waiting as yet), a notice came telling us to advertise in the paper. As we read the communication under the grapevine outside our room, we could scarcely believe our eyes. Then we faced our biggest hurdle. We knew of no one willing to stand in as our guarantor. Marvin went down to explain this to Lucy at the FAB. She made no comment, and he returned rather dejectedly to the hill. But God had not forgotten us. A few days later we were given the incredible news that the government itself would stand in bond for us!

By this time, our household had shrunk drastically. Joyce was going to travel out with us, and Sylvia would join us from the mission home in the city. David and Phyllis Day, along with David Stewart, were the only ones remaining on the hill. Although their names had been handed in earlier, travel procedures had not yet meshed into gear for these three.

We were busy in those last days. Furniture had to be sold and houses finally cleaned and locked up. Our own packing was done and our lists prepared. How we missed Mr. Chen's careful efficiency! Then illness struck. I went to bed with a high fever just as we were told to report to the city in preparation for embarking. Marvin went down to ask if we could postpone our sailing until the next ship.

"If you don't go when you are told, we cannot guarantee when you will be able to leave," they said. So we had no alternative.

It was hard to say goodbye to the three we were leaving, but they faced the future and the loneliness with smiling faces. For the last time, we went down the old stone steps to Hwang Ko Ya, the "Forty-Niners" bungalows empty and silent behind us. In the distance, we could see Chungking's mass of buildings jutting out of the white fog that blanketed the mighty Yangtze. Closer at hand, in the little valley, green rice fields glinted in the sunshine where an occasional diligent farmer was at work. Soon these familiar sights were hidden as we continued our journey down to the ferry, across the river, and up the crowded steps to the CIM home.

Now we lay under the stars, and memories came crowding in. Questions too. Why this whole "Forty-Niners" venture? "To what purpose… this waste?" (Matthew 26:8). Nearly two years in the lives of many people had been spent cooped up on the hills. Thousands of dollars had been expended in travel to and fro, in food, and in lodging. Illness of body had hit some, and tension of mind had affected others. Was it worth it?

It was not for us to judge. God saw the love in the hearts of the "Forty-Niners," just as Christ had seen the love in the heart of Mary as she poured the perfumed ointment on His feet. He also saw their obedience. These were the things that mattered. In the difficult experiences we had passed through, He had taught us precious lessons. The many miraculous answers to prayer had deepened our faith. Times of waiting before God had enriched us all and drawn us closer together as a family. The testing had led to humility, and to honesty one with another. We had discovered for ourselves that God could give peace and patience in strange situations, just as the Bible says. We had come to know God better. No, the two years had not been wasted.

Early the next morning, we were awakened to have our passes examined. When this was completed, we steamed downriver. As we headed east, our eyes strained towards the west to catch a last glimpse of our hills and to say goodbye in our hearts.

That journey proved to be a nightmare. Joyce became very ill with a severe attack of dysentery. If some Roman Catholic nuns traveling with us had not been able to supply her with antibiotics, we don't know what might have happened. Traveling as deck passengers meant we had no protection from the sun that beat on us by day, along with the soot that showered down as smoke belched from the funnel. It was also necessary to keep a constant watch on Rosemary and Peter, as friendly Chinese passengers gave them all kinds of tasty tidbits. Jennifer was shy and stayed closer to us.

At last, we reached Hankow where our party gladly disembarked. We had to register our arrival with the police, after which the China Travel Service arranged for our travel south. First, we had to spend one night in a specified hotel (they wanted to keep us under their eye) where we unexpectedly met some missionaries from the Northwest, also on their way out. The next day, we were ferried across the river to the railway station where all our baggage was reexamined and resealed.

The train journey was quite comfortable and the children were thrilled with this new sensation. The carriages were clean, and simple food was available. The fly in the ointment was the continuous broadcasting in every carriage of the songs of the Revolution and quotations from Mao Tse-tung. However, the scenery was beautiful. Mountains etched the far horizon, steep crags jutted from the middle of lush green fields, occasional walled cities loomed into sight, and yellow brick houses squatted in the shelter of dark green trees. We were surprised at the lack of roads and traffic, and to notice that there were only footpaths between the fields.

In Canton, our passports were inspected. Once again, we had to spend the night in a specified hotel. Very early the next morning, just a week since our exit began, we and our hand luggage were taken to the station and another check was made. We were so near to getting out and were afraid one false move might keep us behind the Bamboo Curtain for good. But we should not have been concerned, for was not God leading us out?

At last, they allowed us onto the crowded train, which steadily chugged nearer to freedom. At the border, the train stopped. We all had to get off for our final inspection at the Chinese Customs. Across the barbed wire barrier, we saw the Union Jack proudly floating from its pole near the British border patrol station. What a glorious sight it was to our freedom-starved souls! The one American girl in our party gazed at it with tears in her eyes as she realized all that the flag stood for.

Our trunks, which we had last seen at Hankow, were opened up again and carefully gone through. We were glad we had been well briefed concerning items the police were looking for: old Chinese paintings, antique carvings, jade, valuable china, and so on. The Communists did not want such articles to be spirited out of their country by foreigners. As each box was examined, it was humped over to the train standing on the other side of the platform—the train for Hong Kong. Then it was our turn to move. We handed in our exit permits and walked over the Freedom Bridge in a daze, Jennifer and Rosemary holding my hands and Peter holding on to his daddy.

A photo taken of our family on August 12, 1951, as we safely crossed Freedom Bridge from behind the Bamboo Curtain in Red Communist China to Hong Kong.

Friends and relatives were waiting to welcome us, and what a joyous reunion we had! They gave us tea (Marvin enjoyed the white sugar), and the children had all the cookies they could eat. We were bundled onto the train and the talking began. Questions and answers flew back and forth. There was so much we did not know.

In spite of the excitement and joy, at the back of all our minds was the thought of those we had left behind—our three "Forty-Niners," as well as Chinese Christians under increasing pressure from the government to compromise their faith, to renounce their belief in God's Word. For the latter, there was no escape, no chance to cross the Freedom Bridge. They were in the valley of shadows, but our comfort was that GOD was with them.

Chapter Sixty

He that loveth son or daughter more
than Me is not worthy of me.
Matthew 10:37 ASV

AFTER THE COMPARATIVE isolation we had experienced under Communism, it took us awhile to adjust to the crowded, bustling colony of Hong Kong. Hundreds of missionaries had poured out of China into this British Colony, and more were on the way. This meant that housing of any kind was at a premium. Miraculously, God provided for His refugee servants through the kindness of the Hong Kong government, and in answer to the earnest prayers and tireless efforts of our mission representatives in Hong Kong.

An empty Army transit camp in Kowloon, edging the harbor, was released for the tide of weary men and women coming out of China. They named it "Free Haven." A few barn-like Quonset huts were filled with rows of beds. Trunks, suitcases, and clothing were piled wherever room could be found. One hut served as a large dining hall. A phone was installed. Here we lived a day at a time. Most missionaries went home as soon as ships or planes could take them. Some remained in Hong Kong—a few to help in administration, a few to work among the many thousands of Chinese living in abject poverty in refugee camps, a few to move on to serve in the countries on China's perimeter where the spiritual needs were enormous.

What did God want *us* to do? Only two years had elapsed since we left Canada. Were we justified in returning again so soon? Mission leaders put no pressure on us, but they did suggest to Marvin that he could immediately fill an urgent need in Hong Kong. As we prayed, we believed God wanted us to stay. Marvin was then asked to deputize for Ken Price in the Christian Witness Press, the literature arm of our mission, as the Prices' furlough was overdue.

Rosemary's schooling now became an urgent matter. She was six and a half and had never been inside a classroom. We phoned and visited various schools in the Colony only to be told there were no vacancies at that time and none in the foreseeable future. The flood of missionaries and business people from the mainland had brought an influx of children who now filled every available space. Thus a conflict arose for us.

Was this guidance for us to return home, or did God really want us in Hong Kong? Marvin's knowledge of the Chinese language, his administrative ability, and his rapport with Chinese people fitted him admirably for this new work. But what of our little daughter? Already, she was behind other children in reading and writing skills. Would she have to leave us for education in Canada? Surely God would not demand this sacrifice of us! How could we let her go? She was so wee, so vulnerable, and she needed us. Yet God had already shown the direction of His will for the next year at least. It was an agonizing time, a tug of war between natural desires and the will of God. He could so easily provide the one opening in a school, but always the answer was, "No room."

We were cast on Him in a new way, and the word "daughter" in Matthew 10:37 pierced our hearts.

"O Lord, surely You don't want us to be separated from our little girl, our firstborn?"

"Do you love Me?" came the tender reply.

"You know we do."

"Can't you trust Me with her?"

There was the rub. We loved God, but could we trust Him? "Lord, help us to trust You more," became our prayer.

My brother John and his wife were booked to sail to England in early September. As we mentioned our dilemma to them, they gladly offered to take Rosemary under their care. Letters flew between Three

Hills, London, and Hong Kong. Quickly, everything fell into place, and on September 6, 1951, the parting came. Of course, there were tears. God understands our human emotions—utterly. Our little fairhaired daughter, clutching a large doll in her arms, cried bitterly when we kissed her goodbye. Our eyes and hearts were full as we stood on the wharf and watched the ship pull slowly away from shore, turn her prow to the open sea, and steam away.

Years later, Rosemary and I were driving through the Rocky Mountains together, talking about that parting.

"I used to cry every night in bed after you told me I was going to Canada on my own," she said, "but I didn't want you to know. You promised me a doll, but I didn't want a doll—I wanted to stay at home."

Even after the passage of many years, a stab went through my heart. Of course, she had wanted to be with us. Had the hurt been deeper than we knew?

"But I want you to know I'm not bitter about it," she continued. "I was talking with a friend recently in the clinic where I work, and she was amazed that it does not seem to have scarred me in any way. She can't understand how that has happened."

But we knew!

Above us, the sun shone down on rugged mountains clothed in green spruce trees, dappled with light and shade. Sparkling water rippled over a stony riverbed. The God who created this beauty had kept His loving hand on the heart and life of a little girl, and no harm had come to her. Yes, He can be trusted with our most precious things, but He does not say we shall not suffer in the process.

Chapter Sixty-One

He took a towel and girded Himself.
Then He poured water into the basin and began to wash.
John 13:4,5 ASV

OUR TWENTY MONTHS in Hong Kong proved to be busy and exciting. The work of the Christian Witness Press kept expanding. Tracts, booklets, books, commentaries, and posters rolled off the presses in increasing numbers. Additional workers were needed to cope with the growing demands. The literature bug bit us then, and has had a lasting effect on our lives.

In 1953, we left Hong Kong for our second furlough, with three children—Peter, Jennifer, and David, our Hong Kong baby who had helped to fill the gap Rosemary had left. He was a big, contented baby who rarely cried, and we all loved him. He was born a few months after news had reached us of the sudden death of my father in England. Upon returning home from a speaking engagement one night, my father had suffered a stroke. His death was the first in our family. 1952 had brought both sorrow and joy in its hands.

We sailed first to England, which was reveling in the pageantry of the Coronation. Being residents of Hong Kong, we were able to apply for tickets in the stands at Hyde Park. When we arrived there early on the morning of June 2, paperboys were already shouting the exciting news of the conquest of Everest. We and thousands of other spectators watched the procession, fascinated by the glamour of the occasion: marching columns, colorful uniforms, prancing horses, and finally the

Golden Coach in which we could just see the Queen holding the Orb and Scepter. One night, we joined the thousands of excited men and women outside Buckingham Palace, shouting, "We want the Queen," until the balcony doors opened and she and Prince Philip appeared, to be greeted by the thunderous cheers of the crowd.

A few weeks later, we reached America. Here our supporting church in Michigan did a beautiful thing. Unknown to us, they had arranged for Rosemary to fly east from Three Hills, Alberta, Canada, to join us in Wayne. How thrilled we were as we saw her walk down the steps from the plane. Our family of six was together for the first time.

Seven months later, on January 1, 1954, we said goodbye to Rosemary and Peter, leaving them both in Three Hills at our mission hostel, and set our faces once more to the east. Peter could have returned with us (and how we longed to have him), but the hostel parents felt strongly that Rosemary should not be left alone again. All the other children living there had a brother or sister with them, and this gave a sense of security and belonging that each child needed. We wondered how we could leave two behind, and it was with aching hearts that we climbed into the car and turned towards the coast. We were discovering some of the costs of missionary service, and could only look to the Lord for strength and peace.

We were on our way to Singapore, where we had been asked to take up once again the challenge of Language School work. Steadily, the Norwegian freighter *Silverspray* plowed its way across the Pacific. On February 13, we docked in the harbor. As the ship slowed down, the heat struck us like a blow.

Eighty miles north of the equator, a kaleidoscope of new sights and impressions burst upon us as we drove through the city. Towering palm trees, graceful bamboos, fragrant frangipanis; sweating laborers, busy streets, crowded honking buses; airy houses, smooth green lawns, six-foot-deep monsoon drains; Chinese, Indian, and Malay ladies in colorful dress.

A large old house with a red-tiled roof, plastered walls, and a hospitable entrance sat at the end of Chancery Lane. Green lawns and tropical flowers surrounded it—the home the Lord had provided for our new work. Fortunately, Faith Leeuwenburg, our good friend of the

"Forty-Niners" saga, was there to greet us and help make preparations for the arrival of the young people already converging on Singapore from different parts of the world. Within one week, two new workers arrived from Switzerland and a few days later the contingent from Australia and New Zealand. On March 2, a large open truck, piled high with baggage, lumbered up Chancery Lane. The big group from England and North America brought our number to forty-three.

This school was so different from those we had helped with in China, for now Thai, Tagalog, Malay, and Japanese were to be studied, as well as a number of dialects of Chinese. The Overseas Missionary Fellowship (new name for CIM) was feeling its way into the lands of Southeast Asia, and its missionaries had to learn the languages of many nations. What a babble of sounds when teachers, students, and tape recorders started the learning and teaching process!

The example Jesus gave of humble service was a lesson I had to learn there. In Singapore's heat and humidity, clothes have to be changed once or twice a day, so for our large family of students, a washing machine was a must! I ran the machine six days a week in the damp passage behind the kitchen. Two Chinese girls hung out the clothes to dry and ironed them. Each week we washed an average of one hundred and twenty five dresses, three hundred and eighty pieces of underwear, seventy shirts, one hundred and forty bath towels, fifty sheets, and innumerable socks. I began to feel sorry for myself, for all the interesting things seemed to be happening on the other side of the wall!

Was this missionary work? Had I left our two children thousands of miles away for someone else to look after and enjoy, just to wash clothes for a bunch of other missionaries? Marvin was enjoying this new life and the challenge of his responsibilities. I didn't find much challenge in mine—standing for hours over a noisy washing machine, sorting sweaty clothes, keeping an eye on my two Chinese helpers.

The Lord reminded me of His many years as a village carpenter, and of His final humility in washing the dirty feet of His disciples. The amazing thing to me was that He set aside His outer garment and took the towel, *knowing that the Father had given all things into His hands* (John 13:3). And what did He take into those power-filled hands? Something with which He could minister to others' needs. The towel of service was not too lowly for Him to use—the washing machine would be fine for me.

After I had accepted the situation, things changed. Arrangements were made whereby Faith and I alternated our duties—planning meals one week, doing laundry the next. This created a more balanced life for both of us, and worked well all the years we were together.

Editors Note: We recognize that this is a rather abrupt ending to Miriam Dunn's memoirs. It was the choice of the editors to primarily conclude the book with Miriam's experience in pre-communist China.

Marvin and Miriam continued to serve with the China Inland Mission (later renamed Overseas Missionary Fellowship) for twenty-three years, eventually retiring in Calgary, Alberta, Canada in 1974. During those remaining years of service they served in a number of capacities, their primary role being that of directors of language schools in both Malaysia and Singapore, helping missionary recruits adjust to the language and cultural barriers of the Far East. The specific skills that they developed while working as directors of language schools in China stood them in good stead for the rest of their years of service with the OMF.

Afterword

Not one (sparrow) shall fall on the ground
without your Father. Fear not therefore; ye
are of more value than many sparrows.
Matthew 10:29,31 ASV

L ATE ON THE night of June 25, 1974, Marvin and I drove through the streets of Kuala Lumpur for the last time. Our destination was the decorative, arabesque railway station. Mixed feelings filled our hearts. We were leaving Asia to retire in Canada.

On the platform were many friends who had come to say goodbye. Sharp on time, the train began to move. As it gathered speed, their faces vanished from our sight. Some we would never see again on earth. We were close to so many people in that part of the world, for much of our lives had been spent in the East. Now God was taking us to the West. Once again, the future was unknown.

On August 31, we reached Calgary, not knowing where we would live, but sure that God would have a place for us. A few days later, we rented a nice little home with room for David, our youngest son, to live with us, along with a spare room for guests. However, it was empty of furniture. To see the different people God used to help us was exciting. Lamps and a coffee table from someone we had never met before; a couch and easy chair from old friends; a rug that exactly matched from complete strangers; a dining table, chairs, and buffet from folk interested in the OMF; a washing machine from old colleagues; even a new clothes dryer from neighbors whom we scarcely knew! With family pictures on the walls and ornaments from China, Malaysia, Singapore, and Hong Kong much in evidence, we were very grateful to our heavenly Father for His loving provision.

Jennifer was teaching in Edmonton, so was often able to spend weekends with us. She always brought Pip, her little blue budgie, with

283

her, and he became one of the family. In the summer of 1976, she went to Venezuela to help with a mission project, and Pip came to live with us. He loved to be free, so his cage door was left open and he flew in and out at will. One afternoon, I came up from the basement and noticed that the house was strangely quiet. I called, "Pip! Pip! Hi, Pip!" But there was no answering chirp, no flutter of blue wings.

My heart sank. Where was he? How had he gotten out? What would Jennifer say? He meant so much to her. How could we write and tell her he was lost? We went outside and walked up and down the sidewalk calling his name. We put his cage on the back steps. We looked into the shimmering leaves of nearby trees. We scanned the blue afternoon sky. We asked the paperboy and the neighbors if they had seen him. On all sides the answer was, "No."

Around seven that evening I decided to phone *The Calgary Herald* to ask them to run a LOST ad in the paper. The girl took my message:

Friendly blue budgie named Pip. Cambrian Heights area.
$5.00 reward. Phone 282-6365.

When I told her we wanted it in the next day, Friday, she said she was sorry, but it was too late for that day. It would run in Saturday's paper.

I was upset. If someone saw Pip on Friday, there would be no ad for them to refer to. *Why didn't God change the girl's mind?* I fumed.

That night, a cold wind blew as darkness closed in. We left the light on outside the back door, shining on the empty cage. In our evening prayers, we reminded God that His Son had told the disciples that not even a sparrow could fall to the ground without His Father knowing all about it. Surely Pip would be with us in the morning.

The next day—still an empty cage.

All day Friday, we kept praying and hoping, but no little budgie came into view. Saturday came, and still our prayers were not answered.

I was cooking supper when the phone rang. A lady's voice spoke in my ear. "I noticed in today's *Herald* that you had lost a budgie."

"Yes, we have," I replied, my heart beginning to pound.

"Well, about fifteen minutes ago, a blue budgie suddenly flew down onto my shoulder while I was sitting in the garden," she went on. "I wonder if he's yours?"

"Oh, did you catch him?" I asked eagerly.

"Yes, I did, and put him in an old cage. Then I looked in the LOST column of the *Herald* and saw your ad."

"I'm sure he's ours," I cried with mounting excitement, "for that's just the kind of thing he'd do! Thank you so much for phoning. Can we come over and get him? Where do you live?"

She gave me her address. We caught up the cage, and hurried to the car. I was so excited—yet humbled, as I remembered my resentment over the ad not being carried in the Friday paper. If I had had *my* way, there would have been no mention of Pip in Saturday's paper. God, because He is God, knew best and He kept His hand on the venturesome bird, protected him from cold and cats, and guided him to people who took *The Calgary Herald.*

The house was nearly a mile away. Quickly we transferred Pip to his own cage. Marvin gave the family some Christian books when they refused to take any reward, and I shared our story with them, including the fact that the ad had gone in one day late. The two children listened wide-eyed. The lady seemed moved. Her husband remarked, "All I can say is that you are very lucky!"

"No, it was not luck," I countered. "We believe in a God who hears and answers prayer."

We thanked them again and climbed into the car. I held the cage on my lap while Pip preened his feathers inside. We drove home with happy hearts. God is concerned for all His creation, even a little roving budgie. How much more is He involved in all that comes into the lives of each one of His children!

As we have looked back on our experiences in China and Southeast Asia, we almost wonder if these things really happened to us. They seem unreal in the pragmatism of life in Canada. Yet we know that God walked with us through the dangers and stresses of our earlier days, and He is still with us here in our retirement in the burgeoning city of Calgary.

How did He want me to conclude this account of His dealings with me? Since leaving Malaysia, a number of things have happened in which God has related some portion of His Word to our need, and how was I to know which to include? I prayed about it, and recently the verse heading this final chapter came in my morning reading. Immediately, I remembered the saga of Pip's escape and capture. I recalled the awe that filled our hearts as we saw God overrule circumstances and bring the little bird back to us. Did He want me to share this experience? It seemed so insignificant. In the quiet of my room I reread many of the verses of the tenth chapter of Matthew. Some had been applicable to Marvin and me during our missionary service in Asia, and some were relevant to our circumstances today. When I read the *Daily Light* the very next morning, there was another mention of birds. I believed this repetition was no coincidence. The subject of my last chapter was chosen.

Not only on the mission field, but also in a modern Canadian city, we found that God has His own message to fit our needs.

About the Author

Miriam was born in Kuling, China, in 1913, to missionaries Joseph and Rosetta Toop, and spent her childhood in Tientsin. At eighteen years of age she traveled to England to study nursing. Miriam's return to China, to her parents' home in Peking, was heralded by heeding God's call to work with CIM–China Inland Mission in 1940. In 1942, she was married to Marvin Dunn. Four children were born to the Dunns', one in India, two in China, and the last in Hong Kong. After retiring from mission work in 1974, they settled in Calgary, Alberta, Canada, where Miriam worked on My Children or the Cross. She died in 1999 after eighty-five years of selflessness, built on the belief that, "Ye have not chosen me, but I have chosen you."

Epilogue

*"They went about from nation to nation, and from one kingdom
to another people… declaring His glory among the nations."
(I Chronicles 16:20,24)*

Miriam and Marvin Dunn retired from mission work in Southeast Asia in 1974, and settled in Calgary, Alberta, Canada. Marvin set up a book-distribution business, selling inspirational literature in over one hundred book racks throughout the city. The basement of the home functioned as his warehouse. Mother spent much of that time working on this book.

Marvin and Miriam moved to a retirement community in Abbotsford, British Columbia, Canada, just outside of Vancouver, to be close to family plus the allure of a warmer climate.

Marvin died a week shy of his eightieth birthday in December 1989. Miriam died a decade later in December of 1999. She was eighty-five. Jennifer Dunn Greenway died in March 2000, at the age of fifty-one from breast cancer.

Rosemary's chosen occupation was also nursing. She is retired and lives in Spokane, Washington. Peter lives in Dalton, Ohio, and is recently retired from P. Graham Dunn. He has been married to LeAnna for thirty-eight years, and they have four grown children. David lives in Vancouver, British Columbia. He is an accountant and for a number of years has been a financial administrator of nursing homes. He has been married to Heather for twenty-five years and they have three grown daughters.

*Peter, Rosemary and David
November, 2010*

Obituary

*The following was compiled by Jennifer Dunn
Greenway, the Dunns' third child:*

In my imagination I can see my mother as she was before I knew her:

A teenager, riding the ponies on the beach at Pei Ta Ho, China.

Being the responsible older sister to two mischievous twin brothers, Billy and John, and a vivacious sister, Peggy.

Adoring Eric Liddell, of *Chariots of Fire* fame, who went to China as a missionary and became the Superintendent of the Sunday School she attended.

Being tied up with ropes to my father, Marvin Dunn, by Chinese bandits before they barely knew each other.

Falling in love and being married six months later… a pink and white wedding dress… a romantic honeymoon on mysterious and beautiful Yellow Mountain, Hwang Shan.

Bearing three children within three years under difficult circumstances as the Japanese and the Communists tried to gain the upper hand in the parts of China where they were living.

Dodging stray bullets while protecting three little children (by putting them under a dining room table covered with thick quilts), on a mountaintop, while my father was away on an errand down the mountain.

In my memory's eye I can see:

A patient mother. I have no memories of her losing her temper or even uttering a sharp word.

A mother who sacrificed being with her children while she carried out what she firmly believed God had called her to.

A mother who prayed and read her Bible daily.

A stamp collector. Being a missionary who wrote and received copious amounts of mail (prior to e-mail days) provided a lot of fodder for this hobby.

A creator of cross-stitch, knitting, calligraphy, poetry, a lover of nature.

A writer who spent many hours organizing her memoirs, using her faithfully scribed diaries.

At Christmas decorating the tree, setting up the crèche, making name tags.

Driving in from Abbotsford every other week to volunteer her time at University Chapel and to stay overnight.

Hanging on to a sense of humor even in her declining years—a twinkle in her eye and a ready smile.

A sheepish grin as I nudged her awake while she was nodding off to sleep at church.

Creeping into Blenheim Lodge after a late-night fireworks display, like a teenager sneaking home after a dance.

Her trademark answer when asked how she was, "Not too badly, thank you!" even when her quality of life was not so good. She often answered my question about whether she was ready yet to go to heaven with "Not quite yet." Life was still okay down here.

In my imagination I can see my mother entering heaven:

Welcomed and hugged by the God she loved, obeyed, and trusted all her life.

Delightedly received and surrounded by those who have gone before her—her husband, her parents, a multitude of friends and fellow missionaries.

Able to walk and run again, and ride the ponies of heaven.

Acknowledgments

This book would not have been published without the continual encouragement and support of a number of people. Copies of Mother's memories were circulated among a group of our friends, and it was from our friends reading the memoirs that the momentum started to build.

Perhaps first among these was our long-term tour guide, Harry Wilkins. We loaned a copy to Harry and his wife Meg a few years ago, and ever since he continues to ask us when we are going to publish the book. He and Meg were both moved by Mother's writing and insisted that we publish it. He even went so far as to say that if the project needed financing he would provide the capital for launching the publication! Harry provided a moving review, and Meg proofread the document a number of times to assure accuracy.

Our sister Rosemary has also been a consistent source of encouragement. She circulated copies of the memoirs among many friends in Spokane. The response was the same: this book needs to be published. On occasion when I became discouraged or overwhelmed with the enormity of the project, Rosemary would gently prod me on. She also wrote a review of the book. Without her constant gentle nudging, daily prayers, and Scriptures that she would forward to me, this book would not have been published.

Ian Grant, a childhood friend and also a son of missionaries under the China Inland Mission, provided wise editorial counsel. Ian has an extensive grasp of the history of China. He is the publisher of the *Chefoo Magazine* based in Toronto, Ontario, Canada.

Our brother David has been supportive of and encouraging of this publication, and for that we thank him.

Barbara Dunn Greenway painstakingly retyped the 84,000-word manuscript in order to get it into digital format. Barbara is our cousin; you will read about her birth on page 130. She also was raised in the foster home in Canada with us. Maggy Dunn Haggberg, Barbara's sister and our cousin, provided valuable input in graphic design for which we are thankful.

We are indebted to Marcus Wengerd of Carlisle Printing, along with the able assistance of Aaron Hershberger, who assisted in providing for the overall direction of the publication. The two of them in conversations with Peter were the ones who arrived at the decision to entitle this book *My Children or the Cross*. We are fortunate to have a printer that embraces the same vision for the book that the Dunn children have. I have lost track of the number of hours of animated and emotional discussion I have had with these two gentlemen as the three of us worked on shaping these memoirs into a book that would appeal to readers in 2011.

We are deeply indebted to Rosetta Mullet, the graphic designer, who painstakingly designed the cover, discovered graphic vignettes from Mother's writings and reproduced them throughout the book, provided able editorial assistance, and created the overall format that has made the book aesthetically appealing. In our effort to make this book perfect we ended up making multiple changes, which would have tested the patience of any normal person.

It has been said that a good proofreader, to avoid getting caught up in the drama of the book, will on occasion read backwards in an attempt to catch every error. In our case, I'm imagining that Marie Kline must have also stood on her head! A proofreader has to be knowledgeable in geography, history, editing, and grammar, to mention only a few. We will always be grateful for what Marie did for us in perfecting Mother's writing.

Reverend Ted S. Rendall, Chancellor Emeritus, Prairie Bible Institute, Instructor, The Olford Center at Union, provided editorial and proofreading suggestions which enhanced the accuracy and flow of Mother's writings.

We are grateful to those who, prior to publication, took the time to read through it and provide reviews for us. This would include Martyn Smith, a childhood friend of mine who grew up in the same CIM home with us, our son, Thomas Dunn, Ruth Amstutz, a faithful friend from our church who has prayed for and taught our children, and

Dr. Joseph Stowell, President of Cornerstone University. The Reverend Bill Detweiler, pastor emeritus of the Kidron Mennonite Church where LeAnna, my wife of forty-one years, and I have been attending for forty-one years, was gracious to read, proof, edit, and write a review. Phil Callaway, a childhood acquaintance of the Dunn children from Three Hills and now Editor of the Servant Magazine at Prairie Bible Institute in Three Hills, Alberta, Canada, compiled a moving tribute of Miriam Dunn's book. He refers to it as a twelve-ounce missionary.

Bob Whitaker of Whitaker House-Anchor Distributing provided wise council on the intricacies of publishing, along with suggestions on marketing. With this being the first book we have published, his encouragement and support were most helpful.

Foremost we would like to acknowledgement Mother and Father. They lived for others, not for themselves. In the process Mother journaled extensively throughout her life and left us children this written description of her and Dad's experiences in Communist China. She has touched not only our lives, but the lives of our children. Her writings have been used as devotional material with her grandchildren. Her memoirs left us a living legacy of a sacrificial life.

If it were not for a one-inch twig in our driveway, I wonder if this book would ever have been published. That twig was divinely squeezed between the front tire and fork of my bicycle on a Saturday morning ride in September of 2010, resulting in serious broken bones that put me in a wheelchair for a number of months but in the process allowed me the time needed to bring this book to publication.

It would be negligent of me if I did not thank my wife LeAnna for putting up with what I would describe as a five-month distraction. A distraction of this magnitude can test the patience of anyone, and yet she supported and encouraged me through the process.

Finally, we are grateful to our Father in heaven, the Great Orchestrator, Who has provided us with such a heritage, for His hand of protection and blessing throughout the years, and for His love which He has "shed abroad in our hearts."

Peter Graham Dunn, for Rosemary Dunn,
Jennifer Dunn (deceased 2000) and David Dunn

Reviews

With China prominently in our news headlines and with reports that the church there is growing phenomenally, we must not forget the army of evangelical missionaries who sowed the Gospel seed from the earliest days in the 1800s until they had to evacuate in the early 1950s. Mrs. Miriam Dunn's story is one of learning to apply the lessons of the Crucified Life: whether raising a family in difficult circumstances, or learning to be a servant to other missionaries, or accepting assignments to difficult fields of service. The secrets of her service are seen on every page: her intimacy with her Lord, her love of God's Word and its promises, and her complete honesty in dealing with matters of failure and faithfulness. Whatever our own calling, this testimony will instruct and inspire.

Reverend Ted S. Rendall, *Chancellor Emeritus,*
Prairie Bible Institute Instructor, The Olford Center at Union

The stories of struggles and victories of missionary pioneers are always exciting and interesting to read. *My Children or the Cross* is no exception. From her youthful days in England to her missionary exploits in China, Miriam Dunn weaves a compelling narrative that is at the same time inspiring and thrilling—think Jason Bourne in China!! This magnificent memoir gives glimpses of her call to missions, the challenge to selflessness, the guiding hand of God, and the joys and difficulties of starting a family in a foreign land. It is also a love story as she tells how she met her husband, Marvin, and how God used them both to spread His love during some of the darkest days behind the Bamboo Curtain. I know you will be challenged and blessed, as I was, when you read this heartfelt memoir of God's faithfulness in pre-Communist China.

Martyn Smith, *Boyhood friend of Miriam Dunn's children,*
Retired School Teacher, Vancouver, British Columbia

The experiences of Miriam Dunn in China were not only interesting, inspiring, and God-centered, they were also very dangerous. After having read an especially dangerous situation in which Miriam's and Marvin's lives were in extreme peril, I walked into Peter's office the next morning and said, "Peter, you should not be here today, I should not be here today, this building and business should not be here either." He was rather puzzled by my dramatics, but after I related what I had read the night before, he agreed. I know you will enjoy reading this most inspiring story of faith and God's leading in the lives of Miriam and Marvin Dunn.

Harry Wilkins, *Public Relations, P. Graham Dunn, Dalton, Ohio*

Our mother stayed soft in times of crushing. It produced a sweet aroma, a fragrance that permeated her life and the pages of this book. Now she has exchanged her cross for a crown! I'm blessed to call her "Mother".

God's Word was a vital and practical part in her life, where she found great encouragement, direction, strength, and comfort. God always honors His Word.

Jesus says in the Bible, "Unless a grain of wheat falls into the earth and dies, it remains by itself alone; but if it dies, it bears much fruit." John 12:24

Rosemary Dunn, *Eldest Daughter, Spokane, Washington*

My heart and soul were deeply touched with the bold message of unshakable faith in this inspiring story! Your mother reflected momentous insight as she skillfully penned everyday joys and struggles. The pages contain important historical facts, but more importantly, there are mirrored lessons to be learned from her profound commitment, first to God, then to her husband and family. This autobiography clearly provides a beautiful, unforgettable portrait of one who chose to follow Christ and invest her life for Him in China where she found her "Calcutta." "To God alone be the glory!"

Mrs. Ruth Amstutz, *Kidron Elementary teacher*
of the Peter Dunn children, Kidron, Ohio

...*Mother's book is not completed.*

It is our hope that the last chapter of Miriam Dunn's book "My Children or the Cross" has yet to be written, and in fact may never be. We would invite you, the reader, to communicate with us as to how this book has challenged you. What stories do you have to relate in response to reading this?

To facilitate this communication we have set up both a website:
www.pgrahamdunnpublishing.com
and an e-mail address: peter@pgrahamdunnpublishing.com
for direct communication.

For those of you who prefer Facebook, we have set up an account entitled "My Children or the Cross," www.pgrahamdunnpublishing.com/facebook where we encourage you to visit for updates, post comments, and discover ways in which Miriam's memoirs are being used years after her departure.

All of the pictures from this book will be posted on both the web site and on Facebook.

We would love to hear from you.
The children of Marvin and Miriam Dunn,
   Rosemary Dunn
   Peter Dunn
   David Dunn